Florida A&M University, Tallahassee
Florida Atlantic University, Boca Raton
Florida Gulf Coast University, Ft. Myers
Florida International University, Miami
Florida State University, Tallahassee
University of Central Florida, Orlando
University of Florida, Gainesville
University of North Florida, Jacksonville
University of South Florida, Tampa
University of West Florida, Pensacola

Fear and Anxiety in the Arab World

Michel G. Nehme

University Press of Florida

Gainesville · Tallahassee · Tampa · Boca Raton

Pensacola · Orlando · Miami · Jacksonville · Ft. Myers

Copyright 2003 by Michel G. Nehme
Printed in the United States of America on acid-free paper
All rights reserved

08 07 06 05 04 03   6 5 4 3 2 1

Library of Congress Cataloging-in-Publication Data
Nehme, Michel G., 1951–
Fear and anxiety in the Arab world / Michel G. Nehme
p. cm.
Includes bibliographical references and index.
ISBN 0-8130-2611-3
1. National characteristics, Arab. 2. Fear—Political aspects—Arab
countries. 3. Anxiety—Arab countries—Psychological aspects. 4. Arab
countries—Politics and government—20th century. 5. World politics.
I. title.
DS63.6 .N44 2003
152.4'6'089927—dc21 2002040900

The University Press of Florida is the scholarly publishing agency
for the State University System of Florida, comprising Florida A&M
University, Florida Atlantic University, Florida Gulf Coast University,
Florida International University, Florida State University, University
of Central Florida, University of Florida, University of North Florida,
University of South Florida, and University of West Florida.

University Press of Florida
15 Northwest 15th Street
Gainesville, FL 32611–2079
http://www.upf.com

To my mother, Nadia, my wife, Sanaa,
and my daughters, Dina, Tania, and Dana,
who were deprived of my true attention
while I was working on this book.

Contents

Preface

The Arab countries have been in a state of radical change. This is noticeable in their internal politics, ideological trends, social structure, and regional and international interaction. Processes that have taken centuries in Europe and in the West in general have been telescoped in the Arab world into less than fifty years, requiring an intensity of psychological adaptation by Arabs rarely matched in human history. Arab countries are undergoing a general transformation from conventionality to novelty, sometimes conscious and planned, often half-conscious and erratic, and frequently occurring despite fierce resistance to change. One of the objectives of this book is to explore the backgrounds and impact of some of these changes, especially on the minds of Arabs.

Aristotle observed that "man is by nature a political animal." By this he meant that the essence of social existence is politics and that two or more individuals interacting are invariably involved in a political relationship. Fear and anxiety have been ignored as human drives. Presumably any attempt to trace political behavior and action of individuals to the impact of their fears and anxieties is to observe inevitably that the foundation of politics is psychology.

In dealing with political socialization and the real and acquired fears of people in the political arena, one assumption is that there remains a deep, residual insecurity in politics. People worry about the consequences of others' political decisions and of their political actions. Political psychologists describe this hidden force as anxiety. Once some degree of political anxiety becomes a component of the motivation system of individuals, it exerts a continuing influence on their behavior. Recent instances of violence and terrorism like the al-Qaeda attack on the United States on September 11, 2001, and the resulting counterattack on Afghanistan are good manifestations. These phenomena and the like illustrate the importance of fear and anxiety at the individual, group, and state levels. In this respect individuals, groups, and governments project diverse reactions. These reactions could be condensed to (a) power seeking, a process where the party strives to gain prestige, possessions, and control over others, a pattern representing a quest for security even if it means depriving others of their security; (b) submission, when a party becomes docile to protect itself; (c) withdrawal, when a party insulates itself from potential harm.

In general, fear and anxiety force individuals in the Arab world and in the Middle East to struggle with the tension inherent in a desire for security (domestic, regional, and international), a struggle most often culminating in submission to local authority, which is in turn submissive to global authority. The submission to authority counterpoints the drive for avowal of freedom and sharing in decisions affecting their destiny. Based on this, one could understand the regime's continuity in Arab authoritarian regimes.

The September 11 attacks produced new political trends and influenced new political and confessional movements in the Arab and Islamic world. These trends are a manifestation of new reasoning in the minds of Arabs and Muslims, who in turn have consistently set up a new profile to their identities, memories, stereotypes, beliefs, discourse, emotions, and actions.

1

Fear and Anxiety as Concepts Linking Psychology and Political Studies

This book uses the diverse components of human fear to explain political dimensions in the Arab world. Although the concept of fear is used without difficulty in everyday language, problems arise when it is used to explain intricate issues and as a force of change in the domain of political dynamics. In this context political studies, as a discipline, if not associated with the learning of psychology, is not able to recognize and subsequently use the concept of fear. The prevalent social and psychological norms that obscure the hidden impact of fear complicate any study involved in the description and analysis of the relationship between the drives for change in society and political processes.

Interdisciplinary research in political science takes many forms. Of the thirty-three organized sections of the American Political Science Association, ten are explicitly interdisciplinary. Political psychology, as an approach that focuses on the individual level of analysis and draws upon psychological theories to understand political phenomena, is one of the largest of these sections, and the use of psychological theories is becoming a common practice among all subfields of political science.[1]

The relative popularity of political psychology research is not surprising given the considerable overlap in social science research topics among political scientists and psychologists. Scholars from both disciplines have long been interested in exploring, for example, public opinion, violence, stability, decision making, conflict resolution, socialization, social and political identity, and leadership.

Then again, innovative inquiries are still desired, a vocation that is challenging political scientists interested in bridging politics to psychology. This task needs to be done either independently or in collaboration with psychologists. The first important concern should focus on the formation of a common language and a set of definitions for all the terminology commonly used. The second involves finding groundbreaking conceptual and theoretical frameworks leading the field of political psychology to better enlightenment of hardcore political issues.[2]

In composing this book, I had tried to use language acceptable to the two disciplines. The only way out was to generalize across contexts. Notwithstanding, and as Greenstein observed, political scientists examine "aspects of the political psychology of presidents that are presidency-specific," whereas psychologists are more likely "to deal with the psychology of leadership as a general phenomenon."[3] For the sake of interdisciplinary bridging, I sought to delimit the general parameters for how psychological and political phenomena interact and tried to explore the conditions or contingencies under which these general parameters produce different effects.

I conducted my research for this book with the belief that real-world events are themselves natural experiments. If they are collected and analyzed, they may yield empirically based postulates. Real-world events are very much like data: They offer speculative meaning and cannot be understood unless observed within conceptual frameworks and academic standards.

Undeniably, recent political trends and the emerging and reemerging of new political and confessional movements in the Arab world are real-world events. They are a manifestation of new reasoning in the minds of Arabs, which in turn have consistently set up new profiles to their identities, memories, stereotypes, beliefs, discourse, emotions, and actions. With the impact of new values resulting from the new global order, and the new political reality of Arab regionalism, the state is perceived as a rootstock of two contradicting feelings. On the one hand, it offers Arabs a stronger sense of security, affiliation, and even personal identity than does any alternative universal assemblage. On the other hand, it is a source of fear and insecurity to Arabs under the strain and shocks of new regional mobilization and alienation from current domesticated political environments. The greater is the fear of people, the greater becomes the potential power of the nation-state to channel both their longings and resentments and to direct their lives and fate. Notwithstanding, uncontrolled fear could undermine social stability and put the state at risk.

Though we speak of human fear from a group perspective, we should not disregard its individualization and that it is a perpetual enigma. People try to hide their fears behind the fears of others and/or try to hide their fears in a group.[4] Whether it is realistic and justified or not, fear plays a major role in most political and social disorder and has a major impact on progress. If it prevails among forces of change in societies, it undermines the ability of plural and mixed political entities to survive a long and durable stability. For this reason, it is a subject that should occupy more attention among political scientists and sociologists. More research should be conducted to explore the effects of fear on political stability and social change. The factor of fear needs to be exclusively acknowledged as important and then in association with other factors to better understand political predicaments in their durability and potential reoccurrence. Once this is done, then, attempts at finding techniques to reduce the fear and anxiety in the individual and among the communities could lead the way to modifying the putative underlying causes of the fear that lead to misery, upheaval, and destabilization of political order.

Although fear pressures people to cooperate and to create order in society, it also sets off a new dimension of social, economic, and political struggle, often resulting in violence.[5] In Arab societies where proper education and democracy are lacking, the rulers, out of fear, develop a need to reproduce themselves as incumbents in authority. Rulers mostly fear the sectors in society whom they have oppressed. They perceive the public as potentially dangerous. Incumbents balance their own fear with that of their subjects. They attempt to subdue crowds by deliberately fostering an atmosphere of fear. They dramatize imprisonment and executions and establish a highly visible landscape of punishment.

Findings derived from observation and research allow me to assert that Arabs are specifically influenced and moved by fear and anxiety.[6] Even when their fear is not justified, they nonetheless, in some instances, cause threat to the prevailing political stability. Definitely, the intensity of their overall anxiety upsets basic elements of their thinking in all proceedings. What does this do to political processes, having people living in continuous fear? As usual in psychology, there is the persistent but less detectable in the so-called normal circumstances. So under extreme stress, the built-in consistency of anxiety is reflected either in violence or reduction in differentiation, realization, and a strong tendency to altruism.[7] The latter explains Arabs' lack of cooperation and their dependence on the "other." Usually the "other" is the religious leader or the state.

With the unfolding of new and inharmonious social development in the Arab world, political systems have become increasingly perceived as responsible for addressing individuals' needs for safety, order, better living conditions. With the steady penetration of Western modernization, for instance, Arab political regimes have become the collective instrument for controlling all forms of grief and for managing fears of cultural death as well. Given the contemporary political involvements with technical freedoms, tension prevention, warnings of pollution, the risks of high speed driving, and homicide, it should be evident that polities have become responsible for preventing most forms of premature, man-made (and hence avoidable) death. But political responsibility now extends to protection from death by the natural order as well. In other words, the Arab state now is alleged to play the role of the parent, and it is becoming the legal custodian of all subjects. If the state is perceived as such, then any failure to meet expectations will result in alienation and the labeling of the state as being bad parents.

Following any given catastrophe in the Arab world, the state is blamed for not being able to predict it before it happens and for not being able to provide sufficient salvation. Most Arabs no longer appeal to God, as did Moses, Job, or the other Prophets. Instead, they call on the government for relief. Even the contemporary manifestations of civilizing death fears have become politicized, including not only the politically sponsored military weapons but fears of disease and traffic accidents as well.

In the rise and relative demise of all nationalistic and sectarian trends in the Arab world, and the Arab intellectuals' demand for political participation, Arab political regimes are perplexed as to how to respond to a "climate of expectations," which includes the public's needs for reassurance, sense of progress, and legitimacy. So far this "climate" featured disenchantment, disconnectedness, and cynicism, leading to the lowest public confidence in the Arab leadership and the state. Another problem of Arab government in our time arises from the fact that techniques for appealing to subrational and even to subconscious levels of human motivation are still in their infancy when applied to politics. Most political leaders have in this respect assumed Arab rationality and discounted the passions. But psychologists and social scientists no longer believe that men are ruled by reason,[8] a notion asserted by advertisers and professional military men.

Arab states maintain that their central function is to maintain order. Routinely, this has been achieved through their use of force. If modern Arab governments cannot control their people by direct force, then they must control their fears. There is a slender tendency in this direction through the establishment of the public relations industry and developing political socialization of the young in their schools' curricula. However, these programs require big budgets and can be paid for only if the economy is dynamic and the government cuts waste, corruption, and unnecessary bureaucracy, conditions that few Arab states can afford.

Most Arabs are depicted as being selfish and aloof from social and political responsibilities. It is natural not to help those who contribute to a state of affairs you perceive as a threat. Arabs avoid responsibility by depicting themselves as being too young and unprepared, yet Arabs' expectations of their societies and state are high. Narcissistic withdrawal is the most common way to escape the overwhelming fear and tension in the political reality in the Middle East, that is, the perception of being underage permits individuals within the state-family to place themselves outside the dilemma. Throughout the horrible and terrifying time of massive bombardments on civilians during the civil strife in Lebanon, people forced themselves to believe that what was happening to others did not concern them, even if they were relatives. The logic is that if they were not concerned, they would not be harmed. This denial of danger together with the personality splitting mechanism employed by individuals when too much anxiety besets them is a common phenomenon well recognized during American bombardments of cities and villages in Afghanistan. In summary, the individual denies the danger and becomes less human and civilized.

Individuals in the Arab world struggle throughout their lives with the tension inherent in a desire for domestic and regional security, a struggle most often culminating in submission to the existing authority. The submission to authority opposes the drive for avowal of freedom and sharing in decisions affecting their destiny. Based on this, one could understand the Taliban regime's continuity until ousted by the United States and the unyielding Arab oppressive regimes.

Although they share a cultural heritage, Arabs have had a history of unpleasant confessional and ethnic rivalries. Recent bloody conflicts regionally and domestically have cost them family, friends, their dignity, and their status in the world. Promoters of Arab unity claim that tension in their region is caused by their distrust of the incumbent regimes and by misperceptions among the diverse Arab communities. These misperceptions open old wounds, casting further obstacles into the path of mutual cooperation. Whether it is a misperception or not, past history is still influencing political strategy. From a political psychology understanding, this displacement of perceptions is a familiar phenomenon. The state in the West through its different propaganda and indoctrination institutions has played the role of the psychotherapist and allowed for minimizing fears emanating from the memory. Unfortunately, nothing of the sort has been palpable in the Middle East.

If groups are like individuals, then in an analogous fashion, a group will enshrine with bitterness the memory of a hurtful event that occurred at a crucial time of its development. I'm thinking, for example, of the ongoing watchful position that the minority groups in Lebanon, Iraq, Sudan, Syria, and Algeria tend to take due to the repeated bloody clashes that they had to encounter with one another. Another example can be found in Shi'ite Moslem history, though it sounds remote, but nonetheless it is real and it exemplifies how unhealed wounds create current events. We can trace the wrath of Shi'ite Moslems to the death in 680 A.D. of the Ali Bin Abi Talib's sons, Hassan and Hussein, the latter killed in battle on the desert at Karbala in what is now Iraq. This created a schism between the followers of Muaawiyah, founder of the Sunni sect in Islam, who became caliph, and the Shi'ia, partisans of Ali. These incidents gave the Shi'ite their emphasis on suffering and martyrdom.[9]

Let me take this issue further to say that it is indeed a powerful and frightening lesson to witness how ancient anger can be unleashed to threaten the present domestic and regional order. The manifestation of the Shi'ite wrath is a convincing testimony that a group's anger or frustration cannot and should not be ignored, even if it originated centuries earlier. Indeed, on other grounds, Arab anger and resentment have simmered for years over the status of dependency on major powers. Arabs fear that, once again, their region is the arena for the most deadly confrontation between Western culture and Islamic faith: American retaliation against Afghanistan following the September 11, 2001, terrorist attacks directed by Osama bin Laden and his al-Qaeda subordinates. Unable to identify or relate to one another, Arabs feel a continuous loss of control.

In their studies of individual fears, psychologists suggest that fears subside as a result of repeated exposure to the frightening situation.[10] Is it relevant to utilize this theory in explaining the relative diminishing of fears from one community to another because of repeated exposure and thus with the subsiding of fear, reconciliation becomes an easier task to achieve? The tendency to adjust to repeated stimulation is a universal characteristic, but there are instances where adjustment fails to occur. Arab communities' fears fall into this category of exception and are therefore considered unusual in the restricted sense of undue persistence despite repeated exposures. They may be regarded as unusual, if the fearful reactions are also disproportionate, and to some extent they fall into vicious cycles of repetition.

Arabs have seen substantial development when it comes to the new materials and technology, including sophisticated weapons of mass destruction. However, tribal mentality has not changed significantly. Acquiring new weapons has given Arabs controlling the instruments of the state greater potential for destruction compared with their previous command over the family, tribe, and village. The bloody clashes in Lebanon, Iraq, Algeria, and Yemen confirm this. Political settlements, or more precisely nonsettlements, in the Middle East are vivid proof that the Arab psychology has not changed much from the tribal instincts. They are anxiously paranoid in their thinking, readily given to projection, splitting into good and bad, chronically dependent on externalization processes such as "it is the enemy out there." What is called Arab modern anxiety is not easy to articulate; nevertheless, it is a constant reality of the region in its sociocultural climate, and in that sense it undertakes a special layer in the political developments of the region.

Individuals in the Arab world are often unclear about whom to blame for the political, social, and economic retardation that has befallen them. Fear often drives them to enlarge their circle of enemies. They accuse others of being either instigators or perpetrators of a secret plot aimed at undermining their national subsistence or at the very least of developing a hostile purpose against them.[11]

People in the Arab world have so many fears, general and specific, and do not seem to differentiate between the two. This is why they are driven by group memories. President Bush's violent reaction to the September 11 terrorist attacks reinstated Arab fears of the other who is out to get them. The other is hostile by nature and different in what are considered to be important values. Because of that, Arabs are afraid of the future, afraid of the bullet that may hit them at any time. This is by no means an attempt to rationalize fear. It is really hard for anyone to rationalize fear. But as a general observation, Arabs are afraid of everything.

Nothing can be resolved by saying to oneself, "I will not be afraid." Fear is one of the hidden emotions. There are strings connected to the conscious fears of which one is aware. Those strings are deep down in the transitional memory, undetectable with simple methods and techniques. How is one to deal with conscious fears as well as with those that are hidden? This is not a simple task, because fear in the social sense is to be afraid of "what is" as understood by the individual. To listen to someone who is living in a state of fear implies that one gives the explanation serious attention. This should not mean that one agrees or disagrees with what is being said. There is no agreement or disagreement when we are exploring an individual's fear.[12]

Sometimes fears are exposed by actions or attitudes. If we analyzed the reasons for fear and we came to understand them and undermined them, would this free those analyzed from fear? All analyses that undermine the impact of fear on politics in the Middle East are inclined for the objective of conditioning. If Westerners analyze Arabs' specific fears by comparing them to their general fears, the analysis will imply the perspective of the analyzer, who is the sensor, and he is going to analyze fears that he has perceived. The specific fears of the Arab people are regionally unique and are related to the pain that they experienced yesterday and the possibility of its repetition tomorrow.

The mind recalls the pain of yesterday, thus it is the thinking that involves the memory of yesterday's pain. It is the thinking that projects the fear of having pain again tomorrow. It is the thinking that can help me in providing ways to avoid pain in the future. How can I be sure that my thinking is producing the best means for avoiding pain? How am I going to be sure that when my thinking produces a plausible strategy for avoiding pain, others are going to allow me to execute my strategy? So it is history, thought and the obstacles for satisfying solutions that perpetuate fear in the Arab world.

While some can escape fear through amusements, drink, and sex, many others in the Arab world surrender to God and religion, ultimately becoming involved in radical religious tendencies. Living in fear, conscious or unconscious, is creating tremendous inward conflict and resistance. The greater the fear the greater the tension, and consequently the greater the neuroticism, the greater is the urge to escape, and at times the greater is the potential for violence.[13]

Arab societies need a strong, comforting, and unifying ideology. Only such an ideology could energize Arabs to actively respond to those in power. But what is an ideology? In part, it is an interpretive framework that integrates and gives consistency to individuals' wide-ranging experiences, beliefs, and values and organizes their social fears and drives. Ideology is the manifestation of the wishful philosophical understanding of the mind collectively and individually.

To illustrate, I offer the traditional religious leaders' and specifically Islamic fundamentalists' logic, based on male sexual fears. To them, working women have contributed to the moral breakdown of Arab society that in turn has caused social demoralization, moral and ethical retardation, children alienation, and increasing disbelief in Arab society. Men are afraid that their wives will be sexually attracted to other men if they leave home to work. This objection to working women comes at a time when the state is strongly advocating the enlargement of the labor force to remedy the shattered economy.

It has been implied that most Arabs are willing to give up some economic revenues to avoid fear resulting from sexual equality. In the same token they are willing to give up a few of their civil liberties in order to avoid anxiety. This kind of relinquishment of freedom and liberties is usually preamble to the surrender of political freedoms to the state.

For most Arabs, civic and political resignation comes as a response to being economically dependent on the state. Arabs have developed far more needs and expectations from their states than ever before. Their sense of tribal security has eroded. The Arab states have grudgingly begun to believe that they have to relinquish some more traditional tribal freedoms in the name of political stability. The state wants some people's support against other people's uprising and wants a free hand in intruding in private lives. There is an assumption that some Arabs have been unwillingly disposed to give in to those restrictions to enhance the sociopolitical system of safety and to avoid fear.

It is believed that too much anxiety leads to riots. In dealing with domestic stability against uprisings, there's a recurrent issue concerning the use of violence. If we are to exercise theories of psychological fear, then we ask, does the government do better to engage in "surgical strike" operations so that only demonstrators and their supporters are hurt? Or does purposely causing "collateral damage" lead to other population segments turning against the demonstrators and their supporters without whom there would be no crackdown? Or does this same collateral damage induce homogeneity out of heterogeneity, resulting in a massive opposition surge sweeping the government from power? These questions merit not only theoretical reflections but also practical research identifying salient and concealed variables of fear and anxiety affecting the consequences of the use of violence.

As described previously, real-world events are natural experiments that only need to be collected and analyzed to yield empirically based theories. One problem with this approach, however, is that, as with research on the political psychology of deception, knowledge of the outcome of such a study can affect reliability and validity for insurgents and governments alike. From the perspective of political psychology, it is recognized that fear is a powerful mechanism used to make people cope and adapt in totalitarian and other oppressive environments. What is not recognized is that fear generates in some individuals fear of fear, thus helping to overcome the impact of that fear. In doing this, they act outside the limits of fear, achieving more personal freedom than formally allowed. This means that they can only lead a freer life by exploiting gaps in the policy making and its implementation. Such individuals take advantage in being outside the circle of fear to act corruptly in society. This is typically the situation in the Arab world. However, with such individuals around inflicting corruption, they best facilitate dynamics for desired change on and throughout the polity.

Many Marxists, Progressives, Leftists, and Islamic fundamentalists who play outside the established circle of fear justify their corrupt actions by pretending to be revolutionaries. They create and nurture images of themselves in fantasy. They protect these images from outsiders through extensive ego investment in other players. They often collect from opponents of the state funds thrown to them as "chump change."

Again, there is the fear among individuals who can be many types of personalities and play inconsistent roles in different situations. A man may have many sides to his personality. He may be religiously inclined in political orientation, an Arab nationalist, humane, brutal, charismatic, schizoid, the "New Man," and the common man. These persons may be accurately diagnosed as manifesting traits of a diversified fear personality. They do not necessarily possess a suspected learning or conditioning inconsistency. They merely leap from one personality to another to protect themselves from the immediately perceived threat.[14] However, in all cases complex fear is a basic characteristic of these personalities.

There is fear among people who are clinically "acting out" (in the psychodynamic sense) an intrapsychic conflict on the external political stage. These individuals are best described as prisoners of their internal psychological dynamics rather than the usual external cues that often can be used to reinforce, punish, model, mediate, moderate, and otherwise condition behavior.[15]

Fear is not a substance or an object. It is a notion; thus, any study of the psychology of fear is subjective because it reflects the researcher's mode of thinking. This book tries to avoid that by benefiting from other scholars' viewpoints, especially Freud's perspective on fear and history. To Freud, fear among individuals constitutes choices in matching assumptions and sentiments of the past with the present and future and in differentiating commonalities and unique aspects of stories that have been passed down, are being passed down, and have yet to be initiated. He who learns something does that to avoid the fear of ignorance and is doomed to repeat what he learns, and learning is instigated by fear of the hidden and unfamiliar.[16] To stick to the core of this contest lays the notion that in the process of leaping away from fear, individuals hold a hierarchy of needs. Once basic needs of a physiological and economic nature are satisfied, fear produces other needs of a social and psychological nature. Fear comes to occupy a new place in the mind and to motivate individuals in a new set of attitudes and behaviors. Accordingly, individuals may display value priorities that put the emphasis on materialistic goods ("materialist values"), such as physical and economic security or on psychological contentment and self-actualization ("postmaterialist values").

The process of value change is derived from fear, which in turn stems from the dynamics of political socialization forces and economic influences. From the socialization perspective, Arab individuals who have grown up in grim poverty will develop a fear of starvation and will prioritize materialist values. Arabs whose basic needs are satisfied may develop moral fears, such as guilt, shame, or social inferiority. They tend to pursue postmaterialist values. However, these generalizations are moderated by the presence of short-term forces such as the oscillations of the economy that may stimulate the upsurge of materialist values in times of high inflation, recession, or unemployment and conversely may encourage a more vocal presence of postmaterial values in times of low inflation, growth, or job stability.[17]

As part of the Arab world has recently moved toward increasing economic stability by relying on the petrodollars and as other parts are moving toward economic instability due to domestic and international market influences, one expects to find evidence of a process of value differentiation across individuals from one region to another. This makes Arab unity hard to achieve, especially as improvements have occurred in communication and social mobility. These differences in the respective socialization environments of classes translate into value cleavages.

It is obvious in the Arab world that oil-exporting countries harbor people who tend to display postmaterialist values in a more intensive manner than Arabs in less fortunate countries. This is manifested in the individuals' fear of what is there after death and their striving to be religious and to meet God's expectations. This explains the perpetuation of the Islamic regimes in the Arab Gulf states.

In the 1970s, the capitalist economy of the Gulf states was booming, and opposition movements calling for cultural change had been decisively suppressed. The issue of the day is to figure out how to assess this reality of the unquestioned religious hegemony of a long persistent culture. This requires focusing on the Arabs' mind and their fear of the afterdeath, not on any particular socioeconomic theory.

Then again, in shifting focus, the real concern now in any study of the political psychology of Arabs who don't export oil is the suffering of the huge, impoverished, and marginal populations, especially the landless peasants and the shantytown poor in the cities. This is taking place at a time where governments have limitations in meeting their urgent material needs. With the adoption of modern development trends, the poor in the Arab world are not part of the dynamic sector of the economy. They cannot be the social basis for progress, nor can the working class be the vehicle for universal values, as Marx had anticipated. This is more so especially after the collapse of the Soviet Union and the diminishing power of the Communist Parties in the Arab world. With this one could observe that progressively the organized unions of the poor are no longer against the employers, they do not direct their threats against the bourgeoisie, and they are critical of the government and its institutions.

The concern now is, do the Arab poor and dispossessed have new fears derived from values of their own that are different from those of well-to-do Arabs? This question is posed not only for ethical reasons but also because stability in Arab societies cannot be explained from the so-called established socioeconomic theories. For why do the excluded having a psychology of their own still tolerate being regarded as "sand in the machinery" of economic development and society at large, at a time when social programs are lacking to integrate them into the mainstream?

Whether or not fear is justified, it plays a major role in explaining stability and instability. If fear prevails among forces of change in societies, it creates friction among the contending groups. This gives the Arab regimes more leverage to use force and prolong their control, thus imposing stability by manipulating the people's fears of one another.

Fear has been a component of culture everywhere in the Arab world. There existed the traditional "culture of fear," which is now associated with the novel fear from the state. Stability and order in almost all of the Arab societies were established by ferocious repression by the ruling elite, and contemporary regimes follow the same course: Just as the Turks have branded the Arabs as savage beasts to justify their oppression and exploitation, so those now in power have sought social and political terror. Throughout the second half of the twentieth century, nothing has been more significant than the role of the state in restructuring the traditional culture of fear. Those who have sought to expose and overcome the culture of fear in their countries have left martyrs, and those who speak of these martyrs have been silenced by the powerful.

By any measure, fear and terror are basic components of Arab culture. How much impact has this had in depressing the expectations of the majority vis-à-vis the powerful few? That is the crucial point; wherever such methods of terror are used, they are justified to subdue the "internal enemy."

The concept of fear as used here actually indicates shared anxieties among the presumably similar groups on the salient cultural dimensions. Such similarity is more straightforward with regard to religion. However, for ethnic groups, fears are more subjective and include groups sharing a common lifestyle and customs, as well as a perception of common anxieties and a link with collective historic frustrations.[18] Do such explanations help us understand or offer solutions? This remains to be judged by scholars after reading this book.

2

The Hidden Drives of Arab Politics

In the Arab world, fear is part of living, and it stems from diverse sources. It is individualistic in the sense that it is encountered within the conscious and subconscious reasoning of individuals. Because individuals' fears are not the same and are constantly changing, their fears are subjective. Some fears are clear to their bearer, especially in a threatening environment, while others are obscure. Fear is burdening Arabs who have been living in stressful societies with unstable political systems. Nonetheless, fear has the same impact on relatively stable societies as vast petrodollar powers.

What is fear? As Vinacke clarifies, it is a complex feeling of which two strains, alarm and anxiety, are clearly distinguishable. Alarm is triggered by an obstructive event in the environment, and an individual instinctive response is to combat it or run. Anxiety, on the other hand, is a diffuse sense of dread and presupposes an ability to anticipate. It commonly occurs when an individual is in a strange and disorienting milieu, separated from the supportive objects and figures of his home ground. Anxiety is a presentiment of danger when nothing in the immediate surroundings can be pinpointed as dangerous. The need for decisive action is hindered by the lack of any specific circumventing threat.[1]

In the Arab world, people are aware of the drastic impact of politics. They inexplicably distinguish between fear and anxiety. Fear is taken to refer to apprehension about tangible decisions and actions by authorities that produce predominantly realistic dangers. Anxiety, on the other hand, is taken to refer to apprehension about past experiences of one's community that are difficult to relate to present tangible sources of stimulation. The inability to distinguish between past terrible experiences and present indicators of potential harm is usually regarded as the hallmark of anxiety. In psychology, anxiety is defined as a warning sign that the psychic system is being threatened and is overwhelmed.[2]

Political anxiety is normally attended by a feeling of being "out of control" and of not being able to affect or avoid the decisions and actions of others.[3] In the case of psychodynamic theories, the inability is said to be a result of repression, hence the sources of anxiety in the Arab communities generally remain unconscious. The division between tangible and intangible fears bears on another distinction that is the historical experience of one Arab community in a previous political environment and its present status in a different political setting.

The fluctuations of fears and anxiety are important to understand, especially their emergence in politically tense situations (regional wars or civil strife) followed by a relative decline in frequency and intensity when a hypothetical solution to the political conflict seems plausible. Escalated and relative degeneration of fears inasmuch as they explain behavior of people in making political decisions raises specific questions in the Arab world. Do tense situations between the communities happen as a result of an existing fear, or does fear take place as a result of the tense situation? Why do fears decline and become dormant? And why at other times is fear awake? The common assertion in the field of psychology is that individuals diverge in sensing and responding to fear.[4]

One might explain that anxiety is crucial at the private level, for it signals that the individual is responsive and that Arabs refuse to deaden themselves to situations they cannot control. On the other hand, it is potentially dangerous at the collective level because it extends the feeling that Arabs will forever be living in a climate of violence and potential jeopardy. The apparent danger is when generations are growing up without a solid sense of safety, without an expectation of a better future, without basic trust that a decent life in their political environment is possible.

Social psychologists have asserted that fear and anxiety are strongly associated with aggression. Various research efforts have been made to explain this association. The intent here is not to summarize these efforts but to illustrate only those that have relevance to this study.[5]

Arab governments have a history of executing political rivals. Fear of death even when others are being executed develops an instinct for self-preservation. Arabs are confined in their toleration of fear. These limitations are not just external; they involve forces within the self that are difficult to explain and hard to control. Internal limitations in the form of psychological complexities have major impacts on the Arab's life in general and just the same on political processes.[6]

Whenever we are dealing with the subject of order and development in Arab societies, individuals and groups are studied in terms of their collective energy and capabilities. Hardly ever do we perceive fear that prevails among individuals and groups as a result of the mere fact of banding together. This kind of fear is inclined to place limitations on their capabilities. Those who don't feel protected by the bonds of society tend to defect from these social bonds in exchange for protection and security elsewhere. This explains the tendency among Arabs to emigrate to non-Arab countries, especially to the West.

If death is inescapable, then security means delaying this fate as long as possible. Humans have internal and external limitations in this respect. Internal limitations are related to the health and physiological conditions of the individual. External limitations are related to the surrounding conditions of survival. The implications of Arab limitations encompass all disciplines of social studies. From the perspectives of psychology and sociology, the fear of death in the Arab would has two manifestations. First, at the psychological level, limitations on the fear of death invoke the likelihood of self-destruction. Second, at the social level, it evokes the likelihood of killing others.[7]

Freudian psychoanalysis projected the idea that fear of death produces what is identified as a "force of death and destruction" or what is commonly known as the "death instinct," and this is something inherent in human nature.[8] Academically, the "death instinct" as a concept was first associated with the sex drive and its destructive consequences. Freud took the issue further and separated the destructive force of death from sexuality.[9]

According to Freud, the mind, not the thinking of the individual, is always in conflict. This, to Freud, is the dynamic view of human psychology. That is what needs to be addressed: How is the conflict to be understood? What forces are in conflict? What are the consequences of opposing forces struggling against one another in the mind of the individual? The death drive struggles against the forces of life, survival, and passion. To prevail, the death drive produces depression, masochism, self-destructive behavior, and suicide.[10] Once this drive at the individual level is transformed to the social level, it manifests itself in criminal and oppressive acts, and if it is at the collective level, it exhibits forcefully, especially in civil strife and wars.[11] Recent violence between the Palestinians and Israelis is a good example of that.

The death drive, especially in very stressful environments, promotes our intellectual reasoning beyond the philosophical linear propositions on the human nature. Individuals in the Middle East are not simply, as the Hobbesian school asserted, bad in nature, competitive, warring, and destructive. Nor they are "noble savages" inclined by the institutions of society, not by their nature, to be good and to be social. In view of these convictions, the philosophical tendency that blames the individual for the evils of society and promotes formal institutions as the best solution loses ground.[12] Then again, the tendency to blame institutions for all evil, because they inevitably become a destructive force for the freedom, good, and flowering nature of the individual, is insufficient in explaining multifaceted reality.

Freud implied that the individual could not be understood in linear suggestive assumptions about his one-track nature. To him, the individual's mind is surrounded by conflicting forces, and the manifestations of these forces to the outside world are perceived by others as either good or bad.[13] The concern here is that Freud has located a drive or force of death, destruction, and annihilation of life within human beings, not outside them. Of course, this projection is incomplete if we are to explain political realities in the Arab world because if this Freudian theory is not associated with sociopsychological theories related specifically to the Arab environment in terms of peculiar Arab social stimulus and responses, in terms of outside forces (not within the mind), then the study is incomplete.[14] The idea of outside forces was not completely negated by Freud or by his followers. Beck, Emery, and Greenberg explain the combination by correlating the instinct theory, with particular emphasis on the death instinct, with that of an object relations approach (outside forces).[15] The outside forces could be visible by producing hatred, aggression, envy, and violence in the individual.

In using this line of logic, both love and hate start operating from the beginning of life. The death instinct operates from within the self biologically and mentally. In order to preserve life from annihilation or overwhelming depression, the death instinct has to be projected out (outside the biology and mind of the individual). However, the residues of the death instincts vary from one society to another and could be observed in the individual through anxiety and phobia.[16]

Because of their stressful environment, the death instinct among Arab individuals is projected in the outside world in the form of aggression. It becomes the "persecuting object." In other words, it is the need of individuals to have enemies in order for them to deal with their projected aggression, which stems from their death instinct.[17]

Freud tried to draw a parallel relationship between the individual and society.[18] Being influenced by the Hegelian mode of thinking, he depicted them in the dialectic of mutual struggle. Again, because of the specifics of the Arab culture, the individual has a tendency to coexist with both instinctual drives that allow for relative social peace and progress. This is an internalization of control and repression of the forces causing conflict. Within the Arab societies, this led inevitably to guilt, self-destructive tendencies, and emotional disturbances. Tension between the individual and society remained always ready to break out in some subversive or destructive fashion unless channeled and controlled.[19]

The death instinct is useful in explaining the Arabs' need to develop their inner power by extending themselves in society through acquiring weapons. In order to make up for the guilt mechanism of projecting death from the inside to the outside, the Arabs worked hard to produce devices of good. Whether created for good or for destruction, most of these involve group function and process. Certain functions among the individual members of the group are produced by group process. The individual finds it comfortable to dilute his inner feelings including the death instinct in the group, especially if it occupies an ego-promoting function. The group provides the individual basic levels of security against external threats. Bion concluded that fear and the need for security are the main reasons people band together in static groups.[20] The Arabs' need for security and protection is central in their lives, but the static banding together in their societies causes developmental stagnation. They are totally dependent on the West for science and technology. Creative Arabs need to escape the group or else face social punishments.

Arabs need enemies. Otherwise, they will destroy themselves. It is frustrating that groups have frequently exaggerated the danger of the "other" to avoid their self-destructive drives, thus multiplying their internal fears as well as organizing the ability and forces of the group to deal better with the perceived enemy. When the group does not find a place to project its anger, it will face serious danger from the inside. A new enemy will have to be found.[21]

The problem for any Arab group is the tendency to believe that members are caring, loving, and cooperative. They are shocked to discover that individuals are inclined to hate and compete in an aggressive and harmful way. Aggression is a much more serious problem in the Arab world than was supposed, and it is not easily accepted and dealt with. The denial of unintentional individual inner aggressiveness impedes all attempts to explain the reality of politics anywhere in the world, especially in Arab societies. The death drive theory emphasizes the powerful innate tendencies toward aggression and destruction. If these tendencies are associated with social frustration, then the whole political reality in the Arab world becomes loaded with potential rage.[22]

The relative calamity that occasionally prevails within any Arab group is related to the connection individuals make between their fate and the fate of their group. There is a tendency among Arabs to suppress hostility toward other members and to mobilize to protect their group for their own sake and for the sake of the group, which comes down to the same thing. If we are to take this argument further, Arabs' belief that they are threatened by a common danger can serve yet another function, which is the feeling that confronting a common threat might lead to increased group cohesiveness and increased social interaction. Then again, it provides a distraction from strictly personal worries, offers new roles and perhaps status to people who were previously isolated, and offers people experiencing some degree of personal distress an external reason for their harmony of mind. This means that, as they evaluate their failure, they do not have to resort to an explanation based on personal inadequacy or illness.[23]

Historically, when Arab groups did not perceive danger from outside their inner circle, the most important element of endurance for them became their ability to construct durable systems of stabilizing institutions to deal with rivalry and envy among their members. This, according to sociologists, is handled by obsessional defenses leading to hierarchy and rules. When this fails, basic group defense mechanisms come into the picture: denial, splitting, and projection.[24] In 1975–90, civil armed conflicts in Lebanon and similar Middle Eastern strife in Iraq, Algeria, and Yemen explicitly manifest the potential among Arabs for splitting and denial in their societies.

In reference to this, psychologists have assessed the behavior of people in such intense situations. They conclude that pushing an individual to the extreme fear of death reduces his actions to the mere life-sustaining initiatives.[25] The individual in such situations loses his civilized behavior because he loses the multiplicity of motives to concentrate only on surviving. The more unfortunate and pressured individuals are, the more they tend to express indifference to others. The aftermath of the Iraqi-Kuwaiti conflict, Lebanese civil strife, and other regional feuds like the continuous wholesale killing in Israel generated a new epoch of anxiety in the Arab world, especially among youth. University students have repeatedly shown that they are apprehensive about their future and frightened by the recurrence of strife and violence in their societies.

For some, the escape from extremely stressful situations comes in mystical proceedings. There is an assertion in psychology that counter to the increase in awareness of fear runs the prospect of denying such fear through mystical proceedings. It is contained in numerous cultures and religious notions that indulge in apocalyptic visions in which only the evil sources of fear will perish while the good, adequate, and reasonable will be revived to live-and-let-live in peace and tranquility. While the thinking of new Arab generations, in measure, tends to rectify the isolating, narcissistic tendencies, the demonization of their fears and the glorification of martyrdom pander to the promotion of an instinctual desire for death.[26]

To illustrate this phenomenon of embracing death, one has to look at all those young men who have volunteered for armed service ever since their clans, nations, or religions have called upon them to do so. Suicide attacks are not new in the history of Arabs and in the Middle East in general. We conclude that their willingness, often eagerness, to do this is a manifestation of the death wish. It asserts itself through the explicit promise that the self-sacrificer will enjoy eternal life—or at least his band will.

Death and rebirth rituals were always linked in the Arab culture. In a common atmosphere of fear and anxiety, these concepts should be addressed with caution. Individuals tend to trace their source of fear, and that shifts with the turnabout of ideologies. To Arab nationalists it is the West, imperialism, and economic penetration. To Islamists before the shrinking popularity of Arab nationalism, it was communism, Marxism, and atheist socialism. Now after the defeat of communism, Islamists are identifying the Western culture as the source of their fears and the source of evil in their societies.

In shifting from the external to the internal sources of fear, it is important to focus on the impact of the state. Arab regimes believe that creating an atmosphere of fear is necessary to control individual behavior. If individuals are afraid of the authorities, the latter can control the former better. Then again fear could be used as a moral pressure. Indirectly, Arab regimes say that fear is the only instrument of order in society and that otherwise the citizens will abuse their freedoms wildly. Fear has become an instrument utilized for stability and control of the masses in the Arab world.[27] Arabs are afraid. Their fear exists as a result of their bloody history and in relationship to the astonishing alterations in their immediate political realities. In addition, Arabs suffer from so many forms of psychological and psychosomatic fears. To explore each form of fear would take an enormous amount of time. But one can observe the general quality, nature, and structure of fear without getting lost in the detail of the psychological scientific form of analysis. When one understands the nature and structure of fear as such, then one can approach the explicit political fear.

Then again, fear creates emotional range that is a gauge of the nervous system's complexity and hence, indirectly, of the mind. Emotional range opens the capacity of the human mind for shame and guilt, which adds greatly to the scope of human fear.[28] In this line of logic, Arabs have frequent sayings: Awareness of pretentious evil enables a person to see and live in phantasmagorical worlds. Betrayal by a relative or a friend is more shameful than betrayal by an enemy outside the familiar circle. To be able to differentiate between your friends and enemies is a graceful blessing. To apprehend is to risk apprehensiveness. Those that do not know so much have less to fear. If such sayings are to be deeply investigated in this realm, Arab imagination and experience could add immensely to the existing knowledge of fear.

It is true that fear is in the mind, but a good part of its origin is in external factors and circumstances that are truly threatening. What are the foundations of fear in the Arab world? They are the manifestations of the forces for chaos, natural and human. Being omnipresent, Arabs have attempted to control forces that could cause chaos, and their continuous efforts are ever-present. In a sense, every Arab construction, whether mental or material, is a component stemming from the spring of fear developed to contain chaos. Thus cosmological myths, philosophical ideologies, and political systems are shelters built by the mind within which Arab societies can rest, at least temporarily, from the siege of chaotic experience and doubt.[29] Likewise, the Arab social gathering and the feeling of belonging by individuals to groups because of relationship of identities are social fortresses built to defend Arabs against the elements of fear. This in itself is a constant reminder of Arab vulnerability. Generally speaking, every state boundary in the Arab world, though created by Western powers, whether material, political, or psychological, city walls, radar fence, political boundaries defended by military devises, are attempts to keep inimical forces at bay. Boundaries are everywhere in the Arab world because threats are ever-present: threats from alien armies, invading culture, hegemonic political wave, and outside economic exploiters.

Many types of fearsome sources exist in the Arab societies. The differences between them, however, tend to blur in the past and in the present experience of the Arab individual because a dire threat in whatever form normally produces two powerful sensations. One is fear of the imminent collapse of the social group and the approach of death, which in turn leads to that final surrender of integrity to chaos. The other is a sense of personalized evil, the feeling that the hostile force, whatever its specific manifestation, possesses will.[30]

Traditional Arab communities have always depicted outside societies as capable beings with deities and demons, powers and evil spirits. This deeply ingrained habit of alienation and being different and spiritually better than others enhanced the tendencies for group solidarity. Because strange people are the most common cause of fear, familiar people provide the greatest source of security. Arabs have maintained in their culture that alien or strange people can be indifferent to their needs, betray their trust, or actively seek to do them harm.

How can we relate the above to Arab nationalism? It is only because Arab intellectuals have realized and convinced masses that strength lies in numbers that some Arabs, though indifferent to one another, approved the call for merger to attain power. By proposing to act together, the Arab communities thought they could master the local environment and create more or less better defenses in a region where they feel at home. Arabs with nationalistic tendencies perceive themselves as living in a pocket of order and safety surrounded by a host of threats.

Arabs experience persecution anxiety. Their feelings are characterized by a sense of indefinite and terrifying threat to the self from something inside.[31] The most primitive defense against persecution anxiety is for the individual to take his inner feelings to the outer world. There in the outer world these inner feelings are still an object of terror, but at least they have become something that can be fled, barred, or attacked and, if possible, destroyed. In other words, an aggression within the self that endangers the self is not any more the property of the self but it is attributed to someone or something else.[32]

Something needs to be explained in relation to the concept of the persecution anxiety or the paranoiac. This concept in conjunction with the concept of political paranoia, a common phenomenon in the Middle East, did so much to produce fear and tension in these societies. Arabs are less likely to be aware that this can play a part in intensifying their own political anxieties and animosities. Although the basic anxiety is felt as an indefinite foreboding, within the Arab mind, it becomes the focus of other terrors that are definite enough at least to the unconscious. These include Arab fear of being socially drained, robbed, starved, or forcibly separated from loved objects. These mechanisms tend to disturb much of Arab political emotion. If the personified abstractions of parties or ideologies other than the Arab individual concerned already stir primary feelings of persecution, this individual shall unconsciously attack them by any or every devise known to unconscious talent, and he shall expect and fear the same treatment in retaliation.[33]

The assumption of paranoia among Arabs is strictly dealt with in relation to politics. Such paranoia stems from both real and imagined dangers. In certain instances the real and the imaginary get mixed one with the other. Arabs tend to overstate the dangers that are there. The victory of another party may cause alarm if it is likely to reduce their wages or increase their taxes, but it also puts them more in the power of employers or officials they have reason not to trust. But their emotional response is often appropriate to a much greater threat. Like all paranoid anxieties, it may have a real basis. But if it were not for the individuals' own persecution anxiety, their own unconscious desire to rob, castrate, and dominate others, they should not be so ready to react emotionally, thus behaving as if there were a real danger of these things being done to them. In this sense, Arabs' fears and hatreds could not be reduced to pragmatic properties.

But again, real dangers in the Arab world are by no means always exaggerated. There is a secondary defense against anxieties from projection that has the opposite effect. The secondary defense against persecutory anxiety, where a real danger is underestimated, consists of a denial of the real malignity of a terrifying object. With these two tendencies, one tending to overestimate, the other trying to underestimate every concrete danger, it is not easy to preserve a balanced judgment in Arab societies.

A common defense against persecution anxiety in the Arab world is for the individual to project the sadistic superego on to another person, group, object, divinity, or cosmic force.[34] What is the gain in projecting the persecutor in this fashion, especially if one seems to be punished in the same fashion and suffering from heightened guilt? One gains, first, by having an explanation for one's guilt or persecution anxiety. The threat of calamity is always worse when its nature and timing are unknown. An explanation always relieves some of the uncertainty, giving the individual some sense of control over what is affecting him. Second, the individual gains by having a course of action prescribed that will relieve the anxiety.[35]

On a parallel configuration of the inner feelings, the Arab feels that he must satisfy the angry God, through devotion and virtuous living, because bad things happen when God intends to punish. The religious projection of the persecutor provides the individual with concrete hopes of redemption, if he acts properly. In the fullest sense it takes him out of himself and gives him greater confidence in control over that self. However, in idealizing the persecutor in the religious way, the individual will probably demand great sacrifices of himself, in the name of a protective God. These sacrifices could go to the limit of self-denial in the individual to protect the God who is protecting him. This leads to splitting defenses in the individual.[36]

Psychologists assert that strong splitting defenses in adults may indicate paranoia. The paranoid Arab has a psychological need for evil in the outside world, whether it is embodied in capitalists, Jews, communists, criminals, imperialists, blacks, women, homosexuals, or whatever. The individual needs to project the bad half of his own character, the one his punitive superego disapproves of, onto the scapegoat group, and then hopes to purify himself by destroying the public manifestation of that part of his character.[37] Thus some Arabs have tried to purge both their own bad conscience and their polluted wishes by eliminating other Arabs, whom they charged with plotting to destroy the well-being of society. Paranoid individuals in general are very aggressive. This is because in labeling anyone who crosses them as evil they can attack them with a clear conscience.

Polarizing good and evil is a form of splitting defense in the Arab mind. The range of examples of splitting in a political situation is almost infinite, and so is the case in social relations. Where one comes across prejudiced stereotyping, one should suspect a defense against persecution anxiety.[38] This kind of prevalence in politics is vivid in religious, racial, and ethnic animosity and in socioeconomic class conflicts.

Arabs stereotype political entities like states, parties, organized political minorities, religious groups, and ethnic groups in the same way a woman is stereotyped. Sometimes a woman is a whore, shrew, or ogress; at other times she is an angelic virgin and earth mother. The woman is split into good and bad. Political entities are depicted in the same way. This way the Arab man can direct his loving impulses toward the former and his hostile impulses toward the latter. He can express his highly ambivalent feelings after having separated love from hate and bad from wrong.

The significance of survival for the Arab ignites in many engines within his mind. Freud concentrated on the sexual engine and elaborated on the concept of sublimation as one of the main defenses against repressed or frustrated sexuality. Energy derived from the sexual engine is displaced into culture-creating activities.[39] Some scholars of psychoanalysis have subsequently come to recognize the sublimation of the aggression engine in the mind as a vastly more important phenomenon for the well-being of both the individual and society. Undeniably, fear is an engine that produces energy sublimated in aggression and violence. At other times it is sublimated in deference, conformity, and responsibility.

For Arabs, there is often something sour, prickly, and fiercely competitive about groups' relations suggestive of a violent nature close to the boil. At all levels, the understanding of Arab culture requires the sympathetic acknowledgment of combined sexual aggressiveness and religious fear. In line with this, confessional groups in the Arab world are affected by the story of Adam and Eve. Guilt is built into their religious culture because they feel responsible for what the first couple did in disobedience to God. Their guilt flows from an internalized fear of God. It follows that the more fear sublimation is directly outwards in good conscience, the more guilt is relieved. The sublimation of fear in socially legitimate and personally approved tasks is generally the most satisfactory means of releasing guilt.[40] The most successful sublimation in the case of persecutory guilt is that of hard, disciplined work. The ego-ideal approves, the conscience does not disapprove, and the high pressure of fear may be released. In this case sublimation as defense works in conjunction with projecting the persecutor, be it God or the incumbent authority.

The more severe the persecution anxiety, the greater the inner tension and the more severe the need to sublimate. A punitive conscience will probably bar any direct expression of aggression, unless it follows the splitting defense. As a result, thoroughly controlled sublimation remains the main outlet. Work and art are not the only examples. Competition is just as important, as it often functions in cycle with aggression, hatred, friendship, and love.

Competition in politics, in authority, in gaining property and status, and in the pursuit of religious virtue provides outlets for controlled aggression. The Arab culture, on the surface, accepts such competitions as morally legitimate. They are usually controlled by a projected persecutor, such as the almighty God, an awesome legal system, or a republic with a book of rules. Where splitting takes place, the opposing team will be seen, in addition, as the personification of evil.

The Arab character, in general, is associated with persecutory guilt. Using a distinction Freud made, it is a character that acts out a fear of conscience rather than a fear of loss of love. Its traits are fundamentally religious and long-suffering, austere and devout.[41] Arabs in this sense tend to be self-controlled, striving for categorization and obedience; hardworking, striving for achievement but only within what they have around. Arabs again tend to moralize all history and action into the working out of the warring forces of good and evil. It may be inspired in an imaginative or religious manner; likewise, it may be driven to probe the deepest metaphysical questions about the meaning of life. In investigating the Arab culture, one could easily find paranoid symptoms, obsessions to the point of the complete ritualization of behavior. Arabs as such may become bravely self-righteous or authoritarian, identifying with the persecutor and lacking the virtue of the depressive, thus concerned more with authority and obedience than with care and kindliness.

This takes us back to concepts of shame and guilt. The common assertion is that they fall into two broad camps. There is an ethnological distinction, and there are shame cultures and guilt cultures.[42] Psychoanalysts explain the difference in relevance to individual psychology. Based on the individual psychology, the Arab world contains both shame and guilt cultures. Failing before his ego-ideal, an Arab feels ashamed. On the other hand, when he contravenes his conscious, guilt is aroused. Thus, an Arab soldier defeated in battle and the journalist who fails to assess a dangerous situation feel guilt and shame at their fallen reputations. This usage combines Charles Darwin's commonsense reading of shame as the result of the sensitive regard for the opinion of others and the individual's moral reflections about his own conduct. The latter means that an individual could become ashamed without "an audience."

Whether they are kingdoms or republics, Arab states are personified as parental figures. The state is something into which Arabs tend to project their superego. In most of the Arab states, the head of the regime clearly typifies the state. In less authoritarian societies, the superego is projected into the collective authority that performs the task of legislative, executive, and judicial functions. If the individual feels that the authority is tyrannical or benevolent, he attributes more of these qualities to authority than it already has. Arab states have or are expected to have the same sort of influence on the character of its citizens as the actual nature of parents has on the character of children. The child's picture of his parents is partly determined by what he projects into them. But their actual nature tends to modify the picture. As the child matures and as the individual develops in understanding the reality of politics and government, a modified picture will be reintrojected to modify the individual superego. Such modification may be very slight in mature, politically oriented intellectuals. But since the majority of Arabs are modified in their superego, this means an increased authoritarianism in the state does produce increased authoritarianism in the morality of individuals. And conversely, it would lead us to expect that an increased humanism in the state, by reducing the strictness of individual superegos, would at least clear the way for the appearance of a more humanist morality.

As depicted in the political culture of Arabs, those parents whose moral character has been influenced by their introjection of the state morality will tend to pass on the same modification to the children, who introject them in turn. The same process of psychological inheritance will also operate, almost to the same degree in the Arab diverse minority groups where the elderly reproduce their thinking in the following generation. The influence of the state's character will be greater on the state employees who are most closely in contact with the state.[43]

In utilizing the above operation of the superego, we must distinguish between the conscious and unconscious forces involved. When the superego of some Arab people on the average becomes harsher, there may appear an increased conscious desire for freedom. But this will be defeated by an unconscious impulse to remodel the external authority until it accords more closely with the internal authority that is projected into it. So in the end they will make the state stricter than it was before and compensate themselves for their actual loss of freedom by identifying themselves with it and so acquiring the sense of a power beyond belief.[44] And, of course, the same result will be achieved, and more directly, if the conscious reaction to a harsher type of superego is not mutiny but a greater tolerance of subjugation.

All forms of corrupting influence in the Arab world are related to the increase in the desire for power that accompanies a decline in the desire for freedom. Because of their new exposure to modern states, Arabs do not have any alternative but to perceive of the state as personified in a parent figure. They try to make it the kind of parent that they want to have or that they want to be. If some Arabs unconsciously want a harsh parent, they tend to make the state harsh, too, no matter how much they may consciously desire the opposite. Notwithstanding, there is a trend of weakening in the severity of the internal superegos among some Arab youngsters who have been influenced by the Western media. If this continues, it will increase the capacity for freedom and decrease the desire for power in parents either actual or sensational. This gives hope to make the state more liberal.

How do we assess the above suggestions in the Arab world? It is possible to evaluate these ideas if we are to assume that the state has tremendous influence over the employees of the public sector. The bureaucrats of Arab states tend to reproduce themselves generation after generation with the same mentality, values, attitudes, and behavior. This means that the effect of the new generation, influenced by new values, will have a linear influence first only in the official classes, then hopefully in the country as a whole.

Contemporary political studies of the Arab world as opposed to the traditional ones are characterized by a commitment to rational criticism. Rather than defer to the authority of class and socioeconomic analysis, researchers are seeking moral principles to determine whether Arab political traditions, laws, and practices are worthy of citizens' commitment.[45] Ideologically oriented research about the Arab world projects implications for a theory of justified obedience or disobedience. That is, if Arab compliance with the demands of the state cannot be justified by valid principles, they have no obligation to obey. On the other hand, Arab states reason that an obligation by their subjects to support and comply with the demands of the state is necessitated by the fact that they receive benefits from the state, although the ways in which the obligation is derived from benefits received are quite different. Arab states, again, forecast utility in asserting that subjects have an obligation to comply with the state's demands insofar as doing so is beneficial to the stability and order of society. Accordingly, an obligation is entailed from enjoying order regardless of whether fulfilling a specific obligation is beneficial to the subject.

Political psychology holds that political obligations arise from consent.[46] While we might need some other principle, such as utility, to decide whether we should consent, the idea here is that if people have obligations, it is because they have voluntarily undertaken them by consenting. If people never consent, they have no obligation. Of course, there are ambiguities within each trend regarding how it is to be applied and whether in particular circumstances it would support either noncompliance or active resistance. My purpose is not to address the details of this debate but to see whether we can add a strikingly different approach to this debate.

Studies of political obedience and disobedience are designed to make widespread adjustments in the structure of society and of the state. Some Arab scholars may find these advantageous. But unless we can also foresee their probable repercussions on national character, we may find we have brought about some unexpectedly unwelcome results. Any social spiral consists of two halves: the influence of the character of individuals on the state's structure, and the influence of the social environment and of the state on the character of individuals. Understanding the second half of any social spiral is the concern here, particularly the part that assesses the social conditions that are likely to be important in understanding the development of political personalities.

For theorists committed to rational, principled criticism, deference to long-standing traditions, practices, and institutions, taking individuals' and groups' consent for granted is but the "worshipping of dead men's bones." For a practice, institution, or law to be justified, there must be some good reason for it, apart from its sheer existence or heredity. Not without reason, psychologists are often seen as opposing the spirit of rational criticism and opposing the construction of a state, as it "ought to be." To determine what is the individuals' duty, they argue, we need to turn not to a one-sided and empty ratiocination but to the existing norms as adopted and accepted in the individuals' minds.[47] There exists rejection to the idea, which surfaces in the work of some contemporary political analysts, that each generation can ignore traditions and start anew. The understanding here is that the political theorist's task is "to comprehend what is" and not design blueprints for ideal states.

It is just as impractical to imagine that any political entity can transcend its history as it is to think that an individual can transcend his own time or culture. If political entities do indeed transcend their own time and build a world, as it ought to be, then it certainly has an existence, but only within a mind in which the imagination can construct anything it pleases.

My argument here in addressing the question of why Arabs obey the laws of their governments is not because it is the law or because there are obligations. It is well known that in general Arab states have unjust laws, and I do not think that Arabs are bound to them merely because they are called law. I think Arabs do not consent to their institutions. They feel obligated to support these institutions because bad institutions are better than no institutions. The new organizational structure, bad as it is, still has come to play a positive role in Arabs' lives. In other words, there are strong and weak senses of consent. To consent in a strong sense is to authorize, or grant permission. When an Arab consents to his government he authorizes it to act on his behalf. However, obligations are not derived from consent in this strong sense.

Historically speaking, Arabs have never as people granted in a democratic way permission to authorities, foreign or local, to author their laws, practices, and institutions. Nor did they have the chance to write a law that would project their convictions. That is why Arabs have weaker senses of consent: for example, to "agree to," which itself has many senses, such as to explicitly agree to something, or agree to something tacitly by just going along. Consent might mean "approve of," which Arabs do reluctantly of something with which they do not agree, as when they would have had an alternative to choose. Still a weaker sense of consent is to "accept," which we can do without actually agreeing or approving.

Citizens of the present Arab states have a duty to comply with the institutions and laws of that state, regardless of whether they ever promised to comply and even if they do not grasp a principled justification for those institutions and laws. However, an Arab obeys laws because he recognizes the laws as de facto, and such recognition amounts to a sort of consent. This could be better understood by turning to Arabs' existing ethical lives. Their laws, customs, and practices dictate their obligations to them. But what justifies these obligations and explains why they are not unfree in discharging them is not the fact of their existence. Arabs comply with the demands of their ethical life only because they think that their ethical life is rational.

To Arabs, the state but not necessarily the government is based on reasons and principles. They do not understand the reasons for complying with the state's demands, but they obey. This could explain why political obligations are based merely on authority. Arabs conform to a principle of commitment. We should distinguish this principle from the "abstract" principle, with which we can make judgments without reference to the rules, purposes, or shared understandings associated with social practices.

Immanent principles have weight only for those sharing in social practices from which the principles are derived and political obligations are justified, and felt to be justified, only for people sharing in an ethical life that engenders shared understandings and standards of right conduct. However, Arabs often carry out their political conduct not from knowing that it is their duty to conform to abstract principles but, rather, from feelings such as love for the object of their duty.

Love of the object of duty brings about the issue of ethics, which in turn is "implanted in the child in the form of feeling." Arabs are brought up with the practices, laws, and institutions that determine what their obligations are. Acting in accordance with their demands has become second nature to Arabs. Arabs are disposed to carry out their duties not because they are dictated by some abstract principle they know to be true but because they are involved in concrete relations that require them to act in certain ways.

From a psychological perspective, any search for those social conditions that impede or strengthen the political behavior of adults, and thus by indoctrination from adults onto children, should be traced to the child's parent and parent's child persecutory and depressive anxieties. For the individual, this complicated process tends to create and to foster a picture of the world, particularly of his society and environment. Anything, therefore, in his real environment that seems to confirm anxiety tends to set up a vicious spiral of character defect, and anything that relaxes anxiety tends to set up a beneficent spiral of greater rationality in social behavior.

The twin heads of deprivation and frustration that generate anxiety fashion most of the unfavorable influences on individuals, especially children. The amount of deprivation a child can stand without harm depends, of course, upon his age. In the early period, he can stand very little. To be kept waiting for the breast or the bottle, or for the satisfaction of any other need, may throw him into paroxysms of rage and panic which, if prolonged, may end in a kind of depressive apathy sometimes mistaken for contentment. Deprivation confirms his sense of living in a world of enemies, and the rage engendered makes him feel that whatever good objects it may have contained are now destroyed.[48]

However, though active frustration is harmful to the child's own surroundings, the child is terrified of his own destructive impulses. Children divert their hatred and rage against an external force outside their small environment, blaming this force as being an enemy of their folks and their enemy. Their parents and their own group cannot provide for them not because they do not want to but because this external enemy is making it very hard. This blame on the external force (usually other people) brings about restraint against their immediate surroundings and reassures them that they are loved and worthy of their family's physical protection, which they cannot do without.

The factors that constitute an unfavorable or favorable environment for the adolescent in the school or, politically speaking, for the adult in the state are much the same, with only quantitative differences, such as those that constitute an unfavorable or favorable home. The state guarantees us a certain measure of protection. It demands from us a certain measure of obedience. It may inspire our loyalty. In short, our relation to it as an object is the same general form as our relation to our parents so that it is inevitably personified as a parental figure. What is important in this analogy and comparison is that the state, like the parent, plays the role in confirming or correcting our earliest fantastic pictures of them. If it is actually tyrannical, the old sense of inner persecution will be increased together with all the distortions of thought and feeling that occur as defenses against the old anxiety. But if it is actually beneficent, all these distortions will be correspondingly diminished.

For example, in the kind of state that the Arab nationalist movement created in Syria, Iraq, and Algeria, even those who had developed political rights seldom maintained their acceptance of others having the same. An external world so persecutory in character reawakens the early sense of inner persecution and so produced in them the paranoid feelings of being ceaselessly observed by an omnipotent and omniscient enemy. And their impotence to defend its victims, whom at least unconsciously they felt they should protect, aroused in them a deep and abrasive guilt. The easiest escape from the strain of this position, to which they were exposed not for weeks or months but for years, was to reverse their values and idealize the authority they so much feared. Since this adaptation to the society in which they lived involved a widespread distortion of the truth about the world, it may justly be described as a flight into collective withdrawal.

In much the same way, though I know much less about it, one might speculate that the monarchical dictatorship in the Arab Gulf states has created an environment in which it is almost impossible for anyone deeply embedded in the system to be socially or politically active. It is remarkable that repressive political systems seem to promote a shift in the type of conscience of their subordinates away from the humanist and toward the authoritarian end of the scale. There is, for example, a noticeable difference between the official conscience of the average Arab soldier or civil servant and that of the average Arab member of less authoritarian professions. It may be that this would affect their private conscience, too. Those who are inspired to obey or who habitually function only within their terms of reference and never question a policy decision made at a higher level than their own tend to become a little insensitive to the more generous, and perhaps rebellious, promptings of the other kind of conscience. They cease to feel so responsible for injustices that fall outside their province and may even commit injustices, without conscious guilt, when told to do so.

Back to the wider spectrum, many observers have reported a general mood of frustration among Arabs. A clear picture of frustrated masses among Arabs is provided by the feelings of a younger generation drafted into the army in peacetime. In the present condition of the Arab world, conscription may be a military necessity, but is it psychologically beneficial? We already know that it tends to produce a shift in the form of conscience in the Arab from the humanist to the authoritarian end of the scale. What we are concerned with here is its effect on the social and political impulse of individuals. In this respect, we can expect it to be helpful only to those who either enjoy and find their natural outlet in the service or are already lethargic about other occupations because their confidence in their creativeness has been lost. The feeling of being part of authority provides security for those who cannot find a creative outlet outside the army. The individuals' psychological remuneration drives them to increase their assertiveness in authority.

Arabs, who have been subjected for generations to the authoritarian regime that permeates and is reproduced in the family unit, acquire strict and indeed ferocious superegos. The external despotism is supported by, and a counterweight to, the internal tyranny. If it is not too severe, this relieves rather than exacerbates the sense of inner persecution. Such people are seldom aware of any widespread wish for freedom. But as a result of defeat in war, or of conspiracy, or even of a voluntary abandonment, freedom may be thrust upon them. Then when their external authority is suddenly removed, they may feel lost without it and more than ever exposed to persecution from within. The result may be a widespread paranoia. Again, the result could be expressed by the disintegration of society into factions passionately hostile to each other. Something of the sort happened in Lebanon after the collapse of the state, and it may happen in Syria, Iraq, Algeria, and other Arab states if the present regimes collapse.

The impulse to worship may express either spontaneous gratitude to what is loved or a compulsive idealization of what is feared. It would seem that the second motive is often stronger than the first and that many of those who believe in the greatness of a leader cease to worship him as soon as they cease believing him to be a threat.

At present, the main competitor of Arab state authority is political philosophy in the form of religious fundamentalism of which there are many forms. And here too we can observe that the sort of welfare state which is both liberal and benevolent seems to inspire a much less intense devotion than most Arab authoritarian states, which are without pity or sorrow in their treatment of ordinary individuals.

This defense against persecutory anxiety, in which a sadistic superego is projected and then idealized, is in my view one of the greatest impediments to the achievement of transparency of vital issues in Arab societies. Again, in using the splitting mechanism of the self in the study of Arab individuals, the child who is sometimes satisfied, sometimes frustrated by parents not only loves and hates them intensely but, in accordance with his own emotions, conceives them in unconscious fantasy to be both loveable and hateful to extreme degrees. These extreme objects, however, are either kept apart from the beginning or split in the process of being formed. The bad half is the prototype of all subsequent persecutors and is made yet blacker by the projection into it of all the child's aggression toward the good half, which in turn is idealized more as a protection against the bad half. In this way two concepts—one of absolute goodness, the other of absolute evil—are built up and remain in unconscious fantasy to distort the individual's subsequent assessments of his role and others' in society.

The idea here is that such early splitting mechanisms tend to distort Arab political thinking inasmuch as this is associated with intergroup relations. The unrealistic exaggerations of the virtue and greatness of Arabs to their own nation and the vices of their enemies is an example of that, and even in relation to domestic politics, one faction may be wiser than another or more concerned with common welfare. But each side often seems to feel, after suppressing their guilt, that it alone has a monopoly on wisdom and virtue and that its opponents are all naive.

Depressive guilt begins, as psychologists recognize, when the children first realize that they have hated, and in fantasy destroyed, the very objects they most need. Such fantasies are usually a direct result of their ambivalence.[49] But it soon appears in a different situation, in which they feel they have deserted or betrayed a good object because of their terror of a bad object.

The projection of guilt among Arabs as manifested in their culture presupposes its denial, another defense that sometimes seems to operate almost independently. Arabs are by nature ferocious. Bedouins used to prey for the most part on their own tribes, developing in the process opposite instincts that made them love and protect. Such contradictions often arouse guilt. Again and again, Arabs have supported the leader who promised the most and the best and indirectly expressed their own greed at the expense of others. Yet when the promised benefits, which often could have been obtained at the expense of others, are not delivered, Arabs claim that they have always wished to live at peace and treat everyone as brothers.

Arab leaders exaggerate their promises, and in the process they ignore the very material limitations in the Middle East. In reality, there has never been enough for all in the Arab world, and people have lived by competition. Competition means suppressing the other and sometimes to the extreme. This may generate a feeling of guilt, yet the defense against this guilt aroused by depriving others is to exaggerate their failings, which serves the purpose of denying that any sympathy need be felt for them.

Arab nationalism is a repressive system of ideas and ideals that explain and dictate Arab life. It does not provide room for separate independent Arab states or allow Arabs to exhibit the characteristics of an independent liberal individual. It does not recognize social classes or the rights of minority groups. Arab nationalism often polarizes Arabs into adherents and opponents, such as materialism vs. idealism in philosophy, mechanism vs. vitalism in physiology, capitalism vs. socialism in economics, despotism vs. democracy in politics. Even when rational in their content and structure, polarized beliefs can lead to rivalry, hatred, persecution, and warfare, which is evident in the account of Arab feuds during the last century.

Arab nationalism has had a strong psychological impact on Arabs, both those who believed in it and those who did not. It has been a double-edged sword. As an ideology, it has brought prospective for development. On the other hand, Arab nationalism has always endorsed the stamp of unreason. It has led to wars of anti-imperialism, anti-traditionalism, sectarianism, and fundamentalism in the Middle East. In its mystical notions and impenetrable local doctrines, Arab nationalism has diminished the Arab world throughout the second half of the twentieth century, causing a psychological retreat to the individual self and giving rise to what is worse, Islamic fundamentalism. The latter is more alarming, especially in regard to their stimulating mass appeal and their ability to produce pathetic omnipotence that results in more fear and anxieties among the Arab minorities.

In addition, along with Kant and Freud, I believe that fear should be judged not only by the criterion of truth and common sense but also by the criterion of science and psychology. Fear can serve the ends of radical evil and lead to abuses of power and violence, culminating in crimes against people. Absolute monarchies before the formation of modern states in the Arab world were not totally despotic. Most minorities were given relative autonomy or freedoms. It was only after independence, supposedly made safe for democracy under the banner of nationalism, that Arab dictatorships achieved unprecedented control over the bodies and minds of the masses, by the use of systematized terror and delusional systems of ideology.

The outstanding phenomena of Nasser in Egypt and Saddam Hussein in Iraq were not just a matter of Arab leaders' psychosis or paranoia, of their omnipotence and grandiosity, or issues of leaders' individual psychology. This political reality began as a romance between the leader and the nation in an ecstatic, orgiastic love embrace, using all the modern paraphernalia of mass visceral excitement, the illusion of being loved by the leader, the common bonds of identification among adherents old and young, the young abandoning parental values to follow the leaders' values. The final outcome of these phenomena demoralized people and materialized in an Arab ideology systematically pursued by a repressive state political system.

Arab leaders have successfully proclaimed that the psyche of the masses is not receptive to half-measures or weakness. They claim that their subjects are like women, whose psychic feeling is influenced less by abstract reasoning than by an indefinable, sentimental longing for complementary strength. The masses, as perceived by the ruling Arab elite, love the strong leader rather than the suppliant. Arab leaders perceive their subjects inwardly as being more satisfied by a doctrine that tolerates no rival. The importance of physical terror against the individual and the masses also became clear in the process. Here, too, we find exact calculation of the psychological effect. Imposing fear, as proclaimed by Arab rulers, could bring about stability in schools and universities, labor unions, the army, and the assembly hall. Stability results from the success of imposing fear. The theory goes on to imply that only those who know the insecurities of people, not from books but from life, can understand such success. When it comes to the use of fear, Arab regimes come into view as masters of mass psychology, and what is called democratic parliaments in the Arab world established to promote freedom and liberty are institutions as corrupted and artificial as the Arab leaders themselves.

3

Arab Political Identity in Crisis

In order to verify, classify, and document the diverse characteristics of individual and group identity (physical, cultural, psychological, and spiritual), one has to link the present with ancient history. The concept of identity at present is increasingly one of concern for scholars interested in political stability. By way of making things simple, the *Oxford Universal Dictionary* emphasizes personality and individuality and stresses the quality of inseparable association between the two as a central element in the definition of identity. However, to indulge in the utility of identity for better understanding of politics, political psychologists assert that identity is usually a reaction to internal and external forces and an array of insecurities.

Aspects of identity are attended by social psychologists dealing mostly with conflicting societies.[1] However, the overall research on this subject does not highlight the link between the psychosocial aspect of individual identity and that of political affiliation. Political identity is hard to define and difficult to assess. It has been claimed that this concept is as indispensable in political and social analysis as it is unclear in its enormity. Despite its complexity and relative ambiguity, the concept of political identity has a significant explanatory value that could not be substituted in the study of intergroup relations, social and political conflict, stability, and predicament of political systems.

It is important to incorporate to the study of political identity the dichotomy between the *I* and the *Me* in defining the self and the neo-Freudian distinction of self and ego. This dichotomy is employed to study the monolithic individuals, especially in how they passively respond to external contingencies.

In identifying themselves as Arabs, most individuals in the Arab regions take pride in highlighting their unique selves and the immediate group to which they feel they belong. Ironically, identity among Arabs is not exclusively a self-definition. It is a feedback to external imposition. Identity is a label used by Arabs to perceive, categorize, treat, cooperate with, or mistreat one another. While no comprehensive study has emerged to bridge this duality between the adherents of self-perceived as contrasted with externally imposed identity, it has become clear from recent events in the Arab world, domestic and regional, that regardless of the identity's true substance, an individual or a group responds cleverly to a sudden and drastic renovation of their political identities.[2]

One of the central problems of current political analysis in the Arab world is the challenge that the individual and group identities pose to concepts of citizenship and attempts to create states and/or nations. The role of the newly emerging social, ideological, and religious groups in politics is at once a question of political identity and instability. Although it is fashionable for the Arab nationalists, communists, and Islamists to implicate support to their political tendencies through the harmony of identity politics, some of their recent writings have focused on the lack of homogeneous identity among Arabs. This approach is derived from political thinkers who stressed the multifaceted, flowing, and romantic character of identity rather than reducing it to separable sociological and cultural categories.[3] However, the writers who articulate this more complex understanding of identity in the Arab world have not yet in their writings translated this into clear implications of the recent political transformation, that is, the impact on the Arab world generated by the disintegration of the Soviet Union.

During most of the second half of the twentieth century, others viewed all Arabs as belonging to one nation. They were secondarily identified in terms of their religion, ethnicity, or state. The repeated regional conflicts that led to population dislocation, devastation, and distrust in the Arab political systems made Arabs less certain of their proclaimed political identity. Several Arab states are no longer clear as to whether they constitute more than a mere minority or exploited and abused ethnic or religious groups. In this sense, all Arabs now are experiencing a crisis of political identity.

By crisis of political identity, I mean a potential threat of drastic change in the panorama of Arab entities, that is to say, a structural disruption of the equilibrium required for all national, communal, and individuals' well-being. The turbulence could produce severe repercussions for the socioeconomical environment, for the psychological comfort of both domestic and regional Arab communities, and for regional unity. The consequences adversely affect the political strength of practically all of the standing sociopolitical institutions, be they party, clan, tribe, religion, state, or nation.

The Arab world is currently witnessing confusion in the meaning and role of personal and political identity. Traditional institutions that have played major roles in the shaping of their previous identity are on the decline. They are frequently replaced by less tolerant, less benevolent, and more militant modalities. Major criteria, symbols, and classes of identity are in a process of change. Both individuals and communities are undergoing painful changes with regard to the definition and consistency of their identities. The results have brought on increased distress, anxiety, and instability within most customary social institutions.

The escalating tensions arising from this identity crisis increase the fear of authority (familial, religious, and political). They also account for the widespread violence and strife, unproductiveness and chaos, the decline of politeness, and the emergence of spontaneous alarm throughout. Among the tasks facing the Arab world that we must investigate is the exploration of the mounting fear inasmuch as it explains the rise and fall of the cohesive role of identity. From these assessments we must determine whether the changes that are taking place are thwarted, detested, or adaptable. Are group will and social and political policies capable of having a significant impact on new developments that are the products of activist socioeconomic and religious forces?

Traditionally, studies of Arab identity were accompanied by an elaborate derivation detailing the major assemblage of human identity. These consisted of families, languages, territories, and cultural heritage. These four categories have long remained the core of Arab identity studies. Before the Iraqi-Kuwaiti crisis, Arab nationalism was a subject of strong elitist as well as popular interest. With modern Arab mass migrations, population dislocations, and concentration in urban areas, established studies on the Arabs barely satisfy simple curiosities of bridging the new reality to social, economic, and psychological roots. By the same token, the study of linguistics has failed not only to unravel the historical mysteries of Arab peoples and civilizations but also to aid with the still deficient aptitude of Arab communications. A new awareness by Arabs of geography and of how people live in Western societies manifests an aspect of the new reality in the Arab world. Increasing overseas travel among Arabs has made the meaning of lands more understandable, yet also produced a growing awareness of how brutally Arab authorities treat Arab visitors and how harsh the divisions of the Arab world through politically or militarily imposed boundaries can be.

The studies of the family, language, country, and nationality, as accepted components of human identity, supply a rich background from which one could seek a broader understanding of the composition of identity. However, it is with political psychology that we understand Arab dramas of alienation, multiple identities, and the identity crisis of being a nonentity. It is through political psychology that scholarship could determine whether predicament's impact on identity is likely to be productive mostly of conflict and strife, or whether it may contribute, instead, to a resentful societal mosaic. Most important, projected social and political studies if associated with psychology could formulate an insight that could help explain the peculiarity of the diverse communities and individuals of the Arab world.

From a psychological perspective, identity originates from fear. The fear of being a nonentity that drives people to desire an identity. Neurobiologists have asserted in their histological and embryological studies that humans are born with an undeveloped brain and with no sense of identity. The baby is unable to perform organized movements, to talk, or to understand language and other sensory inputs. In the absence of sensory inputs, the brain's neurons won't develop and will remain in the infantile stage.[4]

Children first develop by learning how to overcome their fears. Fear is intrinsic but not evident to the child. Children negate their fear by association with their parents. They generate confidence by imitating those who are close to them, thus identifying with their actions, speech, and responses to various situations. This means that the pattern of growing does not reflect an act of the child's individual logic but is an imprinting of complex rational-free behavior in the brain through habituation. Thus, the human self and human identity in the first few stages of development are both intrinsically products of fear rather than of genetic makeup.

The infant brain lacks not only the essential mechanisms for survival but also the capacity to choose sensory information that shapes its own development. It is logical to assume that the impact on personal growth rests on the memory and experience collected from the surrounding group in how to overcome fear and generate security.[5] In most stable societies, success is determined by the group's ability to relax the conditions that cause the duress of fear. In traditional psychoanalytic theory, fear is as basic as the life-promoting drives and does not presuppose an environmental contextual cause.[6]

On the other hand, fear normally is presumed to be a reaction elicited by the hardship of the environment. Dynamically speaking, there is a direct causal link between being hurt and the outgrowth of fear. Thus, we are accustomed to reacting with fear when threatened. Threats drive us to develop defense mechanisms through identifying with groups.

In Arab culture, it is socially expected that a distressed individual should become aggressive toward the causes of his fear. When he does not respond with hostility, his group may speculate that he lacks courage. Rejected as a coward, some individuals react with absurd violence. Such formulation is consistent with the psychological orientation of drive theory, which sees fear as a natural phenomenon and not one that must necessarily be provoked by threats from without.[7] In the case of provocation, surely, threats can be expected as a driving force. Dynamically, however, threats merely facilitate natural preexisting tendencies of fear, rather than representing the cause of the fear reaction, and socially it becomes a criterion for individual refinement and stratification.

Cooper outlines the major controversy in fear-response theory concerning the coming together of the fear and response.[8] Originally presented as an intrapsychic phenomenon oriented at impulse (or drive) derivatives, the construct has been elaborated by object relation theory to include defenses against fears derived from object loss, environmental failure, and poor self-concept. Brenner, moreover, suggests that any process may be classified as fear response if it diminishes anxiety.[9] In drive theory, however, fear responses are oriented primarily at avoiding recognition of anxiety and psychic pain. Self-restraint against the open expression of fear is positively valued in most societies, especially in the Middle East, and precludes negative personal repercussions. The anticipation of negative consequences is often cited popularly as eliciting self-control for the sake of self-protection. Such a formulation does not meet the definitive criteria of fear-reaction within drive theory. It does, however, meet the broader object relation criteria where defense mechanisms may serve to maintain or preserve a view of the self or the object that, without it, would signify overriding anxiety.[10]

In *Orientalism,* Edward Said refers to the fear of being inferior and elaborates on the alternatives of counteridentity, exodus or escape from identity, and national or local particularism. In fact, Arab societies have reacted with kinds of departures in eloquent and nearly passionate language, to the point of almost abandoning the aspect of political counterattack. What motivates these trends, at least in part, is the depressing political performance of almost all Arab countries, especially the rise of opinionated types of cultural and religious fundamentalism in many parts of the Middle East and elsewhere. Said is selective in denouncing this depressing record. Almost everywhere in the non-Western world, he writes, the effort to homogenize and isolate populations in the name of nationalism (not liberation) has led to colossal sacrifices and failures. The rise of nationalism and fundamentalism has led to the upsurge of identity politics of a narrow and intolerant kind. In the Middle East, more energy is spent bolstering the idea that to be Syrian, Iraqi, Egyptian, or Saudi is a sufficient end than is spent thinking critically, even fearlessly, about the Arab national program itself. Hence identity has been a process of coming to know about others. In the broader setting, the insistence on local identity or counteridentity is only the reverse side of the other identity; both are expressions of essentialization, to be an entity, and thus two sides of the same coin.

From their identity perspective and from within their own sectors in society, Islamists and Arab nationalists attack the West, or Americanization, or imperialism, with little more attention to detail. They provide no critical differentiation, discrimination, or distinction to what is good and what is bad and why any of it has been given to them by the West. Edward Said finds that the process of decolonization and national liberation has given way to bad consequences in the Arab world through petty provincialism. Said feels that counteridentity based on fear reaction in the Arab world appeals to pure or authentic Islam, or Arabism. And he says that all had a strong response, without sufficient consciousness, that those ethnicities and spiritual essences would come back to demand a very high price from their successful adherents. It is not clear why the West is to be blamed for that.

Yet again, and without negating the identity derived from a grand sociopolitical movement like decolonization, the problem lies in a national consciousness emanating from all kinds of fear and anxieties. Much the same could be said about the insecurities of a rising religious consciousness. The price is the destabilization of national security and a rise in separatist identities.

Individuals respond to stimulus in their environment as they construe it and not to intellectually assumed reality as such. There exists no absolute reality. They respond to the images they have drawn to typify reality. It should be noted, however, that the social actor is an individual whose understanding of political reality is his point of view. Logically, the actor must decide what to do and how to identify with the nature and sources of his actions.

People live in social constraints that condition their image of themselves and the ways they think and act, without determining them in any complete sense. Recent development in the ongoing revolution of technologies especially in the different domains of communications, transportation, and education facilitate greater individuation of selves leading to more self-psychic fears and anxieties. The impact of that is more evident in Arab cities than in rural areas. Although it is downgrading the institutionalization of the individual, the Arab world is also making individualism optional.

Individualism has a multiple impact on political identity. One is the possible encouragement for personality and character formation ranging from radicalism to deliberate subordination and strong collective orientations. Somewhat paradoxically, this context of identity and value pluralism makes all positions appear more or less as individual and thus somewhat arbitrary choices, even when they are presented as natural, traditional, or beyond human disposition.

It is safe to assert that living conditions shape what people are, how they view themselves, and what they do. Of course, the sociocultural context is not the only factor, although it does condition and it is a prime conjuncture for the possibility of human consciousness, orientations, and behavior. The other factor that could be proclaimed and with considerable evidence as a result of individualism is that the human psyche is embedded in a cognitive structure, commonly known as an individual's perspective or mental ability to perceive. If the individual is individualistic, then this tendency sets the parameters of identity and personality and is defied with difficulty. Individuals are not merely the result of their surroundings. But if they alienate themselves from the mandates of their surroundings, they risk being negated as human beings.

In this context, modern Arab characters are different from those of fifty years ago. They are changing now under the impact of affluence and new technologies. While I stress the role of individualism as a factor, the anticipated changes are the result of a confluence of factors, none of which is fully determinative. It could be argued that the essential differences between the traditional (old) and the new individualistic psyche stem from the development of a powerful superego (conscience).[11] To a group-oriented individual, power lies outside the self, although the boundaries of self and nonself are not clear. One seeks power by following rules set by the gods, through the charismatic leader or tightly knit community structures. The problem is that, unless the gods continually speak, their message dims. Social organization of any kind, therefore, requires rigid and continuous community controls. Communities adapt to their environment, and they rarely attempt to master it beyond that which is necessary for survival. The strange and the different are suspect. Forbidden impulses are projected upon them. The superego of a group-oriented Arab is largely located outside himself, in the form of spiritualists or gods whom he tries to please. He has little sense of himself as an individual who can exercise power over his environment in a consistent manner so as to serve his needs.

The individualistic Arab has proved to be different from an individualistic person in the West. While psychoanalysis tends to emphasize the punitive qualities of the superego, it is not without positive aspects.[12] By providing an inner mechanism of control, the superego permits the individualistic Arab to develop a stronger sense of self. The group-oriented Arab believes that God helps individuals who obey his commands. Individualistic Arabs attempt to overcome obstacles by living up to their inner ideals. The source of power is within and not external. Furthermore, the sublimated energy derived from the individualistic Arab's internal control, of both erotic and aggressive drives, fosters the development of the ego. This enables him to examine and to manipulate nature, to adapt to new circumstances, and to be creative. It also enables the individualistic Arab to recognize fear of the unknown and fear of other groups as he develops rational ideals for understanding nature. In these ways the development of superego and ego strength permit the emergence of the flexible Arab individual to decide on an identity.

Max Weber demonstrates that the unintended consequences of Christianity, and more specifically Calvinist doctrines, included the emergence of the modern world in the form of liberal capitalism, that is, a capitalist economic system associated with individualism and gradual, if imperfect, political identification.[13] Weber emphasizes the capitalist side of the equation, but the contribution of this cultural complex to political identification, although well documented,[14] does not provide a comprehensive assessment fit for all societies.

Perceptibly, none of the assessments drawn is complete in the evaluation of Arabs. Some individualization occurs in all societies. It is also clear that every great historical civilization has been accompanied by a heightening of superego development, usually based on the emergence of a new, more universalistic religious system. It is possible, moreover, that in some Arab civilizations superego development was comparable to that of the West. In line with Weber's argument, however, cultural developments in the Arab world were unusual from the outset. First, the emergence of a prophetic religion gave a peculiar intensity to the superego. Second, the emphasis in Islam rather than in Arab societies was on an individual rather than a communal relationship with God. Third, religious-cultural imperatives stressed general, universal, and moral rules. Finally, great emphasis was placed upon limiting the unresponsiveness in the service of worldly harshness, that is, fulfilling one's obligations through contribution to his religious society. Islamic identity, whatever its limitations, historically has encouraged rationality, emotional complexity, growth, and the capacity for a unique political identity.

As it absorbed and merged with many civilizations, Islam strongly emphasized control of the passions, producing a similar end result in the Arab world via a culture of fear and shame. Indeed, Arabs created a great and long-lasting premodern empire. The Islamic Empire was Europe's superior in wealth and practical technical achievement until the seventeenth century. However, the Ottoman Islamic view of nature did not encourage a breakthrough to a modern scientific worldview. They exercised the element of fear to contain the Arabs. This practice surrounded Arabs with a network of kin and other social obligations inhibiting the growth of that individualism which played so important a role in the break with tradition in Europe. It also encouraged, or at least did not discourage, magical solutions to problems among the general populace.

Again, in demonstrating a reallocation in the general approach of Weber, individualism as a concept has become sufficiently pervasive today that using it carries a certain risk of being misunderstood. The most everyday meaning refers, but not in a precise way, to recent developments in urban finance, individual accounts in banks, individual trade, and the actions of business corporations in reshaping society along an individual division of labor. Other senses focus on the spread of civil and criminal law, which essentially deals with the individual as its basic party. In dealing with political identity in the so-called modernizing Arab states, my use of the term *individualism* seeks to include these meanings while not restricting it to them.

Systemically, Arab individualism is developing by the creation and spread of several differentiated but interdependent societal structures. The main organizing principles of these structures center on function, technique, or instrumentality. Important examples of these structures are a capitalist individualistic economic structure, an individualistically state-centered political structure, an individualistic scientific-technological structure, a structure for mass information media directed to individuals, a medicinal health structure, a school-centered education structure that deals with the individual as its basic component, and an individually centered religious structure. Each of these individualisms has its typical cultural dimension on political identity.

The development of service structures in the Arab world is not easy to summarize. Arabs have responded to the spread of the initially Western technical structures because there has been a great deal of variation, much of it centered on precisely the identity and character issues under discussion here. Essentially, as the Western powers spread their influence, their greatest success was in extending the reach of the service structures, particularly the capitalist economic, the scientific-technological, the academic-educational, and the political structure as entities in the form of the territorially bordered and sovereign states. The development is most striking in the case of the political system where various nationalist movements have created an array of nationally identified states, comparable to those forming and already formed in the West. As a transporter of these developing individualistic service structures, the West is still in the process of perpetuating the spread all around the Arab world, not in any sense evenly, but certainly for the most part effectively.[15]

The capitalist economic system that essentially promotes individualism is an accepted tendency in the Arab world, even in the proclaimed socialist states. These service structures associated with the capitalist system actually promoted change in the political identity tracks in the Arab world. In a capitalist system, anything could become an individual economic commodity; even people could become commodities. The personal or group identities of the producers and consumers become secondary in the sense that what is important is the economic capacity to offer for sale or to buy, not as such one's family, one's level of education, one's religious behavior, and so forth. In this sense it has become accepted, not necessarily practiced, that political qualification generally does not depend on ascribed or achieved statuses. Although wealthy individuals have advantage, nonetheless, educational attainment is in principle, and very often in fact, open to all willing individuals. Laws are developed on the assumption that all individuals are equal, and scientific or artistic achievements depend on the quality of the individual producing the science and art, not on the social background and group affiliation of the artist or scientist. This means that the prospects of sublimation of intrinsic fears are assuming new individualistic dimensions.

It is worth asserting, for the sake of prospects in political identity deviation, that some Arabs are more capitalistic than others and thus have more of the characteristics of individualism. Rich Arabs can send their children to urban and highly qualified schools, and in many cases these children develop economic independence from their parents. Educated Arabs have better access to the legal system and have greater influence over what is produced in the media. We can make similar observations about specific Arab subgroups within regions where most people lack good access to the systems and about regions where the majority are relatively well off. There are privileged Arab individuals and groups in underprivileged regions as well as privileged ones. Yet these advantages accrue because these people and groups have been given leverage to participate significantly in their systems, not because they are better people.[16]

In the power centers in the Arab world we see a strong desire for independence, and the service structures are concerned only with those aspects of a person which are functionally relevant: ability to pay, ability to learn, state of health, willingness to be an audience, and so forth. Service structures therefore undermine the strong tendency in a fair number of personally and socially relevant matters, including the formation of personal and group identities, and thus much about the reaction of personal and group fear. Moreover, the total effect on identity and character of all the service structures does not exhaust such determinations, although it obviously will play a significant role in most cases. Arabs in urban areas have become predominantly occupied with a lower-scale identity reflecting themselves as professionals (managers, professors, doctors, politicians, artists, etc.). In all these cases, the service structures force Arabs to spend more energy on their professional identity than on their time-honored political identity.

Individualism is not new in the Arab world; it had its origins in Islamic religion. Islam, like Christianity, preached that the individual believer was fundamentally on his own in a direct relationship with God. The ultimate judgment of God is going to be on the individual and not on his group. Again here, if we are to focus on the development of individualism in children, at least in principle, what are called modern schools in their system of education develop the individualistic aspects in the personality of the student at all stages of education all the way to the university level. Students are graded and are held solely responsible for their conduct; the social class of that child is irrelevant. All these developments, although from one perspective constituting the rise not only of the individual but of individualism, were also manifestations of the exceedingly complex process of the increasing dominance of the newly introduced service structures in the Arab world.

The shaping of Western individuation in the Arab world as a consequence of the rise to dominance of service structures in urban areas did not just bring individualist and rationalist attitudes in its wake; it marginalized the old structures. Counterstructural tendencies were always part of the picture, not simply as deviance and thus with moral condemnation, but as positively valued and integral aspects of the overall Arab development. Thus, alongside or perhaps in vibration with the emphasis of many Arab thinkers on individualism, we see the search for the more rooted and communal but still from an individualistic perspective. In an attempt to rationalize their standards, individuals who claim Arab identity or any other regional identities in the Arab world referred to tradition, but in a highly selective way, taking only those stories, traits, heroes, territories, and other elements suitable for their ideals, leaving out other possibilities and adding new innovative characteristics where necessary. These were imaginary traditions, not in the sense of pure fabrications but in the sense of discoveries that responded to the requirements of the day.[17]

Arab identity and concomitantly Arab nationalism, however, would not have had a great impact if they had not echoed the development of the modern system of a sovereign state that is based on the equality among all individuals. In terms of identity and character, the Arab culture has certainly been an important source of both. The promoters of Arab identity and Arab nationalism typically include in their self-descriptions ideal national individual identities—above all, the patriot. Nonetheless, the other systemic sources of identity and character remain, as does the incompleteness of such determinations.

We might therefore speak of at least three competing sources of personal identity and character in the present Arab societies. There is the imagined community, most notably the nation, but not just the nation, because different ethnic identities without nationalist aspirations also fall under this heading. There are the technical structures, including the political, the economic, the mass media, sports, education, and the religious. And there are the fears and idiosyncrasies of "self." Identity questions have played a significant role in the overall spread of the modern Arab state systems and thus contributed to the formation of individualistic societies, at least in the urban areas. I focus again on the idea of nation. Without doubt, the greatest impetus for the formation of Arab nationalist identity over the last century has been the spread of the service structures themselves. When we examine such movements within the Arab world, the prime motive has been anticolonial. That is, the different urban individuals, not necessarily by origin, most often are led by newly arisen elites in local major cities who have sought to take local control of the levers of modern power that is derived from economic, political, educational, artistic, and media institutions originally owned by the imperial West. Or they have sought to increase local power and influence to match that of the local colonizer. In doing so, Arab nationalism was undermined to give rise to regional and state nationalism.[18]

Regional and state identities were promoted in the name of the Arab nation at large and for the supposed benefit of the people deemed indigenous to the region. In other words, the collectivity of the nation or its equivalent served as the justification for the efforts to appropriate the techniques of service structure power. Identity, far from being a game of idle introspection, is a strategy for control and for power competition.

Then again, from the perspective of group-oriented individuals, the Arab world is not simply a capitalist economic system from which we would conclude that it favors the individualistic and rationalistic entrepreneur as the paragon of virtue and character. Nonetheless, the Arab world is by no means fundamentally Western in a broad cultural sense unless one insists that anyone who masters the levers of service structures is thereby already Western. Individualism and what we deem to be Western cultural styles are indeed possible in the Arab world. But the rugged individual who depends on his own resources is not the only such possibility. What are sometimes called Arab values, referring somewhat imprecisely to a more group-centered orientation with a greater sense of community, are also possible and just as modern. Individualism does not necessarily mean isolationism; rather, it means a plurality of different and justifiable personal conduct that has individual of liability both in identity and integrity.

Arab societies depend on a balance between communitarian and individualistic orientations.[19] Current trends of analysis assert that Arab values assume that Arabs are more collective whereas Westerners are more individualistic. Although the comparison is undoubtedly to some extent acknowledgeable, it does point indirectly to the possibility of conceiving difference in terms of individual and group memory of perceptive identity and its corresponding influences on the political reality of Arabs. The assumption here is that one basic dimension of identity is derived from anxiety. Some fears are derived from the individual's memory, which plays a primary role in psychological continuity accounts of personal identity.

However, in claiming that memory is constitutive of personal identity, one faces the objection that since the concept of memory presupposes personal identity, it should not be used in the analysis of that concept. Parfit responded to this obstacle by devising a new criterion of personal identity. He stated that memory connections are replaced with quasi-memory connections.[20] The phenomenon of quasi-memory is best explained by the following: When an older member of a group speaks in a gathering about stressful experiences, younger listeners may remember these as events they experienced themselves. They forget that these were stories told to them.

When it comes to the psychology of memory continuity, claiming that an Arab remembers a past episode does not mean that this person has experienced this episode, though someone must have experienced it. Thus, the issue of common identity is related to the question of what makes part of a person's memory the same as another's memories. Imprinted memories at an early age are mechanical in the sense that the brain acquires them unreservedly and they do not need to be fed through indoctrination or conscious personal effort. For example, we imitate our parents' practices to the best of our ability without even knowing that other practices exist. In doing this we are adopting a mixture of other individuals' experiences and memories as our own.[21] Pursuing other practices and adopting a new system of action at a later age, though it is plausible, nonetheless requires a great deal of determination and effort.

The rational processes of abstraction usually begin to develop after age seven. Normally, this process is characterized by appreciation and conformity to the existing patterns of one's culture. At this stage of development, a child begins to demarcate his own identity and culture. The assertion here is that it is the time frame of specific social environment and not personal preference that determines the ideological framework of the individual mind. We are not born free. We must learn freedom, replacing automatisms and instinctive responses with intelligent choice based on learning rational behavior. Cultural conditioning, ideological indoctrination, and education in general are transformed into differential characteristics. To put it in pure scientific terms, these differential characteristics modify the anatomy, physiology, and biochemistry of neurons; thus, the experience of each individual leaves material traces stored in intracerebral memory.[22]

Psychologists assert that memory is linked to personal identity. People project their identities through the reflections generated from personal experiences. People do seem to remember doing things that they did not do. A friend once told me he seemed to remember being involved in an armed clash against a militia trying to liquidate his family, even though he did no such thing. He seems to remember doing something that was actually done by his uncle.

In this regard, attention should be given to examining the possible relationship between personal identification, that is, the extent to which he retains the memory generated within his ethnic or social group with all its manifestations of attitudes, values, beliefs, and behaviors as his own, and the level of psychological distress, fear, and anxiety experienced as a consequence of that. The possible impact of psychological distress on identity has received little attention in the available literature.

However, there exists parallel literature to this dimension of identity, the Social Identity Theory and the Self-Categorization Theory.[23] Literature springing from these theories has emphasized that personal identity is only possible when it stems from social identity. The relevance is suitable for studying Arab individuals. It is observable that Arabs realize their personal identities in identifying with a particular social group. It is through interaction with others in a group that the individual comes to realize his personal identity. The significance of this is apparent in the stress and anxiety generated when an Arab changes from the group through which he has developed his personal identity. The individual's inputs in the new group and reflections on him become confusing. This forces the individual to reshape his personal identity. Arabs believe that changing personal identity will lead to a new political identity.

Changing political identity is very stressful. In most cases, Arabs lose proper levels of self-esteem and respect in both their old and new groups. The impact of this is negative on their inter- and intragroup cognitions, attitudes, and behavior.[24] Social scientists articulate the phenomenon of changing one's personal identity as acculturation processes. The central idea here is that when Arabs realize that their political identity is not appropriate to a changing reality, they painfully face the following alternatives: either maintaining or disqualifying their current political identity, and either adopting or rejecting the new reality. The nature of the individual's psychic mentality plays a major role in pursuing a strategy to adopt. The specific Arab factors of fear and anxiety are strong influences in all cases. The degree of fear is always a variable. It is this variable which concludes the level of conformity and admiration derived from belonging to one's exclusive group through a belief in proclaimed group protection. This may carry over to feelings of efficacy, contentment, and good standing to face new dangers and threats in society and environment. On the other hand, if the degree of fear is high, then the individual is compelled to adopt a new political socialization strategy. Options are integration, assimilation, separation, segregation, or marginalization.

In mapping social and political groups in the Arab world, one realizes that within the same Arab society groups have managed to establish sociocultural and ideological islands for themselves, refusing to carry on with the rapid changes and development around them. They maintained their old social and political identity. Yet for practical purposes they cannot detach themselves completely from their wider environment. In this respect the importance of social and political identity is that it provides isolated people with strength and inner resources that enable them to cope with the demands of a new political atmosphere and hence minimizes psychological distress.

However, although sociopolitical identity has been shown to be positively associated with self-esteem, recent research suggests that self-esteem might provide a crucial link between sociopolitical identity and psychological distress. In short, researchers have demonstrated a causal effect of a change in the political environment with special concomitants on the self-perception of individuals who are secondary to these changes.[25]

By the same token, conceptual analyses of responses to self-esteem items suggest that at least two semiautonomous processes operate in judgments about the self. Despite some overlap, the individual facing a new political reality pushes himself through a process of self-evaluation of worth and efficacy at the same time he reflects self-derogation and negative feelings about himself.

Such a prevailing situation in the Arab world is producing multiple personality disorders and problems of morality choices. This is better known as problems of personality and identity coherence. Indirectly it reflects political socialization incoherence. Stability in society is linked to the coherence condition in the political identity of its individuals.[26] The reason is that *citizen* is a term not restricted to the metaphysical; it is a moral or normative and political term as well in the modern state systems. Persons are not only self-conscious intelligent beings; they are supposed to be moral and political agents whose actions influence society and polity, which in turn accords with certain rights. So what I am interested in is what the lack of psychological, political, and identity coherence could tell us about stability in the different states of the Arab world.

Multiple personality disorders among Arabs are associated with the phenomenon of quasi-memory. It is common among Arabs who are witnessing rapid environmental and political change. Socially it is understood as a dissociative disorder in which a person appears to possess more than one distinct personality and sometimes several.[27] Typically there will be a core personality and a number of alternate personalities.

It is important to indicate that multiple personality disorder is a condition that varies drastically. It is only those who suffer from an extreme condition of multiple personality disorder who are considered sick. When a switch occurs, a personality other than the one previously in control will manifest itself. It is mild personality disorder that I am bringing into play where the core personality is always aware of the alternate personalities. The multiple personalities may differ in their behavioral characteristics and even in their social and political responses.

By the same token, it is asserted that most individuals do suffer from multiple identity incoherence. Socially and politically it is understood as a dissolute derangement in which a person appears to possess more than one identity. Commonly there will be a center identity and a number of other identities called convenient convert identities. It is consequential in the context of this analysis to repeat that multiple identity disorder is similar to multiple personality disorder and very much associated together. When a switch occurs, an identity other than the central one will manifest itself socially and politically. The central identity lies in a dormant stage but will stay very much alive.

As already expressed, in mild multiple identity disorder (the use of the term *disorder* is questionable), the different identities are aware of one another's existence. Yet they cannot exclude one another because the individual's center identity needs the other identities to protect it in difficult situations or to meet certain needs. In a society of multicultural groups bound to exist together and in societies witnessing rapid sociopolitical changes, the tendency is high for most individuals to develop multiple identity disorder.[28]

Multiple identities have become common among Arabs. What is relevant for this study is how the notion of coherence informs a moral or normative concept of the person. An orderly way of exploring this phenomenon is to consider what happens during unification therapy for multiple personality disorders and to compare that with the role of governments and the media in trying to unify personality and identity disorder in individuals (social entities) or in citizens (political entities).

In rationalizing what caused the identity fragmentation, one has to look at the total and the particular of the environment within which the individual lives. How does an individual deal with bizarre and extreme political and social oppression? And how does an individual carry on social relations outside his own group and attune to the norms and social life of others? Fragmentation of identity may be an unconscious survival mechanism in response to fear. A system of multiple identities may develop to deal with an environment changing from one of extreme hostility and terror to one that is apparently normal, familiar, and unthreatening. Equilibrium in the manifestations of different identities is essential for psychological sanity. Such equilibrium does involve the trauma of internal revelation of one identity to the other, but the equilibrium sought aims at some form of coherence between the individual and his alternate personalities. It is in this way that Schechtman's coherence condition may be viewed.[29] It is a necessary part of psychological continuity that accounts for personal and political identity.

Through its institutions and propaganda, the government ought to convince all citizens that they have no reason to fear one another because the state protects all, by eliminating motivation for one to hide behind a different personality for protection. If the state accomplishes that, rarely the case in Arab countries, unification of personalities and sociopolitical identities becomes easier. In retrospect, Arab institutions are a source of fear and oppression. It is difficult to see governments in the Arab world capable of reconciling fears because of the political and ideological structures that they sustain to protect continuity of the political status quo.

Because of its significance for the present research, it should be noted here that positive self-esteem partly reflects self-worth, and this is directly related to political identity, that is, pride in cultural group membership or state membership. What is notable here is that negative self-esteem, being partly driven by self-derogation and negative feelings about the self, might be directly related to psychological distress and violence. That is, feeling positive in a group membership identity and negative in self-esteem in a political system and social environment leads to violence. Collective violence is usually the result of the group's sense of self-mastery or self-efficacy in relation to its sense of trust in other groups and the general community.

When a person compliments other people by showing them that he trusts their behavior in a social setting, it is an affront on his behalf to calm his own fears. This starts in the inner circle of social settings. The more that individuals identify with their distinguished group, the more they will believe that they have recourse to external sources of coping.[30] These external coping resources might include, for example, the belief that others are bound to respect a man because of the power that he derives from belonging to a solid group. Reliance of the individual on his own group allows him to solicit advice. In being able to fit in his own group, the individual generates confidence that he will be successful in fitting in society. If all of these feelings go well, the individual demonstrates increased personal and external coping resources and thus a decrease in the likelihood of psychological distress and potential violence.[31]

The primary motive for identifying with a particular social group is enhanced self-esteem. Indeed, unless the individual's social self-esteem is improved, he will not continue to identify with a particular social group.

In the process of development in Arab societies and knowing that societies do not develop unless they change, concomitants have come about in the form of industrialization and urbanization. This has led to the relocation of Arabs outside their immediate group. Most Arabs must relocate to obtain a better quality of life or better job opportunities. It is a potentially stressful change.[32] They leave their favorite group to enter a new, ambiguous social setting. On these grounds, it is plausible that although they might be understandably proud of their cultural heritage, it would also be important for them to be accepted as members in the new location. As part of this process, they would also try to adapt to their new environment.

For the past fifty years, Middle Eastern states have been going through alarming changes in their social structure and witnessing drastic demographical changes. Cities and urban areas have grown to absorb between 60 and 70 percent of the total population of the Arab countries. Although the relationships between the different groups that come to the urban areas remain to be fully assessed, social psychologists have reported that regardless of the level of contact between the newcomers to urban areas, some evidenced a more positive mood, less anxiety, and less irritation, hostility, and aggression toward each other. Yet there are significant instances where the reverse was true.[33] An example of that are the thousands of Egyptians who were killed by Iraqis when they settled in Iraq.

The implication here is that dislocated Arabs who share considerable cultural similarity with the dominant cultural group in the new urban place of abode might be anticipated to be accepted more than groups whose cultures differ markedly from the dominant group. Furthermore, it might be expected that such groups would have a higher relationship between sociopolitical identification and self-esteem than would those with distant cultural orientation.

In sum, the preceding implications indicate that the dislocated sociopolitical identification exerted a major impact on migrant psychological distress. The effect was mediated by the migrant's level of self-esteem. If we correlate between psychological distress and violence, then we can understand why the urban people in the Middle East have the readiness to rebel and undermine their regimes.

Dislocation stress partially stems from memory and quasi-memory. The parent-child relationship with regard to this is linked to the apparent memories that one might have in quasi-remembering the experience of others in similar circumstances. In this sense, quasi-memories can sustain or defuse sociopolitical and personal identity. The condition, roughly speaking, is that the content of the psychological states crucial to all forms of identity must include some element of self-reference. Schechtman thinks that if someone fails to recognize in his memories (or q-memories) experiences that he seems to have had, those states ought to be considered irrelevant to personal identity.[34] Should psychological coherence be regarded as essential to exploration of a person's identity or merely as something central and important to it? It is essential to explore the effects on multiple personality disorder. The point I have in mind here is allegiance to leaders (father image) in the old sociopolitical setting and allegiance to the leaders of the new sociopolitical reality.

From the perspective of identity, the question is how an Arab living among diverse minority groups in a state-oriented political environment can identity with leadership at a time when traditional Arab societies accomplish that through nonrational means like tribal rituals and stories. Arab nationalists have been critical of the masks and agendas of religious and tribal societies and the nature by which Arabs rally around the traditional leader, yet they have failed to provide an adequate process for leadership away from the tradition into modern statehood.

The essential premise of selecting, accepting, and maintaining a leader among Arabs is related to identity that has to be accomplished with pride, and culturally speaking, one cannot have pride without having a known legitimate father. In the Arab culture, illegitimate children face a traumatic chain of painful experiences. This explains the association of father-leader veracity of defense mechanism that the individual constructs so that intrapsychic maneuvers are devised by the ego to avoid the negative psychological effects of the anxiety of having no father. From an analytic perspective, identity is a virtual redress to an event that elicited the anxiety response. Remorse does not modify or ameliorate the anxiety/memory constellation that resulted from psychological injury. In this respect, identity for Arabs is not a matter of option; it is a matter of being or existing, whether we look at it from a religious or cultural dictate.

Phenomenologically, identity is related to past and present events. By the nature of things, events become inaccessible in the sense that they cannot be modified as soon as they become known. All that is left is the memory of the event and its repercussions, whether fantasized or actual. The only tool available to the Arab individual ego in coping with past events and its emotional casualties is through the defensive function, since the only residue of the event is the experienced pain.

The precipitating factor of the defensive maneuver is usually a disturbing emotion, but it does not imply a substitute, especially for Arabs in terms of perceiving themselves not under the shield of a father or a leader.

Typically, the dynamic agent is fear, shame, or some other related threat to the ego. It can therefore be expected that defensive mechanisms will be concentrated in the affective domain as well. As a rule, defenses that are associated with normal functioning do involve the modification, distortion, or predication of emotions.

Defense minimizes the effects of a threatening experience by shifting information from the conscious to the unconscious and vice versa. Oppressive actions by a father or a leader prompt the individual not only to mobilize his defense but also to relegate oppression to the unconscious. But the very mechanism involves a process that is unconscious as well. Repression as a form of defense is dynamic inasmuch as it corresponds uniquely to the development of the individual's goals and process of implementations. Colloquially referred to as "forgetting," repression typically focuses on affect or memories that have the potential to disturb the individual. The unconscious stores memory that individuals can recall when similar occasions occur.

Stability in such disturbing political conditions in the Arab world and the continuation of rule of the oppressive ruling elite are related to two well-known mechanisms that are in turn associated with psychological repression: denial and suppression. Literature of psychology generally depicts denial as an unconscious mechanism, whereas suppression is described as being conscious or semiconscious.[35] Differentiating among these constructs is crucial to the conceptualization of defense and thus explaining the identification with leaders in the Arab world.

Freud originally formulated denial, as a concept, in describing the scenario where the little boy sees a little girl in the nude but denies her lack of a penis.[36] Psychologists often use denial as a synonym for repression. Subsequent theorists, however, circumscribed the term to refer only to the distortion of actual (perceptual) reality, in contrast to memory distortion. As such, denial is a primitive response often associated with early childhood. While denial may be seen as adaptive, suppression is a mechanism that blocks memories and perceptual reality. However, it differs from repression significantly in that threatening material is not repressed; it is simply denied attention. In this sense leaders are not confronted, especially if they could not be replaced; they are simply denied inward attention. Cognitive psychology refers to this as preconscious vs. conscious. The preconscious refers to the domain that can become conscious merely by having attention directed onto it. Suppression can be conceptualized as interfering with the attention that would bring threatening preconscious material into the conscious.

In that formulation, an Arab frustrated by an aggressive leader with whom he identifies expresses his hostility in an aggressive drive naturally and without defensive distortion elsewhere, such as in displacement or blaming the self or finding someone to blame, preferably a perceived enemy. Displacement is a basic defense mechanism where the ego substitutes a new object instead of a threatening object.[37] The hallmark of displacement is the nondistortion of the original impulse with the defensive strategy oriented solely at object substitution. In altering the direction of hostility, the defense is derived from a movement away from the original object rather than a movement toward the substituted object. Indeed, the substitution is apt to engender secondary problems, as the role of the aggressive object is reproductive. In a threatening situation, acting out can serve as a defense by shifting conscious focus from affect to activity. Acting out is often featured in the literature as a form of resistance to analytic treatment. In a less analytic and more pragmatic approach, some social theorists differentiate between situations where the target of hostility is the objective cause of the problem and situations where it is not. From one point of view, the overt expression of aggression toward another might be thought to indicate the absence of defense. However, Hilgard pointed out that the direct expression of hostility is defensive when the object of hostility is considerably removed from the object of original conflict.[38] In a similar line of investigation, acting out has been operationalized as turning against the object, which operates by transforming the experience of being threatened into an experience of making the threat.[39] Is turning against the object limited to aggression?

Anna Freud conceptualized the defense mechanism of identification with the aggressor to elucidate the phenomenon where one joins with his persecutors in attacking himself.[40] An example is the typical resolution of the Oedipal conflict, where the boy identifies with his father in an attempt to counter his own instinctual expression. While introjection is the mechanism of the identification process, this style utilizes intrapunitiveness as dynamic. Moreover, the process of attacking oneself also brings relief from threat-utilizing dynamics that are congruent with those of acting out, since the activity of self-attack precludes the emotional experience of persecution. Some theoreticians have therefore classified identification with the aggressor as a subset of acting out.[41]

Tracing the defensive evolution of identification with the aggressor in the Arab world elucidates further its differential classification. Given that experiencing aggression from an oppressive source that cannot be dealt with functionally precipitates the response, the question nevertheless remains: What is the affect that is being defended against here? Assuming that it is the anxiety resulting from the aggression, which is the primary object of defense, then identification with the aggressor can be conceptualized as combining the dynamics of fear, anxiety, and protection.

Researchers who deal with responses of persecuted ethnic minorities, however, stress that the most threatening feeling in such circumstances that precipitates defense is the hostility toward the oppressor, rather than the aggression coming from him.[42] This was most clearly evident in the civil war in Lebanon, when most of the minority groups under severe stress manifested a violent act of turning against themselves, since the victim defensively becomes the object of one's own hostility as a substitution for the oppressor against whom aggression is impossible.

4

Nationalism

From the Power of Fear to the Fear of Power

Nationalism is a disordered cognitive reality defined by a number of constraints, and its study consists of a vast arrangement of models, approaches, and techniques. The diverse definitions of nationalism can be widely shared or idiosyncratic, action oriented or observer based. Many of the constructed nationalism models make sense in relation to each other and can be linked to form a complex, innovative study. *Nationalism* is an elastic term and could be theoretically recognized in both the minds and actions of individuals and empirically observed in social settings, economic systems, political institutions, and other formal and informal organizations. Again, nationalism could be exposed through human behavior and linguistic expressions.

Political psychology is still in the process of developing new reflections on the study of ideology—the individuals' psychic impact on the notion of nationhood and visa versa. Thus far, such reflections have been exclusively conducted on the study of leaders' idiosyncrasies. Such studies, though, are widely addressed; they are more propositions for solving methodical problems than they are comprehensive trends. On the other hand, one must admit that political psychology has been an interdisciplinary enterprise. It is not at home in any of the academic or professional disciplines, and as the literature testifies, its epistemological status is notably ambiguous. Consequently, its relationship to the organized yet anarchical political world is always somewhat peculiar and even at times opinionated.

Nationalism at its base is a power relationship among larger groups. Individuals empowered by their groups redirect their anxieties to the intersubjective world by assigning themselves the value of self-mastery, albeit one in which their limited ability to master the self is fully acknowledged.[1] If we are to explore the social and political context of nationalism from a psychoanalytic perspective and we focus on the tension between authority, power, and freedom, I believe that Freud's vision of the political world could provide insights and analogies. Freud deals precisely with the theories of psychical conflict. This brings us to our central concern in nationalism: fear, anxiety, and the conceptualization of the self.

Again, I present Freud's open-ended thinking about the ego and the general tendency to see any unification or synthesis of the self as a falsifying and/or violent imposition. The starting point in this argument is monadic, that is, the elementary unextended individual isolation, and the great enigma that has to be accounted for once we find ourselves within the imaginary representative molten rock of the unconscious. This marks the emergence of separation and at the same time self-realization of being an extension to others. Thus we have, in virtually its purest form, the antinomy of individual and society. But who comes first—the individual or society? Is sociality added on to us from outside, or does it emerge from our inner needs?[2]

The question of who comes first could be passed up if we recognize that the monadic experience of the self is a defense against our unavoidable immersion in a sea of fear and anxieties. We do not come into the world enclosed within an impermeable shell. The most that can be said is that we are protected from the bombardment of postnatal stimuli by a kind of sensuously encoded residue of intrauterine experience. From the outset, this psycho-physiological womb is a defense. Moreover, this relatively global defense is not impenetrable, and as the infant rapidly gains the mental ability to experience some elementary forms of fear and anxiety, his awareness of his surroundings increases.[3] Interaction is then experienced as persecutory and paranoid, the absence of interaction becomes a schizoid or even autistic (relating to mentation that is more or less subjective) retreat, and the mediating link between the two conditions is broken. This, in its most primitive form, is the antinomy of group and individual that is played out among psychologists.[4] But again, being outside the womb for a long time, the individual mind is infiltrated by the experience of resistance and resistance overcome—in short, a tendency for subsequent relationships of power. It is also a situation where the womb becomes the size of a large territorial entity (nation), but the only way to attain protection within this entity is through nationhood and nationalism.

The individual has always been a member of a group, even if his membership consists of behaving in such a way that reality is given to an idea that he does not belong to a group at all. The individual is a group animal in competition with others. Struggle with the group and with those aspects of his personality constitutes his group-oriented mentality.[5]

This contention is important for the interpretation of both nationalism and politics in the Arab world. Arab groups could be distinguished at two levels of functioning: the work group (which is instrumentally rational) and the basic assumption group (which is not). Basic assumptions are the group equivalent of transference configurations. There are three such basic assumptions: dependency, in which the group exists in order to be sustained by a leader on whom it depends for material and spiritual nourishment and for protection; fight-flight, in which the group exists to fight something or to run away from it; and pairing, in which the group exists to witness interaction of a couple, from whose union a messianic leader is expected to be born.[6]

Arabs adapt to a state of nature, taking it in its mysterious sense. When they enter a group, they try to leave all this baggage of mine (the total self) outside the group, within the self.[7] This is an example that psychologists label as the schizoid compromise. In this sense individuals withhold one part of the self from the group, for fear that the group will destroy it, while simultaneously entering the group with another part, in the hope that the group will promote it. This is the case somehow of Arab minority individuals in large Arab cultural settings. Such individuals feel that their false self is created to comply with the demands of a nonconformity environment, while the more spontaneous, authentic, vital part is withdrawn so that it will be less damaged by misunderstanding, disturbances, carelessness, or neglect. The withdrawn self is relational. It seeks a perfect attunement with its intersubjective environment. It is failure of compliance that results in its schizoid (split personality) or monadic status.[8]

Nationality is desirable among Arabs. It provides the means for diminishing fear, attaining security, and promoting capabilities. But fear of whom from the imposition of whom? Nationalism is a double-edged sword as understood by Arab minorities. It may promote security; it may also allow one group to deprive another of its autonomy. To avoid generalities, I must stress that the question of nationhood among Arabs is unique given the special conditions of the Arab world. Again, my analysis of the psychological nature of nationalism and nationhood is discussed only insofar as they cast light on overall understanding of the Arab world.

Readers of Middle East politics have assuredly noticed that there exists a problem of semantics resulting from the different and frequent use of nationalism as a concept. Arab nationalism embraces perceptions of national identity, nationhood, national self-determination, national aggrandizement, nation as state, and nation as people. However, recognition should be given to the early development of nationalism as ideology evolving from the eighteenth-century doctrine of popular sovereignty.

Notwithstanding, this recognition in turn is problematic because in stating the concept of sovereign people the idea is not complete unless we define the constituents. The reference here is to what? Is it to an ethnic group, a cultural gathering, or a multiethnic/religious consensual society? It is worth noting, nonetheless, that a sense of nationhood, of national identity, can be experienced without a commitment to the ideology of nationalism. Concomitantly, a nation can exist without nationalism.

Whereas a nation can exist without nationalism, nationalism cannot, by its mere ideological connotation, exist without identifiable nations. One of the most exciting and challenging effects of research about nationalism is the two traditionally hostile ideological visions, welfare nations addressing economic fears, and socialist nations addressing equalities and social status fears, engaged in a massive struggle to control the divergent trends in polity.[9]

As communism and the Soviet Union collapsed, a veil was lifted revealing Arab states and societies whose political development has been frozen for decades. The severe impact of the Soviet Union disintegration was not only on the Arab states and governments, but more on the Arab societies as well. It is true that Arab governments were embarrassed in trying to find an alternative to their old alliances; however, the jolt was the collapsing of communism not as a political trend but as a world political and economic satellite system. Major groups, especially intellectuals, in the Arab world witnessed a keen shock in their political orientations toward the concept of nation-building. Recent events have largely destroyed the Soviet Union's claim that it has solved the task of satisfactorily enclosing diverse ethnicities, nationalities, and religious communities within a single political framework. The nineteenth-century process of nation-building resumed. Peoples previously defined as nations by monarchies, religion, art, literature, conquest, and defeat emerged into a vacuum of having things disappear and not be replaced.

Arabs are jolted back to their old fears of religious and minority conflicts. To most scholars religious conflict either has a distinctly historical ring or a variety of obscure fanaticism. Both connotations defeat the reality. Like ethnic nationalism, religion at its psychological base identifies peoples. These religious identities were never negated among Arabs who have found a safe refuge in God.[10]

Sometime religious identities hide behind nationalism, universalism, or any other mandate ideology. They surface when ideologies fail to promote the well-being of societies. The second half of the twentieth-century Western European materialism has penetrated and eroded some Islamic values and practices in core geographical areas in the Arab world, something that Marxism-Leninism materialism and communism were not able to do as effectively. However, religious sentiments and identities still serve to rally and fortify Arab peoples whose safety is threatened by the harsh order of the new political systems. The fact is that Arabs still are differentiated by religion as much as by race and ethnicity. As newly Arab states struggle through their ruling elite to establish national identities and as minority groups try to assert their rights, religious institutions and organizations will still play a great role.

Group consolidation along a religious identity does not necessarily mean immediate, nonstop confrontation, though it holds that potential. Arab states have used religion to undermine the authority of foreign governments as they tried to expand their own influence in the region. In doing this they stirred and irritated the existing different religious insecurities and fears among other minorities, creating psychological drawbacks among confessional minority groups. The cases of Sudan, Algeria, and the Arab East in general are flagrant examples of diverting religious minorities from nationalism. In the process minorities started to calculate the risk in their status and to take into consideration the price of assimilation that they have to pay to coexist.

The Arab East case has encouraged the rise of other religious and sectarian fundamentalism, which has had local roots and which historically has had confrontations with ruling regimes. In this sense, non-Muslim fundamentalism and militant Islam, which are not homogeneous in nature, do not organize under the incentive of fighting against the status quo. They have a variety of political reasons to choose to force political and cultural change in their own societies. Their basic endeavor is to change the rules of the political game set up by one powerful group in their own societies. They think that it is their religious duty to rearrange Arab societies and establish new tracks of developments that have roots in equality, which is the most important component of nationalism.[11]

Two major political ideologies, namely, Arab nationalism and Islamism, have dominated political life in the Middle East for over a century. These ideologies, bred on the broad and specific fears of Arabs, promised social and political solutions and power through national awakening or religious revival. In the 1980s and 1990s, the rising force of Islamic fundamentalism contended with Arab nationalism. Despite their appeal to the fear of Arabs, the two ideologies have been traversed with contradictions and are being detached from the realities of the Arab world politics. In their inabilities to relieve fears and anxieties and at times quite the opposite, they both carried the essence of their own failure. In the end, neither movement delivered on its promise of individual and group psychological stability or put in order a clear track to Arab-Muslim liberation and strength. Rather, Arab nationalism bred oppression, division, and dictatorship; Islamic fundamentalism fomented intolerance, sectarian fratricide, and religious authoritarianism, and if we are to look at Iran and Afghanistan, the picture is really self-sufficient.

Arab nationalism, as conceived as a cause of liberation from foreign Turkish rule following World War I, is not the same. It grew increasingly radical and antiliberal after the partition of Arab lands and the implanting of a rival to the land, that is, Jewish nationalism in Palestine by the European powers. Radical nationalism crested after World War II with Nasser and the Ba'th Party propagating revolutionary pan-Arabism, Arab power, and socialism. After suffering defeat in the 1967 war with Israel, the ideology lost its allure and has been in retreat ever since. Its proclaimed goals are now a legacy of a former era imitated by a few isolated pockets of revolutionary dreamers in the Arab world or those Arab scholars in the halls of Western universities.

In recounting the tribulations and failures of Arab nationalism, the suggestions that it is a mistaken identity or a myth are probably close to reality. The reason for saying this is derived from Arab nationalism's claiming to embrace the loyalties of countless millions of diverse Arab peoples from Morocco to southern Arabia whose multiple identities and fears are shaped by various ethnic, communal, regional, and religious disputes. Arab nationalism as an identity was thought of as a solution to the discrimination of one minority group to another and as a medicine for ethnic anxieties. However, many of its original inspirational ideas, which are Sunni Islamic distinctiveness and greatness, distorted its objectives. Arab nationalists tended to ignore the psychological aspects of fear and insecurity among minority groups. Unless well tended to, the psychological aspects would undermine Arabism's very claim to legitimacy.

However, the lack of psychological acknowledgment by Arab nationalists should not come as a surprise, in view of the European origin of the very idea of Arab nationalism. Ironically, though nationalism per se is European in origin, Arab nationalism has assumed an anti-Western trend without recognizing the drastic changes in the political reconfiguration of nationalism in the West. Yet, in saying this I am not disagreeing that Arab nationalism could be a source of cultural identification for millions in the Arab world who consider themselves Arabs for lack of any other identity or based on some common cultural, historical, linguistic, and religious ties. Surely we must be cognizant of the fact that Arab nationalism is not a reciprocally based identity.[12]

Perhaps in suggesting that by equating Arab nationalism with the notion of a single political Arab destiny, the champions of Arabism were deluded, confusing what is real and what is ideal. Unable to achieve the elusive goal of unity, Arabism today lies totally discarded by a triumphant state system in the Middle East, a militant political Islam, an ascendant liberal democracy and market economy, and a peace process with Israeli forces that contains in its agenda giving up Palestinian land, thus negating the basic premises of Arab nationalism.

The talk is now about a new Middle East order, superseding the old ideologically unsuccessful Arab national order. Such a concept is all the more irrelevant in a geopolitical area that is neither coherent nor susceptible to political, social, and psychological stability. But the term *Arab world* is used in this book to replace the Arab nation as a defining framework of identity that would constitute the real detachment of Arab societies over the imaginary Arab nationalist notion of one land, one people.

Another challenge to the new Arab world order is the emerging psychological force of Islamism. It is not homogeneous, but then again it is a philosophy that entertains the fears of large segments of Muslims. In this sense we deal with the rise of Islamic movements as political and psychological movements trying to replace Arabism as a political ideology of salvation from fear and produces self-confidence and potency. Just like progressive political parties, Islamism as a religiopolitical force seeks to dissolve existing regimes and reinstitute Islamic governments in accord with Islamic law. It has swept across the Arab-Muslim lands from Morocco to the Arabian Peninsula, shaking Arab states' politics to its foundations and calling for a revival of true Islamic governance and culture.[13]

But has the pull of Islamism provided the push toward the renewal of Muslim power? The answer is no. Arabs maintain that Islamism is insufficient to redress valid solutions and thus will suffer from flaws similar to those apparent in Arabism. It is itself a movement pierced with fear leading to oppression, authoritarianism, and sectarian divisions. Its message of a unified Muslim community stands in sharp contrast to the old sectarian divisions and identities and sectarian strife between Sunni and Shi'a Islam, which it helped reawaken. This was manifested in the 1987 bloody clashes in Mecca between Saudi police and Iranian pilgrims, flaring up a religious-political struggle between Khomeini's Shi'a revolutionary Islam and Saudi Sunni conservative Islam. It is also reflected in the political struggle waged in the late 1970s and early 1980s by the Muslim Brotherhood in Syria against the Alawi-dominated regime of Hafiz al-Assad, which took on a religious sectarian connotation, and again in Iraq when the Shi'ite rebelled against Saddam Hussein in the aftermath of Iraq's invasion of Kuwait. Sunni Muslim orthodoxy considers that the Alawaiites is a dissenting faction. But the most significant outcome of intense sectarian identification and militancy in the wake of the Khomeini Islamic revolution of 1978–79 was the rise of Hizbullah in Lebanon and the increasing assertiveness of the Shi'ia community following the Israeli invasion of Lebanon in 1982. Shi'ia separateness and militancy reverberated in other quarters across the Arab lands. Indeed, one of the major consequences of Khomeinism was to divide the Muslim world more than ever before. Thus, the bequest of Islamic fundamentalism is not national unity and strength; it is a source of more fears, group and minority isolationism, and thus social and political predicament.

Equally important, the Islamic fundamentalist movement generally coupled traditional mode of living with violence for the restoration of Islamic power, thus awakening old fears among the different minorities and ethnic groups. Violence is legitimized as a form of jihad (holy war justified by God) against Western and local trends of modern and worldly inclinations and values.

The issue has always been that of Islam and Muslim Arabs longing for security, relaxation of fear, and recognition of their regional-oriented anxieties. Counter to the Arab nationalists' and contemporary Islamists' propaganda, we could state that recognition of traditions alone cannot solve the deep social and economic crises facing Arab societies. In an age of pragmatism, the politics of identity and ideology championed by the Arab nationalists and Islamists appear to have failed to provide the desired economic solutions, and with the exception of petrodollars, the Arabs are not any stronger or more significant on the world scene than they were a century ago. The Arab world persistently is becoming a prisoner of one's past fears and anxieties, unable to open up to renovating remedies.

When an individual in Arab states compares himself with all those around him, he feels that personal pride is attained when he is equal to all others. But when individuals of minority groups come to survey the totality of their status, and to place themselves in contrast with so huge an Arab world, they are instantly overwhelmed by the sense of their own insignificance and weakness. The same equality that renders an Arab independent of each of his fellow Arabs exposes him alone and unprotected to the influence of the greater number.[14] This inclination at the level of the individual and thus small groups is explained in psychology as an articulation of the schizoid compromise, and psychologists consider this to be a fundamental problem of small and large group life. As part of psychoanalysis, the field of mother-infant interaction is the ontogenetic prototype of the small group. The group situation is not simply dyadic (pair of individuals maintaining a sociologically significant relationship), however, but triadic. The functions of leadership are the third element brought into focus precisely by the pretense that structures the group process. Literature in psychology delineates five dramas that group members enact, each of which is a primitive emotional attempt to deal with the missing leader: the leader who must be sacrificed so that the group may be saved; a state of despair, deadness, and hopelessness now that the leader is dead. In stating this I am trying to say that some of the Shi'ite's rituals are similar to Hegel's drama of lordship and bondage in which the world is divided into the fateful and often (in political life) fatal relationship of Us and Them.[15]

It seems to me that Hegel's drama overlaps substantially with the basic assumption that the group processes are enacted in small groups and large (including political movements, social and religious organizations, polities, and nations). Moreover, I think one should focus on the role of projective identification (the projection of affectively laden components of the self into an other, often in such a way that the other feels compelled to enact the projected parts of the self) in the production of these group modalities. Moreover, one should take seriously the contention that group development beyond a primitive level is both difficult and extremely important, especially for the study of nationalism and politics, and that certain kinds of active leadership are necessary if such development is to occur.[16]

In term of application on Arab nationalism, and in terms of parallel textual interpretation, when the logic of argument about the essentials of Arabism becomes problematic, we turn to historical context. In doing that it is necessary to establish collectivity; to disguise individual and collective interests; to acknowledge motives and desires; and even to broaden the conceptions of Arab cultural nature. When we proceed in this fashion, we address the Arab conditions for mutual recognition or, to vary the expression, to study the environment within which Arabs interact. In my view, analyzing Arab leadership is essential to understanding group development and status.

To Freud, the unconscious is a battlefield where contending forces interact through various strategies of conflict. That is the source of not only the distinctively human imagination but also the monster of unifying madness. Bion views the basic assumptions as having the characteristics of defensive reactions to psychotic anxiety, hence as having something in common with mechanisms described as typical of the earliest phases of mental life.[17] Thus, we can contend that groups can regress beyond the paranoid-schizoid position to the autistic-contiguous position, in which the struggle is to make emotional contact with an entity to which one is already joined at the skin.[18] And so we come, at the end of a descending line, to the experiences of madness evoked and analyzed in terms of power. These concepts are not just different ways of saying the same thing. They have in common the identification of psychological and by inference political health with the ability to experience rather than to repress, split off and project the disturbing, hateful/hatred-filled, and even psychotic parts of the individual or collective self. If we consider these concepts more closely, however, they are characterized by the loss of coming to terms with reality through psychotic fantasies, that is, a loss of the capacity for reality testing and secondary process thinking, alienation from historical reality, and a lapsing into psychotic time.

In political life, secondary process mental operations appear as the values of negotiation, tolerance, and limitation. Nationalistic values are primary process operations that take shape as intolerance, jingoism, racism, and tyrannical appeals to action and repression. Psychologists go on to assert that the psychotic self, almost totally regressed toward infantile identifications and feelings, lives in delusional or psychotic time. Similarly, an ideologically oriented society that has lost contact with its historical and therefore consensual foundations may find itself overwhelmed by belief structures or actions that have devastating effects.[19] This formulation is problematic in studying nationalism in the Arab world in at least two ways. It identifies ordinary conscious state of mind with nationalistic values, when it is clear historically that Arab values were compatible with a variety of regional political norms and systems. Arab nationalistic values have proved to operate with an all-too-Platonic parallelism of psyche and polity. But when we compare Arab ideologies, we might be inclined to grant the heuristic and psychic analysis its prescriptive value. In simple terms, the play of power forces us to interpret the personal as political.

The influences of nationalism have major impact on power relations in any given social setting. Despite wide recognition by scholars that nationalism promotes cooperation among forces of society, cooperation has received more attention from economics and business than from other disciplines such as psychology, political science, and sociology. The idea here is to place the influences of trust and time dimension on cooperation. Specifically, when trust and time dimension jointly determine the extent to which one group is taking advantage of another, if the victimized group concedes, it encourages opportunistic behavior by other groups. Apprehension and temptation, in turn, shape fear and greed. The amount of fear in a relationship is commonly known as the size of loss when one individual or group is victimized by the opportunistic behavior of the other party.[20]

The amount of greed refers to the magnitude of the immediate gains reaped from opportunistic behavior. Trust is a psychological and sociological concept that is associated with cooperation. Trust, one might argue, is essential to produce social cooperation among different groups in a national setting and to avoid inefficient noncooperative traps. One might argue that an element of trust exists in every transaction, and without trust there can be no cooperation.

However, in the Arab world trust is more community oriented, and individuals' lack of trust for others not only alleviates the concern for being mistreated but also contains their own scrutiny behavior. Thus a stream of security derived from cooperation with a trusted partner is safer and more valuable. Time horizon constitutes another important variable in cooperation, and again one might argue that self-enforcing agreements are not feasible if the sequence of actions has definite known last elements; termination must be uncertain to sustain cooperation. The chronological dynamics of cooperation are important because the future casts a shadow back upon the present, as the past does to the present, thereby affecting current behavior. In this respect, the forces that trust and time horizon exert upon apprehension and temptation among Arab minorities' relationships are not the same.

A better understanding of how trust and time horizon determine apprehension about victimization and temptation to behave opportunistically permits answers to the following questions: How do trust and time horizon collectively shape greed and fear and hence cooperation? How sensitive are apprehension and temptation with respect to changes in trust and time horizon? Why are trust and time horizon individually necessary but not sufficient for cooperation? How do benefits from cooperation in a relationship come into play in addition to greed and fear since cooperation is evidently unattainable without benefits?

Arabs cannot escape the feeling that their past, in part, will be a compo-nent of their future; thus trust and time horizon influence the robustness of their cooperation. The point here is how this prospect jointly determines the level of temptation and apprehension, which in turn shape greed and fear. Consistent with previous analysis in this book, nationalism is unat-tainable when there is no trust in a relationship.[21] On the other hand, trust among the different minorities in a nation is not ensured even with full cooperation. This implies that cooperation is not sufficient for trust. Arab nationalism has for some time bridged cooperation among the different Arab states and communities, but this in no way suggests a trust relation-ship. Fear can be provoked, even with full cooperation, if trust in the future is not assured.

Furthermore, by tracking the impact of time horizon across alterna-tives, trust situations among the different factions in the Arab world, that is, no trust, some trust, full trust, we are able to delineate the influence of the temporal dynamics on nationalism. It is found that the shadow of the future does not affect either greed or fear under the condition of no trust. The shadow of the future shapes only greed but not fear when full trust exists; the shadow of the future influences both greed and fear when some trust exists. The diverse Arab groups feel that the power of a longer time horizon mirrors that of conflict in its ability to pass on apprehension.

In addition to the condition of no trust that renders true and effective nationalism impossible in the Arab world, current political trends show that cooperation is also inconceivable when there is no plan for building up trust in the future. Although the prospect for future interactions is necessary for cooperation, this is not sufficient. Time horizon is not suffi-cient because distrust alone can induce apprehension and temptation even with an assured future. It is noteworthy that cooperation is certain to take place under only one particular circumstance: full trust together with an assured future. Of course, the prerequisite for cooperation is that benefits from mutual cooperation, however small, must be present.

Arabs suffer from the temptation to be gluttonous because it would be a rare coincidence for complete certainty of the future and full trust to occur simultaneously in their societies. The concurrence of an assured future and full trust is needed for temptation to cease to exist. As such, defection may indeed be in the culture. Without a doubt, all Arabs recog-nize that all of them would be better off if none of them were greedy. Unfortunately, Arab individuals, groups and states, almost always face temptation to behave opportunistically. We may argue that all influential nationalistic tendencies, from early Islamic patriotism to twentieth-century Arab nationalism, emerged in implicit recognition of this central problem facing Arabs.

A nation's existence is very much dependent on groups' conviction that their safety lies in accepting nationalism. There is no doubt that Arab nationalism is philosophical, ideological, economical, and cultural. It is nonetheless a phenomenon where if in reality the notion of Arab unity is materialized it is less likely to satisfy the philosophical or any other notion behind it. If this is so, then what is Arab nationalism and how should it be evaluated?

The Arab world now is witnessing a division of vision between three groups of people; the first, in the absence of any suitable alternative, have interest in keeping the status quo with its national symbols and institutions. They admit that major revisions and reforms are needed to be able to promote the well-being of society. The second group have good impressions about the old system of society and they would like to revive this old system with its institutions and religious symbols. The third group, and the largest, stand idle and do not sympathize with the first two groups, but they do not have an alternative. Suffice it to mention here that with the failing of the socialist-communist experience in the Soviet Union and Eastern Europe, the Marxist factions in the Arab world have joined the third group. Adopting a new system and a mode of life requires first a reshaping of one's identity. You cannot be a Marxist-Leninist communist and identify yourself as belonging to a nation; you cannot be a nationalist and identify yourself with your religion; and you cannot feel at ease until you choose a scheme to identify with. That is why most Arabs have a crisis of identity.

After World War I, adopting a political identity in the Arab world was problematical. The Europeans had reorganized the old Ottoman Empire into states and introduced new forms of political and social institutions. Even after World War II, the extent to which individuals or families thought of themselves as Arab may have depended on local traditions or ties of kinship. It was just as likely to have been affected by state-inspired schooling, conscription, nationalist propaganda, popular literature, newspapers, or songs. The search for any sort of national identity or national character was therefore as fruitless an exercise as it would be if carried out in any other developed country. If nationalities have an identity or a character at all, it is always changing under changing circumstances. The circumstances of people struggling for their independence created a particular type of image that became difficult to dispel. It is, however, important not only to determine the nature of the Arab image but also to understand why many people came to identify with this image.[22]

Few Arab intellectuals in the late nineteenth and early twentieth centuries ventured to introduce the concept of Arab nationalism. They were very much influenced by Western political values and the strength manifested by radical national European states. However, the concern here is with the popular consciousness of being an Arab in the second half of the twentieth century. Is there concomitancy between Arab identity, Arab nationalism, and being an Arab? Who could lay claim to it, and how it is going to fulfill itself? How do we assess the factor of deeply entrenched parochial loyalties, underpinned by common religious affiliation? For many years, minorities living in the Arab world have adopted the Arabic language as a second language for convenience and to facilitate their interactions and communications with the dominant Arab-speaking population. Arabic as a language is important to both Arabs and Muslims. It might have doubly fortified value for Muslim Arabs.

The most striking aspect of four hundred years of Arab history had been the conflict over being a Muslim and consequently accommodating the Ottoman rule or being an Arab and thus having an independent identity. Confessional bonds were seen as more important than ties of nationality. This factor remained significant until the rise of Gamel Abdel Nasser in Egypt in 1952, when the confessional divide among the groups became dormant by the rising mood of Arab nationalism in the face of Muslim brotherhood and militant Islamists. Why then did the idea of being an Arab assume such overwhelming political significance in the second half of the twentieth century?

Nasserism and other Arab nationalist movements like the Ba'th parties were able, probably unintentionally, to calm the old fears of some minorities. They clouded the image and identity of the Arabs. These clouds were so effective that a search for the roots of Arab nationalism were implicated, without major difficulties, with socialism and the drift of middle-class rising power in most of the so-called progressive Arab states.

Something went wrong with the visualization of those who were supporting nationalism. Arab nationalism overwhelmingly meant resisting Western domination and imperialism. It assumed a meaning of being antitraditional and opposing conservative governments like monarchies and emirates in the Arab Gulf. This explains the rising and declining political crises in Lebanon, Jordan, and other Arab traditional governments, where Arab nationalists fought relentlessly against the incumbent rulers.

Nevertheless, it has been less unusual during the rise of Arab nationalism. The masses, which proclaimed Arab nationalism, have had this after-glow of being Muslims, which became common during the struggle with Western powers. Arab nationalism in its hidden reality was conceived as being part of the revival of the Arab-Muslim golden age, when Islamic militants penetrated and dominated large estates way beyond the Arab world's boundaries.[23]

However, if one is to look at the Arab world from the plebs' psychology, or if one investigates the decision-making process in the milieu of ruling elite within the circles of the dominant parties and high-ranking bureaucrats that take most of the blame for all the civil and regional wars, an atmosphere of fear constantly creeps up and calls for evaluation. When seeking to understand the rise and fall of Arab nationalism as an identity, we certainly have to make much more effort to understand the psychology behind that.

It should not be denied that Arab nationalism contains good foundations for survival, and the Arab world was not something that sprang from a utopian vision of a philosopher. It is less likely that Arab nationalism came as a conspiracy by the West to fight against the Ottoman Empire. The existence of the Arabic language and the consciousness of being a Muslim go back well into the Dark Ages. What is important, however, is that at a time when literate and politically self-conscious individuals in Europe were questioning the nature of their own national communities and subjecting their political and social institutions to the sort of security that might be seen as psychologically reassuring, the Arab world was under the direct control of the Ottomans and the indirect control of a group of Western powers.

Before reassurance as manifested in the concept of democracy started to entertain the mind of Western political thought, anxiety among majorities vs. minorities within a common unified political entity did exist as a political issue. With the development of the state as a concept and in reality, the examination of majority vs. minority began to find a premise among the public and educated discourse. If the idea of a democratic neutral state is empowered to act by the results of universal franchise, responding to the concerns of all members of society within the borders of the state, then all inherited problems of interest-contrast between majorities and minorities will reappear. This is to say that democracy, inasmuch as it is reassuring, is attractive to the intellectual mind. But unless correctly put into operation, it amplifies existing problems in plural and pluralistic societies. The state as perceived by the Middle Eastern elite is by its very nature confessional, that is, it is restricted and dedicated to preserving the position of the adherents of the dominant religious creed. This means that states should be formed along religious lines. Political liberties are the exclusive prerogative of the individual members of established religious institutions. The criterion of loyalty is subscribed in the criterion of identity and is the precondition for the exercise of rights. Therefore, refusal of submission or adherence to the prevailing articles of faith is seen as an act of disloyalty and denial of identity.

The essential feature and characteristics of identity among Arabs was and still is religious-confessional uniformity, which all religious elite sought to attain throughout until they were faced in the second half of the twentieth century by new modern ideologies like nationalism, socialism, and communism. Before that, any defiance to the existing mode of interaction among confessional groups meant rebellion against one's identity and submission to the competitor. Preserving an identity was never a personal initiative. An individual has to be accepted by his peers and his community. Living among the group is a prerequisite for recognition of loyalty and identity. Individuals in the Middle East found themselves compelled by these rules to stick to their own confessional group, since they are not welcomed by others. As long as the terms of allegiance were so conceived, any idea of a legitimate minority sharing equal political rights remains impossible. The question of confessional groups interacting in an established manner did not arise until the second half of the twentieth century, with the introduction and acceptance of nationalism and the beginning of the undermining of the confessional institutions to strengthen the secular institutions of the state. However, a long historical pattern and mode of living does not become totally negated in a few years.

Whenever nationalism is depicted in thinking and action, there has to be a form of authority. In its essence, national politics stems from the issues of authority. All studies in politics, implicitly or explicitly, address issues of authority. Authority is a concept that is hard to identify and analyze. Whatever unit of analysis and whichever range of issues are in question, virtually all human experiences involve pressures arising from or shaping the various forms of authority. No matter what manner of polity is in question, the subject is to some degree always a part of authority.

Authority starts from one's ability to control his own activity in what is known as freedom. An individual freedom means an authority enjoyed by an individual to exercise liberty of making and implementing decisions. The self is never alone in a society. The self is realized only in a group. Thus the authority that individuals have is bound to spill out to clash with other individuals' authorities. In order for one to realize full authority over others, one is bound to deprive others of their right to self-decision-making. How to fulfill one's authority and deprive others of the same is politics. The right for one to make decisions for others has to find forms of institutional expression. Only thus could life, groups, and societies proceed on anything called polity.[24]

The individual has to learn that he is at once, in the jurisprudential sense, a resultant of and part force in political powers manifested through both stated regulations and discretionary uses or abuses of them. Even children are aware of what authority they are part of, though frequently remaining in partial or substantial ignorance as to its extent or actual liability. The first identity that a child develops is the submission to accept an authority that decides for him. This submission becomes his identity. If a child is compelled to submit to two contradictory authorities exercising their powers on him, the child all too often becomes confused and loses respect for authority.

By the same token, national identity for an individual is his acceptance of an authority that fulfills this identity. In the Arab world, state identity appropriates Arabs' national identity, because submission to state authority is all too often confused with submission to the nonexisting Arab nation's authority. The notion of legitimate authority is confused because it stems from a part of the whole (nation) and not the whole itself. This situation undermines the feeling of identity, and all forms of authorities become unappreciated.

Perhaps the first step in studying Arab politics is to recognize that authority exists, whether it is democratic or dominating, appreciated or not. It is evident in the family, the group, society, and the state. Powerful individuals and groups practice authority in all realms. Authority is never absolute (though some will try) and not always successful. Beyond the dominion of small families and in the arena of society, authority is best achieved through well-organized concerts of individuals. All types of agreements are apt to play effective roles in social affairs. In reality, agreements inevitably leave unresolved some of the problems they would like to resolve, or they fail to solve them really well. Authority in these instances will be undermined. Most of the time such failures occur because no one agrees about what should be done, or a solution is inherently too difficult to achieve. In instances like this, a tendency arises to exercise dominating authority. Dominating pressures are not exercised at random, and there is a perceptible general doctrine toward which they are predisposed. When solutions are persistently too difficult to achieve, there is thus a long-term continuity in the general direction of dominating pressures.[25]

Philosophical and psychological theories about domination have not come very far in spelling out the standards that explain hierarchy of politics in the Arab world. Attributes are adopted often from the writings about institutions of control, in contrast to a justification of egalitarian justice that requires equality in the distribution of resources. However, these writings fail to provide a guide on how the notion of equality ought to be applied in circumstances of conflict over certain indivisible goods. That is precisely the problem of Arab nationalism, especially when it comes to allocations of resources among the diverse groups whether within the boundaries of the state or across borders.[26]

Nationalism, national boundaries, and the nation-state system in the Arab world, in this respect, present to the student of politics a unique set of paradoxes. Whereas perceptive scholars would treat Saudi patriotism or Islamic fundamentalism with a degree of seriousness, social scientists who study politics of the Middle East, even those who would expose the pragmatic value of the doctrine of nationalism, cannot deny the aspiration that commemorates the linguistic, ethnic, or historic ties among Arabs. Nevertheless, past attempts at unification have proved to be disastrous and potentially dangerous, such as those that culminated in disappointment from of the United Arab Republic uniting Egypt and Syria. By the same token, contemporary attempts by such figures as Libyan leader Muammar Qaddafi to resurrect Arab unity are generally greeted with bewilderment. The fact is that the boundaries of Arab states are designed by the Western powers not only to separate political elite but also to separate wealth, goods, and natural resources. Prosperous groups are in no way willing to share their wealth under the banner of Arab nationalism or any other ideology.[27]

The sharing of common goods by a wealthy incumbent ruler is associated with fear of losing power. While Syria has historically presented itself as the vanguard of Arab nationalism and promoter of Arab unity, Syria has found it politically, economically, and strategically advantageous to defy all that and to support non-Arab Iran in its war against Arab and Ba'th Iraq.

Although most individuals find themselves compelled in espousing hierarchical allegiances and loyalties to cities, regions, nations, religious communities, and others, yet only within the countries of the Arab world does the dominant political discourse grasp and endorse challenging loyalties to pledges at the size of a large nation. This seeming contradiction can be attributed to the peculiar history of the diverse religious and ethnic groups that struggled to maintain their identities in the region, particularly in the area of the Arab East. My point is that Arabs are living unhappily in a state of irregularity, and they endlessly seek identity in some kind of secure belonging. Such secure belonging is generally organized around centers of gravity that have long been concrete communities but can also be part of an abstract community. Psychologists all along projected an understanding of politics as organized around the friend-versus-foe tension. This view is that humans can only interact together as social animals in terms of us-versus-them identities. Us-versus-them is not always hostile and warlike, but it does imply coming close and substantiating the circle. It implies, in other words, a drawing of boundaries to separate others from those who are considered part of us.

Entry into an available community is a psychological need. Strangers are those who cast loyalty to other groups and are unwilling to cooperate to the point of challenging the very laws of the group that hosts them; in doing this, they are bound to elicit fear, rejection, and hostility. Tensions between regional and local groups are a fact of political life in the Arab world. Official discourse condemns these tensions as relics of regionalism, tribalism, and clannishness, but local feeling keeps them alive. Algerian regionalism is especially peculiar in that the various regional groups are arguing over which is better in using nationalism as a springboard. The objectives of Algeria's various regionalisms have nothing to do with regional autonomy and still less with secession. Instead, what is being sought is hegemony within national ruling circles. Local patriotic feelings are flattered when individuals from a specific group are named to national office. The local members of this group can feel more secure and can then get rich. The internalization of national feeling does not abolish local loyalty and psychological affinity, which remains vibrant and stands firm against the affirmation of nationalism.[28]

The inability of Arab nationalism to ensure political support and psychological security calls into question the relationship between groups and the nation. Social scientists have been too quick to embrace the notion that as soon as a country becomes independent, it constitutes a nation. It may, of course, but most often a nation is the result of a long historical process during which consensual values emerge to furnish grounds for national concord and civil peace. This is not the picture presented today by the Arab world, where obedience to the central power even within the state system is secured by force or the threat of force.

The fact that the sectarian, ethnic, and national groups in modern Arab politics do not like each other does not mean that there are feelings of dislike. Not to like is different from dislike. The most remarkable example of not coming to terms with some disliked groups is found in the Palestinian-Israeli case. But the case of groups that simply do not like each other is found in Lebanon. The 1991 political agreement marked in Lebanon a new measure of conciliation among groups that do not like one another. The different groups in Lebanon are reduced to the do-not-like level and thus are bound to forgive all crimes and violations of human rights committed by one group against another during the civil strife of 1975–90. There is an attempt to neutralize the period of strife, including acts committed by the very members of the cabinet that had issued the reconciliation pact.

To become a victim of cruelty is debilitating, but it can also be emotionally transforming. It hardly seems possible that anyone can sustain protracted suffering without becoming aware of the radical contrast between what is and what ought to be. The experience of cruelty can turn those who are subjected to it in on themselves, or it can help them reach outward in the urge to remake and affirm life. Such an affirmation extends cooperation into the very world of cruel facts that constantly threaten to dismantle it.

Iraqi novelist Arif Alwan believes that Iraq has a future only if its diverse minority groups can somehow maneuver a leap from a republic of fear to a republic of tolerance. He argues that if half a century of ruling elite violence could not clamp the country together, then no amount of centralized repression is ever going to do the job. A dramatically different approach is needed to ward off future violence, one that recognizes reasonable limits to the pursuit of homogeneity and loyalty and accepts differences as a point of departure for political practice and reflection. By the same token, moderate Islamist writers are exploring the ways in which representatives of various currents of Islam can hold respectful dialogues among themselves and with non-Muslims, especially Christians.[29]

Arabs have never been very comfortable with the language of large ideological nations or universal fraternity; it is just not in their history.[30] Arab nationalists worry that group differentiated rights will undermine the sense of shared collective identity that holds a nation together. They realize that the cost of retracting these themes are the most important issues of their political and cultural life. But which religious principles should be recognized in the parliaments, bureaucracies, and courts? Should each ethnic or confessional group have publicly funded education in its mother tongue? Should internal boundaries (legislative districts, provinces, states) be drawn so that cultural minorities form a majority within a local region? What degree of value-oriented integration can be required of immigrants and the Palestinian refugees before they acquire citizenship? These are hard questions that need to be answered.

Arabs now are saying that different times require different answers to the same questions. With great drama and at a terrible cost in human suffering, especially in Iraq, Kuwait, Lebanon, and Algeria, war and bloody feuds highlighted the failure of so many Arab nationalist trends. In the worst cases, like those of Iraq, Algeria, and the Arab Gulf states, a more or less complete psychological change in political mentality is taking place. Coming to terms with such harsh truths is difficult; the emergence of widespread disillusionment, frustration, and fear of the future is not surprising. Cynicism and despair are alarmingly common in the Arab world today. Yet, for a number of reasons, the outcome of the Arab-Arab feuds meant that it was no longer possible for politics to continue as before. A whole ideological structure, its nature typified by old trends, began to disintegrate.

Arabs are stepping into the resulting vacuum of ideology and asking questions. Often their tone is shrill. They are weary of the big questions and consumed with genuine fear for the future. Mostly, however, they are disillusioned. They have learned the hard way that there are no more grand solutions out there. Looking around, they can observe the world-wide decline of ideologies that obliterated the distinction between revolution and democracy and that ended up in dictatorships or worse. This is a whole new cultural-ideological landscape, one full of grave political threats as well as new political opportunities. It might breed extremism of an even more hostile type. However, there are early signs that Arab psychology is beginning to give rise to a new, more pragmatic, less ideological politics in the Arab world.

While toleration may not have been needed at earlier stages of Arab sociopolitical development, growing numbers of Arabs appear to be finding it necessary today. Neither modernization nor national liberation from foreign rule incorporates the principle that one should, for the sake of social peace, put up with things that one actively dislikes. And indeed, whatever the strides of nationalism and technical modernization, this idea has been absent as an active force in Arab political practice. But in the wake of the recent Arab crisis, that may be changing. Somehow, as the cruelties mount, a psychological notion is taking hold that differences between groups and individuals are an inherent feature of any society and can be accommodated.

Then again, there are now two kinds of political communities in the Arab world: those that have pacified the realm of the political, thereby creating a public sphere, and those that have not and maintain power solely by force. The existence of a pacified political arena in any Arab country does not mean an end to all conflict; rather, it means only that power is not taken by force. Observers of Arab politics would not be surprised if they heard that an uprising was hitting the Syrian, Iraqi, or Algerian government, for in these countries the only way to change the government is by force.

Traditional structures in the Arab world may have lost their political efficacy, but they continue to influence the local political culture and people's behavior. The outcome is usually a state of mind that betrays the degradation of a tradition that has lost its coherence in the face of modernity and its agents, Western domination, and the market. From a psychological perspective, there is the acknowledgment that group variation in behavior in the Arab world should be commonly marked and given significance. Groups do appear to have patterns of behavior that are specific and somewhat distinctive. The logic here is to reveal as much as possible the ways in which nationalism and the psyche feed one another.[31] The ideological perspective of nationalism assumes that psychological processes, in this case the nature and functioning of different groups, are not just influenced by culture but are culturally constituted. In turn, the cultural perspective assumes that groups behaving in concert create the culture. Nationalism and groups are most productively analyzed together as a dynamic of mutual constitution; one cannot be reduced to the other.[32]

From a social psychology perspective, the communities, societies, and cultural contexts in which people participate provide the interpretive frameworks. They provide the theories, images, concepts, and narratives as well as the means, practices, and patterns of behavior by which people organize their actions. The claim is that with respect to the psychological, the individual level often cannot be separated from the cultural level. Any psychological approach to study the Arab world has to assume that personality (most broadly defined as the qualities and characteristics of being a person) is linked with the meanings and practices of the particular Arab sociocultural contexts. Arabs have developed their social and political personalities over time through their active participation in various social groups. This psychological perspective implies that there is no person without culture; there is only a biological entity. Being a person is a social and cultural achievement; it requires incorporating and becoming attuned to a set of cultural understandings and patterns including culture-specific understandings of group realities and behavior. As a consequence, the different groups in the Arab world have systematic diversity in the nature and functioning of their personality.

A special study of the political psychology of Arab personality is now more imperative than ever. Such a study probably would show that most current theories of personality are rooted in Western philosophy. As typically understood within a Western theoretical framework, personality may be an indigenous concept that works well in the West but may be of little relevance in other cultural contexts, especially in the Arab world. Alternatively, some notion of personality, particularly when defined in a somewhat more region-oriented way (e.g., one less tied to specific Western philosophical and ideological commitments), may prove productive in analyzing and understanding variation in the qualities and attributes of people in the Arab world. One could argue that cultural groups in the Arab world diverge in their understandings of selfhood. Anthropologists come close to this distinction in providing that the person is a unique, more or less integrated motivational and cognitive universe, a dynamic center of awareness, emotion, judgment, and action organized into a distinctive whole and set contrastively both against other such wholes and against a social and natural background.[33]

Thus, an Arab maintains a dynamic center in his mind and a unique configuration of attributes that are the constituent elements of Arab social and political reality. The idea here is that there are different definitions of a person, but these are much more than philosophical or ideological differences used to explain behavior. Political ideologies as contexts diverge in their cultural practices and in their ways of activity. The ways of being a member of an Arab group are patterned according to the means and practices of a given cultural community, and communities are maintained by these ways of being in the Arab world. That is, in describing the culture-specific nature of self, cultural psychologists suggest that cultural and social groups in every historical period are associated with characteristic patterns of sociocultural participation or, more specifically, with characteristic ways of being a person in the wider environment. These characteristic patterns of sociocultural participation are called "selfways." By extending the notion of selfways, we can also suggest that there are culture-specific ways of having or being a personality.

People do not live generally or in the abstract. They live according to some specific and substantive sets of cultural understandings. Thus, selfways include definitions and ideas of what it means to be a self and how to be a good or acceptable self, but they are not just a matter of such beliefs. Selfways are also manifest in political episodes, both formal and informal, in religious practices, in the media, and in patterns of caretaking, schooling, and work.

Collective construction of personality in selfways of Arab-Arab relationship is manifested in the cultural shaping of personhood and can be most obviously revealed in Arab cultural contexts, where interdependent models of individuals are elaborated. Arab social customs and institutions foster relationally, that is, being a part, belonging, and improving the fit between how one is doing and what is expected. Children are taught to appreciate the virtues of small group life, and this comes short of learning the virtue of a nation. Instead of celebrating individual accomplishments, special events recognize the accomplishments or growth of the small group in contrast to other groups. Attention to and sympathy for others that are similar could be fostered in many routine practices.

Arab cultural contexts that emphasize persons as fundamentally interdependent with others do not incorporate the tacit understandings and implicit assumptions that are central to Western analyses of personality. Thus, they are not committed to an ideological framework of individualism in which the sources of behavior are rooted in the distinctive attributes of the individual. Instead, in these cultures, even if they are diverse, there is a greater appreciation and emphasis on the relational nature of one's behaviors and patterns of such behaviors.

Accordingly, already incorporated into the very model of the person is some aspect of the larger social unit in which the person is participating. These aspects involve roles, status, and group membership. In the ideological framework of individualism, a free and autonomous person is contrasted with external, constraining social roles and forces. In the interdependent cultural framework, the fact that one takes on a particular social role or a certain social position within the family or group does not imply that the person has lost his individuality. To the contrary, an Arab can become many kinds of manager, father, mother, friend, or student. There can be many distinct patterns of behavior within the framework defined by each of these social positions in which a person can be engaged.

It is important to note that individuality is clearly recognized within most groups in the Arab world as an influence of religion. However, because of religion, recognition of individuality does not require commitment to the ideology of individualism that is the basic unit of nationalism. This acknowledgment of individuality comes instead with a commitment tied to the recognition that the person has strict commitment to his immediate group (that is, an individuality that is made meaningful within a small social unit). The different Arab political personalities result as Arabs engage in particular roles with specific people. Behavior incorporates the demands of others.

Within the Arab interdependent model of the person, the integration of social role and individual distinctiveness is accomplished by a sort of psychological conditioning. Individual differences (e.g., diligent or lazy) are defined within a semantic framework or model of human action that corresponds to a pertinent social position or role (e.g., student, bank teller, or secretary). This conditionality of personal distinctiveness in a social context reflects the relational nature of any behavior in the Arab model of person.

Specific ways in which this psychological conditioning of individual distinctiveness on social position is accomplished have to be explored in Arab cultural contexts. Research so far is lacking. It is important to note that in Arab cultural contexts, socially shared, consensual images of ideal people in different social positions organize daily discourses, images, and practices, thereby constituting the entire group culture.

Like all forms of social structure, the nation is both an interindividual and a transindividual relation of social life, that is, a structure of living beings participating in various complexes of meaning with one another. In contrast to other creations of the mind, for example, the work of art whose meaning, while requiring interpretation by the observer, is nonetheless enclosed within the form of the work, the structure of the social relation, in this case nationality, is open.[34] It is open because individuals enter into the social relation of the nation and leave it upon their death: the social relation is constituted by the existence of these living individuals. Without them, the nation ceases to exist, just as Babylonia no longer exists because there are no living Babylonians. Thus, the nation is a form of life, albeit social life. The work of art, in contrast, once it is created and even though its interpretation is influenced by the viewpoint of the observer, lacks this living component, which is necessary for the existence of the social relation of the nation. The form of the work of art is, relative to the social relation, entirely objective.

Even though the Arab nation is a structure of living beings, it does not really exist merely or primarily because it lacks the experiences and expressions of feeling and belonging together. In addition to the necessary elements of living beings, the social relation has another element necessary to the constitution of an Arab nation. In order for the social relation to exist, the meaning of nationhood around which the relation is formed and sustained requires from the individuals an acknowledgment of the specifics of that meaning of nationhood. In the case of Arab nationality, that meaning includes, above all, the temporally deep image of a territory and all that is implied by the existence of a territory, such as territorially bounded patterns of conduct (national customs) that are perceived as a property or quality by which one classifies others. By acknowledging ever anew this meaning, the individuals constitute and sustain the nation.

The recognition of this paradoxical dual character of nationality, its living objectivity, is crucial to our consideration of the persistence, or lack thereof, of nationality. On the one hand, there is an objective element that is borne by traditions and the constitution of nationality. The latter is reflected in the historically evolving image of a territory as a referent in the relationship. On the other hand, that shared image exists primarily in the minds of the individuals who, as such, are members of the nation. That is why the nation is primarily a phenomenon of collective self-consciousness. Of course, that shared awareness also finds expression in various patterns of conduct and the formation of specific institutions. Nonetheless, if the members of the nation no longer recognize the legitimacy of the nation and its traditions, then the nation ceases to exist. This necessary subjection of the objective traditions constitutive of a nation to simulation by subjective life means that intrinsic to the nation, as with all social relations, is a capacity for instability. It thus should come as no surprise that the Arab nation is undergoing change, even as dramatic as fragmentation.

5

Arab Minorities

Individuals' Fear Absorbed in Groups' Anxieties

Irrational aggression by individuals or groups against an alleged opponent could be explained by fear. In addition to biological and love needs, people have a symbolic appetite for ideas and suitable actions and reactions to reconcile their fears. Rational and irrational fears are like an obsessional system or a paranoid system; they are translated into method whereby normal feelings of sympathy are denatured, numbed, or killed so that people can act with cruelty toward others. The victim is dehumanized by being a source of their fear and converted into a subhuman, a despised animal. This is what has been happening in the Middle East.

Psychiatry and psychoanalysis contribute to the understanding of the consequences of fear, anxiety, and the dynamics of violent power. However, concepts like mania, paranoia, omnipotence, neurosis, and psychosis—elaborated in the realm of individual psychology and useful when dealing with the neurotic conflicts of the person in life and in the psychoanalytic situation—should be applied with caution to political fears of groups and societies. Thus, one should emphasize the difference between harmless paranoid daydreams and the paranoia of a group seeking to eliminate another group.

The pretext here is how to use psychology to explain the authoritarian states in the Middle East and their fear/hate ideology. Again, how can we explain why ethnic and minority uprisings and religious fundamentalism are creating a climate of violence and terror?

When violence surfaces in the political arena, minorities tend to be perpetually watchful, thus recycling manifestations of their rational and irrational fears. Usually this is evident in the hate propaganda and violence promulgated as a response to such a fear. Minorities have always expressed themselves in sayings: Not to forget is to remember. The desire to forget prolongs the banishment. The secret of salvation is called memory.

The understanding of fear involves, then, an understanding of tolerance, consensus, dissent, conflict, and violence. I would like to review these concepts and explore the notion of community. Fear is by no means associated with lack of sympathy. If we are unsympathetic, we are uninterested, and that defeats fear. Nor does tolerance presuppose approval. We have our beliefs, and yet we concede to others the right to have their own beliefs. In this sense toleration in the Middle East is always under strain and is never complete. People have fallen into a vicious cycle, and three criteria are involved. First, people have reasons for considering something intolerable. Second, we cannot tolerate harmful behavior. Third, when we are tolerant, we expect to be tolerated in return.[1]

The bottom line thus appears to be that the ongoing vitality of fear and anxiety rests on the tension between conviction and toleration, not on the still waters of indifference or relativism. Now, let us look further at consensus. It has yet to be noted that consensus is not actual consent; it does not require that everyone give active approval to something. Thus much of what is called consensus may simply be acceptance, that is, diffuse and basically passive concurrence. Even so, consensus is a sharing that somehow binds.[2] It is in the context of such a loosely conceived consensus that fear finds its most agreeable soil.

Understanding consensus is equally crucial for understanding Arab communities, minority tension, religious intolerance, and the acceptance of chauvinism. This chapter assumes that the perception of the social actor is necessary and fundamental in dealing with such concepts and that the understanding of social and political reality is in the actor's point of view. There is some logic to the argument that totality is more than just an autonomous level, and it is the one that dominates a lower level of analysis, and that the explanation of the actions of individuals will be in terms of properties of the encompassing system. Nonetheless, the actor decides what to do and how to understand the nature and sources of action.

The controversy between these two lines of methodology are the concern of social scientists who summed up the difference in terms of structure vs. agency.[3] They call this a prior adoption of a concept of social psychology's character, and they pose the question: Can social reality be reduced to individual actions? Can the apparent properties of the social whole be explained by individual action? It may seem that social psychology is best understood as falling squarely on the agency side. However, the approach still considers that agents themselves are socially produced fictions and that their study is an essential start that one cannot do without.

In trying to deal with minorities and explore individual political identifications and affiliations to groups, answers are not to be found solely in the psychology of group juxtapositions, but they cannot be understood without psychologically taking account of the cognitive and emotional concomitants of individual traits and interactions. To pose purely objective inquiries, such as whether increasing intergroup contact accelerates or retards individuals' separate identities, is to miss the decisive impact of the quality of that contact.[4] It is also to ignore instead of attending carefully to what individuals say about themselves and others. Without antipathy, there can be no individual identity or group affiliation.

Social psychology readings reflect that the self is mainly delimited, incomprehensibly identified, in terms of both relative positive images of who we are and negative images of who we are not. Identity is formed by knowledge of the self as well as of the nonself. Group identity, in particular, is constituted both by positive identification with one's group and by negative identification with the other groups. What is the relationship between these two sources of identity? If the self is well grounded in positive images, might it rely less on sustaining a negative other?

Aversion among individuals of different groups can cause fear as much as it is a result of fear. By the same token, fear becomes a dimension by which conflict-producing comparisons can be made. It is obviously the most powerful and widespread dimension in the Arab world and especially in the Arab East, given the history of group interaction. Without individual fear, group conflict would be less important in the contemporary world. Exploring individual fear helps clarify an otherwise puzzling phenomenon in group conflict: Despite the similarities of groups in an environment like the Arab world, individuals still identify themselves by their religion. Implicit in this is a modification of a commonly articulated proposition derived initially from Freud's narcissism of small differences.[5]

It is often said that the greatest conflict arises between groups who are only slightly different from each other. Comparison is then thought to be more plausible; small differences are an implied individual's self-criticism.[6] It is only logical that individuals of one group compare themselves only with those that they believe, in relevant respects, to be comparable.

A minority is defined as any group with a sense of cohesion who compose a significant proportion of the population of a political entity. A minority is a psychosocial group that synthesizes the general setting in which the individual develops and which determines directions in the perception of his self-identification. Whether integrated in the larger social setting or not, a minority maintains discrete characteristics that are labeled by its members and nonmembers as dissimilar to the norm. In political studies, the word *minority* is the specific and peculiar marker of particular groups living in plural societies, groups that are diverse in culture, faith, or ritual from other groups in these societies. A basic characteristic of a minority, besides being a distinctive social group, is an inbred psychological anxiety informing their conduct that in pragmatic terms makes them feel abhorred and rejected by others. Fear touches almost every aspect of the lives of minorities. It makes politics and society more complex and contributes to alienation, aggression, and revolt. Its continuation is nurtured by the persistent efforts of its members to influence laws and public policy concerning discrimination, physical punishment, the undermining of social values, and constraints on ritual and religious freedoms, marriage, divorce, and inheritance. Moreover, minority groups pressure their governments to pursue a foreign policy favoring their views as a group about the outside world.[7]

Again, from the social studies perspective, minorities may include political factions, social or economic classes, religious or confessional communities, sex and age groups, occupational groups, and language or racial groups. In this chapter, my concern is with only the basic social-political identity that individuals ascribe to themselves in the Arab world via confessional, racial, and national convictions. In this regard, I would like to assert that fear in the Arab world has been a valid force. It has fortified minority identity and provided the backbone of resistance to any other assimilative identity. In this sense, loyalty to one's distinctive minority is often more authentic than proclaimed loyalty to the local state or the Arab nation. Governments and especially minority-dominated states in the Arab world frequently make decisions with a view to retaining this or that group's conditional allegiance, and in the process they perpetuate the minorities' identities and become hostages to specific minority interests. This is evident in Syria, Iraq, Jordan, Sudan, and the Gulf states, and it is institutionalized in Lebanon.[8]

In the presence of several communities, nationhood has only a secondary resonance in the Arab world. The manifestations and expressions of minority politics are in some respects different from those observed in developing nations. The outstanding difference is twofold. The first element is the pattern by which the various minority groupings construct complexes of associations and institutions in nearly every sector of society. As a consequence, most of an individual's essential social, political, and economic life is conducted within the limits of his own minority circle. The second element is the greater prominence and salience of a religious definition of communal solidarity. This could be a legacy from the Islamic and Ottoman periods when communities and peoples were defined and registered according to their confessional or ethnic traits. All attempts to secularize the modern Arab states were unsuccessful; instead, confessional and minority solidarity was perpetuated in the constitution, the legal system, or political activism.[9]

It is worth indicating that minorities of the Arab world have diverse bases. Using Arabism and the Sunni confession of Islam as the axis, minorities could be grouped as Shi'ites, 'Alawites, Druze, Maronites, Orthodox, Catholics, and splinters like Protestants and others as non-Sunni proclaiming Arab identity; the Kurds as Sunni non-Arabs; the Jews as non-Sunni semi-Arabs; the Armenians as non-Arab non-Sunnis; Berbers as Sunni non-Arabs; black Africans in Arab states of North Africa as Sunni non-Arabs and in South Sudan as non-Sunni non-Arabs. These minorities have long had their own communities. New identity groups are emerging that are considered alien in nationality or origin. That is, although Palestinians are Arab Sunnis, they are considered aliens in all of the Arab countries. Wherever they settle, they are unwelcome.

Confessional, ethnic, and national differences are especially thorny political problems in the Arab world. Ethnic diversity along religious, confessional, linguistic, or national lines has resulted in long, bloody conflicts. After independence, the development of different political trends, some of which were sectarian or ethnic, made it inevitable that minority groups remained in their established particularistic consciousnesses. Such groups experience real threats to their identity, welfare, and cultural heritage. The minorities of the Arab world have lived in fear for centuries, inculcated by four centuries of Ottoman non-Arab Sunni rule. The Ottoman Turks were hegemonic, which compelled minorities to withdraw to their inner circles of social interaction, to establish their own institutions, and covertly to devise methods to resist all attempts at assimilation. The successors to the fragmented Ottoman polity, European First, and then the Arab elites aroused even more fear and sensitivity among minorities in the Arab world.

Minorities make no secret of the fear that permeates their social and political lives and of the profound influence that it exerts on their attitudes. Minorities in control of their state (Alawaiits in Syria, Sunnis in Iraq and a few Gulf emirates, and until recently Maronites in Lebanon) have an even greater fear of any future reversal of political fortunes. They think it would mean the physical and brutal oppression of a large number of their members and the end of their political existence. The fear in whose shadow minorities live governs what they do and what they refrain from doing. It dictates their psychological reactions, which may appear incomprehensible and sometimes irrational to friends and foes.

Everywhere in the Arab world, but especially in the Arab East, where the sphere of politics is unusually broad and its impact is powerful, collective security is conferred by political affirmation. For this reason, struggles over relative group power are readily transferred to the political system.[10] In the Arab world, political affirmation confers something else that religious groups seek: minority identification with the polity. Identification can be cast in terms that are exclusive or inclusive. Some minority groups claim that the state and/or the region ought to be theirs and the political system should reflect this fact. Other minority groups merely claim the right to be secure and to be included in the system on equal terms.

Arabs commonly use minority group standards to identify themselves and to analyze politics. They seek power within their own minority group before they can attain power on a national level. Whereas individuals in the West are culturally constrained by the feeling of guilt,[11] individuals in the Middle East are constrained by both guilt and fear. The fear of being subjugated, expelled, or annihilated is the supreme force that lies behind the individual political attitude in the countries of the Arab world. A significant distinction between lifestyles in the Arab world and in Western society is how the individual relates to his environment.[12] In both the actual and the cognitive sense, the person in the Arab world is dominated by the vicissitudes of political nature, that is, group identity, and feels he has little control over his political environment. Arabs lack confidence and a sense of power in their ability to manipulate either their system or their social environment, an attitude reinforced by the historical experience of religious, sectarian, national, and ethnic feuds. This sense of impotence and of danger in the environment induces them to rely each on their own people and leaders for decisions.

This vicious cycle of fear makes individuals of the same group stick together as the only way traditionally available to protect themselves. Arabs experience life in community as a group. A community has a common informative configuration that links people. It reinforces in the individual's behavior a set of stable, habitual preferences and priorities. This could affect his thoughts and feelings. As a result of learned habits, common memories, operating preferences, symbols, events in history, and personal associations, communities become used to certain views regarding others; they have similar ideas about good and bad and they bring up their children to behave in similar ways. Hobsbawm defines community as a collection of living individuals in whose mind and memories the habits and channels of informative traits are carried.[13]

The social and religious beliefs and values that give individuals of all societies a sense of security from those fears have been a source of insecurity in the Arab world.[14] In line with that and by using Freud's reasoning, one could argue that the essential differences between the traditional and the modern psyche of Arabs stem from the development of a powerful superego (conscience). To Arabs in the past, power lay outside the self, although to the individual, the boundaries of self and nonself were not clear.[15] The Arab sought power by following rules set by the gods, the appealing leader, or the tightly knit community. The problem was that, unless the individual felt he was worthy of divine attention, his dependence on deriving power from the divine entity dimmed. The other source of power lay in the social organization of any kind; this allowed for rigid and continuous community controls. Within communities, the individual wanted the gods to protect him from perceived enemies.[16] The modern Arab is slightly different. By espousing the new technologies introduced to his own society, he tends to emphasize the disciplinary qualities of the superego, with all its positive aspects.[17] By providing an inner mechanism of control, the superego permits the individual to develop a stronger sense of self. The source of power is relatively within, not totally without. Furthermore, the accomplishment derived from the modern Arab's internal acceptance of uncertainties and relative control of aggressive drives fosters the development of the ego. This enables him to examine and to manipulate nature, to adapt to new circumstances, and to bring creative energies to bear upon them. However, it does not enable the Arab to overcome fear of the unknown and of other groups.

Drawing upon Max Weber and others, we can trace this development to cultural doctrines and, more particularly, to the role of religions. The modern Arab world demonstrates that the unintended consequences of adapting to a new understanding of religion, and more specifically modern Islamic doctrines, allowed the emergence of a capitalist system associated with economic individualism but not necessarily with political individualism. Weber emphasizes the economic capitalist side of the equation, but the social and political aspects are still not well researched.

Although I treat group psychology as the aggregate of individual perception, the analysis provided here does not negate the autonomous domain in which group psychology operates. At the same time it is acknowledged that a regularity cannot be explained by a single factor and that it makes sense to seek links between phenomena like collective fear and individual fear. A Lebanese Christian leader once said to me in confidence, "Merely by their solidarity as religious groups (the different religious sects), they create fear in me; I could become secure only through the solidarity and security of my own group; the history of sectarian bloodshed in the region does not encourage me to feel at ease." Herein hangs the clue to this chapter. If a sense of security is fundamental, it is attained in considerable measure by belonging to a group that is in turn secure. By embracing the new educational techniques and acquiring the new technologies introduced to his own society, the Arab tends to emphasize the positive qualities of the superego, but only at the economic level.[18]

By providing an inner mechanism of financial control, the superego permits the individual to develop a stronger sense of economic individualism, but not necessarily social and political individualism.[19] The identity and behavior of the individual with regard to social values and politics are primarily and spontaneously a function of his identification with a group.[20] Theories of self-categorization were developed on the assumption of individuality as the primary psychological reality, which is prone to seeing collectivism as the phenomenon to be explained in terms of some failure to attain individualism in certain cultures. In this respect, the self-categorization of Arabs is somewhat a product of social and political individualism.

Social and political individualism in the Arab world is fashioned by the process of communication. In a community group, habits, historical experiences, and preferences are the basis of the coherence of minority groups and even the personalities of individuals. The process of communication within a group reinforces the value system and reproduces patterns of political and social behavior. The history of the Arab world exhibits the value system of sectarian groups as what is commonly known as prescriptive. A prescriptive system is characterized by the comprehensiveness and specificity of its value commitments and by its consequent lack of flexibility.

Compromises are less likely in such a system because of strong commitment to a vast range of specific norms governing almost every situation in life. Most of these norms, including those governing social institutions, are thoroughly integrated with a confessional religious system that invokes ultimate sanctions for every infraction. Thus changes in social and political behavior of the group, not to mention the individual, tend to have ultimate religious implications. In the Islamic faith, sometimes small changes will involve supernatural sanctions, yet when Arab minorities began to face grave dislocations consequent to contact with more powerful groups, they were bound to make changes in their displayed attitudes to survive. What changes must be made in the behavior without undermining the value system?

We may say that the value system of such groups was changing from a prescriptive type to a principle type.[21] Religious groups tend to have a normative system, in which a comprehensive, but uncodified, set of relatively specific norms governs concrete behavior. Ultimate group values lay down the basic principles of social action. Such a normative system is called principle, but the group system does not interfere in economic, political, and social life in great detail, as it did when the group was prescriptive. If we look at this distinction in a different way, we may say that there exists a division between religion and ideology, between ultimate values and proposed ways in which these values may be put into effect. Thus sectarian groups under pressure tend to tolerate the distinction between religion and social ideology that makes possible greater flexibility at both levels.[22]

When facing pressure, how does the normative system of religious group change from prescriptive to principle? In reading history, one could assert that only new movements that claim religious superiority can successfully challenge the old value system and its religious base. New movements that arise from necessity to make drastic social changes in light of new pressures from other groups are essentially ideological and political in nature. However, any new movement must take on a religious coloration in order to meet the old system on its own terms. Even when such a movement is successful in establishing major structural interaction with other religious groups and in freeing initiatives formerly frozen in traditional patterns, the problems posed by its partly religious origin and its relation to the traditional religious system may still be serious indeed.

From a psychological perspective, structural interaction has an impact on the minds of individuals, and that occurs in all societies, even the most primitive. All civilizations have been accompanied by a heightening of superego development as a consequence of structural interaction. In some instances this led to the emergence of a new, more universalistic religious system. It is possible, moreover, that in some parts of the Arab world, the superego development was comparable to that of the West. As Weber argues, however, cultural developments in the West were unusual from the outset. First, the emergence of a prophetic religion gave a peculiar intensity to the superego. Second, the emphasis was on an individual rather

than a communal relationship with God. Third, religious-cultural imperatives stressed general moral rules. Fourth, God was conceived as standing
apart from nature, and his workings could be comprehended through reason and empirical observation. Finally, great emphasis was placed on re-
pressing the passions in the service of worldly asceticism, that is, fulfilling
one's obligations through activity in this world.[23]

Some of these themes were present in the predominantly Islamic Arab
world. This was a unique combination. It is undoubtedly true that Islam,
as it absorbed and merged with the diverse civilizations in the Arab societies, strongly emphasized control of individual passions, producing a
contradictory result in the different minority groups via a fear culture.

Indeed, Islam created perhaps the greatest premodern empire. The Islamic civilization was Europe's superior in wealth and practical technical
achievement until at least the fifteenth century and perhaps even the six-
teenth century. However, the Islamic view of nature did not encourage a
breakthrough to a modern scientific worldview. It surrounded the individual with a network of kin and other social obligations inhibiting the
growth of that individualism which played so important a role in the
break with tradition in Europe. It also encouraged, or at least did not
discourage, supernatural reliance and magical thinking among the general
populace.

Thus Islamic regimes, especially those that adopted the Koran as their
constitution, were and still are highly conservative. The Arabs, for example, use the energy derived from social and cultural self-discipline in the
service of national causes. However, the different Islamic doctrines were
such that neither of the Arab societies could bring the modern world into
existence despite their need for that.

The following points of view are derived from the various psychological instruments mostly developed by Lichter, Rothman, and Lichter.[24] Although they compared American businessmen to journalists in the United
States, their work is applicable to the Arab world. They demonstrated that
group leaders exhibit a low need for achievement and a high need for
power. These leaders are also more suspicious of others than normal men
and are considerably more narcissistic.

All of the known characteristics of leaders of Arab groups lead us to
assert that they seek to denigrate other powerful leaders in the society,
especially their political views. Their ability to engage in this kind of activity, regardless of its limitation by custom, the law, public attitudes, and
their political deference, has recently increased exponentially. Even if we
are to assume that not all of the minority leaders are like this, a sufficient

number set the tone of interaction. The result is a powerful drive for all leaders to engage in such behaviors, whatever one's intention, because such defense mechanisms become necessary for survival and success.

My observation of minority leaders in the Arab world allows me to say that their creative efforts in undermining one another result in a picture of reality that is critical of existing national institutions for reasons that are not well defined. This picture is most effective when leaders are part of the day to day action rather than developing explicit and central ideological discourse. The boundaries within which leaders of minority groups express themselves are the medium that in turn has been one emphasizing the legitimacy of expressive individualism as against the limitations imposed by a previous Arab cultural view that emphasizes group solidarity. And so far the impact of such presentations has been quite significant. Most of the studies of such influence have dealt with television, legitimately because it has been the medium with the greatest impact.

The process of how Arab leaders feed individuals through television (government elite in the Arab world occupy substantial time on television news) proceeds somewhat as follows: With its powerful psychological impact on viewers, television contributes to the construction of values and the likelihood that such values will be exhibited in action. Individuals construct their values by interpreting the social and political dimensions of their leaders' comments and speeches. This provides experiences that form an individual's knowledge base from which to draw inferences of his world. From this knowledge, the individual determines what behaviors are valued and what his responsibilities are to his specific group.

By virtue of its growing accessibility and its appropriation by group leaders in the Arab world, mass media assume an increasing heterogeneous influence on the construction of a person's identity and reality. For their own commercial purposes, statistics released by the media establishments show that individuals spend more time reading and viewing the different channels of the media than with families. All media contribute to the construction of an individual's knowledge base and perception of reality. The visual forms seem to have the greatest influence, partly because of their accessibility (e.g., television, film), and partly because people retain visual information with greater accuracy. As a result, individuals are vulnerable to grossly inaccurate representations of reality.

To fuel up already feuding societies, the interactive nature of media contributes to the isolation of the Arab individual and causes new dimensions of fear and alienation as reported by young Arabs. Moreover, this trend toward an individualistic and idiosyncratic medium undermines any attempt to give young Arabs a reference point for establishing values and boundaries of behavior with a larger group or the Arab world at large.

Media attract Arab consumers by drawing on their natural affinity for novelty. The problem is that people also develop a tolerance for novelty. Therefore, to maintain their commercial influence, the media must also increase their presentations of violence and vengeance. Thus, as the media play a greater role in the lives of individuals, they also widen the gulf between what is reality and what is media reality. Recent violent actions in the Middle East were based on the new reality of expectations. When the new Arab generations accept the validity of media reality, they are more likely to act in a manner characteristic of the violent models found in media.

The media do not accurately portray the demands of responsible living. Indeed, for many individuals, the media contribute to feelings of alienation and incompetence. The result is that some people may not act on the values that they know are ethical.[25] Even if the media do not intend to contribute to the formation of values, they do. Unintentional learning is just as effective as intentional learning. What matters is the number of relationships Arabs draw from presented information. The media are teaching violence to Arabs, whether they want to learn or not.

Research shows that television and other media have had a powerful influence on attitudes toward individual responsibility and restraint, sexuality, and aggression against other groups, especially with young viewers.[26] The cultural changes spread by the new elites have consequences for both personality and social action. As usual, such changes have produced structural shifts in the Arab society to include new group-oriented patterns and changes in social and political character.

Hate, aggression, and violence have become experiences in self-realization and at times duties and obligations, and this fundamental reality has had far-reaching effects in Arab societies. Young Arabs are disciplined in the present condition mode, both because parents want them to conform to what is and to be similar to them. Added to this is the high rate of divorce and single-parent households among Muslims. This leads to new cultural behavior that stresses both estrangement and violence. Individuals seeking protection within their own minority groups exemplify the character of such a cultural behavior stemming from the family. Usually individuals feel safer expressing their violent attitudes in society through a group, especially if this group criticizes the existing social and political environment.

Some might argue that a large part of the Arab world now is witnessing political stability at the expense of social stability. But Arabs have projected the ability to express their social grievances and to bring their political passions under some control. Social and political stability in the Arab world has been achieved at a high cost of pain. In line with Freud's thinking, men and women have always rebelled against the price that has had to be paid in any revolution seeking change.

Paradoxically, there are limits to toleration, and even if people do not immediately rebel, they extend a genuine effort at condemnation. Once group feelings become confined to the role of their leaders, their effort in spreading condemnation is entrusted to accepted inner circles. Individuals within the confinement of their groups regard any form of authority that comes from without to limit their choice of life as a form of oppression. They want to be completely free to satisfy their impulses, whatever these may be.

What I see in the Arab world is not promising. Religion in its consecrated influence has declined in its magnitude, yet it is promoting political segregation among the minority groups. Evidence suggests that, whatever Arab rationalists may have believed, losing that internal sanctification which gave the lives of previous generations structure and meaning has left the present generation in a gloomy and empty life. Increasingly, Arabs feel torn between the desire for power and gratification, on the one hand, and the fear of losing control, on the other. They sway between longing for complete individual autonomy and wishing to drop in something that will give their existence order. If political authority lacks order, then this drive is sought in religious institutions.

This perception is best explained when Freud aligns omnipotence with self-love and the love of others. Freud connects the capacity to know reality with the capacity to love, and he outlines the ethics of renunciation.[27] He sees mankind as evolving according to the following developmental outline: How can the human give up the pleasure principle? Inefficiently, caught between the pleasure principle and the reality principle, the individual still craves the illusion of omnipotence as a way out. With this we pass to the social uses of omnipotence in groups, nations, and masses.[28]

Freud was aware of the contrast between the social and narcissistic levels of the individual's state of being. In *Group Psychology and the Analysis of the Ego*, Freud explained that in the individual mental life, someone else was invariably involved, as model, object, helper, or opponent. And so from the very first, individual psychology was also social psychology. Possibly echoing Nietzsche's saying the *Thou* is older than the

I, Freud reasons that the psychology of groups is the oldest human psychology. It is only recently that scholars isolated individual psychology by neglecting all traces of the group.[29]

Again, Freud emphasized the unconscious state of group fascination, derived from imitation and suggestion into which members of a minority could be hypnotized by their group leader. Freud continued to reflect that, first, the individual forming part of a group acquires solely from numerical considerations a sentiment of unbeatable power, which allows him to yield to instincts, which, had he been alone, he would prefer to keep under restraint. A group is characterized as being anonymous so that the individual's sense of responsibility disappears entirely within the group. The second cause is contagion, which is classed among phenomena of a hypnotic order. A third cause is suggestibility: When it is isolated, a person may be a cultivated individual; in a group, he is a barbarian acting by instinct. In this sense the individual possesses the spontaneity, the violence, the ferocity, and also the enthusiasm and heroism of primitive beings. In the group, the individual throws off the repressions of his unconscious impulses, all that is evil in the human mind, leading to a disappearance of conscience. The group has a sense of omnipotence; the notion of impossibility disappears for the individual in a group.[30]

Individuals merge in the group to lose their sense of limits; this takes place within what is psychologically known as the principle of direct induction of emotion. The individual loses his control of criticism, a feeling intensified by mutual interaction. When an individual is immediately in a group, he subscribes to collective impulsiveness, violence, fickleness, inconsistency, and extremity in action. Freud adds to these characteristics the pattern of becoming extremely suggestible, careless in deliberation, hasty in judgment, easily swayed and led, lacking in self-consciousness, devoid of self-respect and a sense of responsibility, and apt to be carried away by the consciousness of its own force. If an individual seeks power in a group, the end result is a tendency to produce all the manifestations we have come to expect of any irresponsible or absolute power.

If well isolated, minority group behavior in the Middle East is like a disorderly child, a wild beast, or an untutored passionate savage.[31] The blood that minority groups in the Arab world have shed testifies to such descriptions.

Then again, to be fair in our analysis, one has to look at the other side of the coin. Another factor that appears to have a definite positive impact on an individual joining a group is personal happiness derived from social relationships. In the Arab world where material happiness is lacking due to cultural and economic factors, to love and to feel loved are certainly perceived as important to one's happiness. Also, to be a member of a large family and affiliated with a group may compensate for extreme poverty.

Furthermore, finding meaning in life is also important, and it can be considered a motivational component of minorities' solidarity in the Arab world.[32] The Arab feels that he must be committed to something or someone in order to experience a sense of meaning. Hence a member of a minority group in the Arab world recognizes that personal goals will be perceived as contributing to happiness, if they are shared with others having the same cultural background.

When it comes to happiness and group solidarity, other conditions seem to have a positive impact. The political system may influence a person's happiness. It is expected that individuals with unstable political conditions will be inclined to consider happiness in their minority groups as a substitute for the anxiety derived from the whole be it a state or a nation.

Freud argues that a group impresses the individual as possessing unlimited power, and this is another source of happiness. In an unstable political system where the individual is reluctant to extend obedience to the state, he offsets their guilt feeling by adhering to the new authority of the group. He may put his former conscience out of action.[33] In this sense one could address the all-important connection between power and love in Arab minority group dynamics.

Again, to speak of the power and love among minority groups, Freud's overall concept is that love relationships and emotional ties also constitute the essence of the group mind.[34] A group has a mind of its own, and it is an essential ingredient in the life of a minority group to find a role, work, and action. The saying "The family that prays together stays together" holds equally well for the primitive hunting horde that preys together, as well as for its modern counterparts: the workplace, the corporation, the team. This is also an essential source of that force which makes for group cohesion, and it manifests itself as a dual love bond among the members of the group and between the group and its leader.

From a sociological perspective, a minority group is popularly conceived as a set of intellectual distinctions in beliefs, habits, social conduct, and so forth. Some discourses claim physiological distinctions among large, historically connected populations. With its common history, language, customs, and self-identity, a minority group is distinctive in culture more than in nature. A distinctive group is not, however, a concept easily broached in the Arab world. Arab nationalists claim that it is foreign in origin and consequences. Notions of group superiority are said to be at the root of the push by foreigners (Western powers) to impose their values on Arabs. However, they have hardly produced compelling evidence for the creation of a special category of group conflict different from other conflict types, that is, intrastate, interstate, and extrastate conflicts. Furthermore, by basing their categories on ambiguous criteria such as elite rationalizations for conflict, they have created a biased population of cases. These problems pose real difficulties for research on groups or, better, intercultural conflict. Because culture is a constant in human conflict, scholars interested in the impact of culture on conflict must analyze the observable relations among Arab minorities as distinctive groups with varying cultural characteristics. Although case studies of group conflicts are instructive, they often assume the salience of cultural factors when, in fact, one should employ analysis on the extent to which cultural similarities and differences are associated with conflict.

Recently, scholars have focused their research on the argument that cultural or ethnic differences are at the heart of group conflicts. Notwithstanding, there are often great commonalities across intercultural fractures and long histories of cross-cultural cooperation among many of the present-day antagonists.

Sudden convulsions of ethnic violence, such as in the case of Sudan and Iraq, often are viewed as resulting from historic cultural gulfs. However, as historians note, to explain an antagonism that sprang up suddenly and died down suddenly, one need not discover, and cannot effectively use, a factor that has been constant over a long period as the cultural difference between the two groups. Often the image of culture groups in conflict is an ideological construct of nationalist historians and politicians attempting to portray ethnic groups as actors and parties to the spoils and/or sentiment arising from ethnic conflict. Analysis of interethnic conflict provides empirical substantiation for the conclusion that even in the most ethnic conflict–ridden parts of the globe, that is, Arab African societies, interethnic cooperation is much more prevalent than its antithesis.

One could argue, in comparing the Arab world with Eastern Europe, that the cold war did not put a lid on a boiling cultural cauldron; it simply poured dressing over a multicultural tossed salad. It provided the subtext for the ascendancy of power politics over concerns of cultural identity. The end of the cold war has focused academics away from power and toward ideational constructs including culture as potential explanations for the ascendancy of soft politics in the post–cold war era. What has not accompanied this refocusing of attention is a reconsideration of some basic assumptions of minority conflicts.

Minority conflict is a confrontation at any level: political, social, and/or military in which the contending actors or parties identify themselves or each other or are so identified by outsiders in minority terms, that is, using cultural criteria. These criteria include any self-defined combination of shared culture, nationality, language, religion, and race. Sociologists define minority conflict as a dispute about important political, economic, social, cultural, or territorial issues between two or more minority communities. Again, sociologists attempt a more operational definition of minority conflicts because the traditional definition comprises threats to values based on a minority boundary between in-groups and out-groups. These threats have the potential to give rise to group mobilization and politicization via separate community, society, or state. These threats to values encompass cultural, political, social, religious, and economic factors.

Scholars have been less attentive to the process by which cultural boundaries among minorities in the Arab world are created and maintained and even less so to how in-groups come to violence against outgroups. Scholars who rely on the statements of elites as to the salience of minority factors in disputes as justification for labeling them minority conflicts concede this point.

Any study of Arab societies and politics should begin by acknowledging the existence of multiple groups within the Arab world. The predisposition as such is to assert that the group is a central unit of the social order and individuals are important to study in the context of their group memberships.

It is worth trying to place Arab politics on two tracks: the relations among groups and the politics that transcends groups. It goes without saying that the institutional structure of political decision making and the resources necessary for groups to participate in the Arab world systematically privilege some groups at the expense of others. In this sense, the public goods are not neutral; rather, they tend to mask conflicts and to favor the interests of those who control political, economic, and communicative resources. The normative weight given this supposedly common interest makes the critical perspectives of less powerful groups appear partial and selfish.

Thus, what characterizes multigroup societies like the Arab world is not mere diversity but rather inequality in group difference whose meaning is produced, mediated, and sustained by oppressive power relations. What distinguishes one Arab group from another is the account of what kinds of groups are political and how close they are to the arena of politics.

Broadly speaking, it is important to focus on groups in terms of economic self-interest and opinions on particular issues. Whether, or in what ways, the character of Arab political groups is distinctive is a matter of some argument. Although some writers have argued that groups could be distinguished by their egalitarian organization and nonmaterialist values such as cultural identity, others contend that such distinctions between groups are indefensible. But it is undeniable that contemporary Arab minority groups have brought to public attention the significant powers, interests, activities, and inequalities beyond the economic or occupational and beyond the formal political realm. These groups hold a particular kind of operation precisely because the primary site for political action is the state. The way in which contemporary groups have politicized practices and relationships previously screened into a so-called private realm makes possible a politics that extends the terrain of political contestation to the everyday enactment of social practices and the routine reiteration of cultural representations. Conceptualizing politics in terms of group sites for action makes it possible to sustain and enact multifaceted political identities.

This caution about accepting the state as the primary site for political agency might lead us to question whether rethinking institutional representation is a useful democratic project. Certainly the dangers for minority groups of working with or within the state have been much discussed by concerned scholars. In the literature on transitions to democracy in the Arab world, these concerns might also seem to offer a caution about using the language of citizenship to talk about group identities and their political significance, since citizenship seems particularly to invoke a primary relationship with the state. The understanding here is that citizenship is a powerful legitimating label for political action and political association and that it can and should be seen in the context of authorized rights of expressions and actions given to minority groups. Political action by groups in the Arab world indicates the deep plurality of citizenship, as a set of practices in various places that are not reducible to one core membership, principle, or purpose.

Minority groups influence politics with regard to the impact of citizenship. This influence is designated as a multiplicity that highlights the heterogeneity of meaningful forms of political action. There are countless ways and sites in the Arab world in which minorities engage worldly power and negotiate their presence and their relatedness to the power-laden authorities. But in addition to asserting an expanded and multifaceted sense of citizenship, I would like to emphasize that an overly exaggerated conceptualization of the state does not work. For example, there exist in Lebanon and similar plural societies in the Arab world fairly broad constraints for minority groups to act within the state without getting co-opted or draining civil society. Thus far, minority group claims cannot be tied to the state imperatives of accumulation or legitimacy. Engagements of claims are considered unworthy of the effort. Arab minorities and in that respect Arab states have not learned from the West where all groups as actors populating all sites in the state act to further imperatives of accumulation and legitimation. In the West, the processes of coordination and aggregation of actions within the state invariably support these imperatives.[35] Yet again, the contemporary Arab state has a more complex character, composed of multiple and irregular phenomena and characterized by multiple modalities of power.[36]

The challenge is to mediate between overly diffuse and overly unified concepts of the different Arab state powers, because the state should be understood in its capacity to fuse material and ideological elements. Again, the sociophysical presence of state institutions is bound up with diverse and often conflicting discursive understandings about the identities of the state and the principles on which it is legitimate for the state to act. The multiplicity of Arab state identities means that actors can struggle against particular aspects of state identity while mobilizing others. In the process, some state organizations try to maintain a distance from certain aspects of state identity, especially those that represent elite interests and produce minority groups' inequality. They link themselves to other policymaking power. The success of such struggles is affected by the contextual limits, that is, historical, institutional, and discursive to the state identities that can be coherently embodied.

It is important to note that different state identities are effects of actions and processes within and against the state. One such effect can indeed be the notion of a coherent state as an exercising agency capable of advancing and implementing a specific agenda. Thus the state, as a functional entity, is sometimes solidified, coherent, and purposive. At other times it is permeable and changeable, often complex or contradictory. The intuitive possibility worth pursuing is that within such a state, citizen identities can be enacted in ways that are more complex than those of the unitary rights-bearing individual or the member of bounded and distinct groups. The questions here are how and why?

The very multiplicity of the state in the Arab world makes it almost too abstract as a site for answering how and why. This is not to argue against using the structural-functional concept of the state, but rather to suggest that the dangers and efficacy of state-related actions and interventions need to be evaluated with respect to specific institutional contexts. The different kinds of groups where each could have a claim to political place force us to face not simply the multiplicity of individual identity but the obscurity of the concept of group itself. Groups are based on or constituted by a variety of factors. Are groups based on race, religion, or ethnicity? From a political perspective, is it possible for groups to share interests, opinions, needs, experiences of oppression, and practices? Which of these is to be the privileged political bond that defines and designates groups? What is the significance of different levels of belonging among individuals in Arab societies to their groups?

I raise these questions not to suggest that political psychology can provide objective answers to them. What has also distinguished minority groups and other social movements in the Arab world is the recognition that the drawing of boundaries between groups and the sorting of individuals among groups are manifestations of social power. So underlying these questions about group membership is the question of who decides. What are the social mechanisms that the group maintains, and what are the political consequences of those groupings? And how is identity orchestrated?

This argument—that power produces group identity—has been made in a different theoretical register as well and precisely to criticize the assumptions of representational politics. The very concept of representation invokes something outside itself, to which it refers.[37] Scholars influenced by poststructuralist theories of power have argued that this outside, this object of reference, is illusory. The illusion is not about the material existence of the outside but, rather, about its character as outside. The illusion is that the represented object is given, natural, inherent in the order of things independent of the practice of representation. On the contrary, these critics argue, the identity to which representation refers is an effect of the representational practice itself. Copts in Egypt, for example, have been labeled as a category of subjects by the very structures of power materialized in laws and other forms of regulation that purport merely to represent them. This can be articulated as an argument for identity fortified by procedures and practices, which impose a collective unity on groups and individuals and put into effect a categorization that produces outsiders or others.[38]

If the Arab world is different in its structural makeup, then one could devise two perspectives on the meaning of variable politics that have been imagined and enacted as a response to these understandings of power as productive of Arab minorities' identity. The first perspective is suggested and pursued by a variety of social movements that engage in group self-definition to redefine and reclaim the meaning and value of the group identity. This is not uncontroversial, of course, because such strategies either perpetuate the category that should be challenged or obscure its constructed nature. Thus the second perspective is to resist the very notion of categorization. This can be undertaken in a liberal individualist mode refusing to treat group difference as significant, or with a postmodern sensibility refusing to speak in terms of fixed groups, and enacting multiple and fluid identities.[39]

My point in recounting these debates about minorities and group identity is to underscore that our answers to them determine how we analyze Arab politics, practices, and institutions. This is done to emphasize that those Arab practices shape members of minority groups and produce and preclude various versions of what they are. Any attempt to change by collective effort of minorities will be an act of power, which is to say, in agreement with the analysis of power as productive. That will develop group identities in the Arab world.

With respect to the why and how questions raised earlier, then, the major reason why it is important to analyze state processes is that current Arab institutions have major impact and power to shape citizens' identity and social manifestations. Social scientists have created a category of minority group conflict that focuses on discrimination as a precursor to elite mobilization of groups in pursuit of collective interests. Clearly, such scholars' use of elite rationalizations for violence is done to justify the promulgation of new categories of conflict, that is, minority conflicts.

Another course of argument that I would like to pursue is the linkage of Arab cultural factors with other conflict-inducing issues to ascertain the extent to which the cultural factors are significant predictors of conflict among Arab minority groups. However, given the sectarian and ethnic diversity in the Arab world, it is not apparent in the obtainable literature why one cultural factor, like religion, is more significant than another, like ethnicity. Do elites find it easier to mobilize against religiously dissimilar groups? Or does ethnic difference breed ethnocentrism, making it easier for elites to mobilize their ethnic kin to war against ethnic others (i.e., the case in Iraq, Sudan, and Algeria)? Although the parties to the conflict will always consist of culture groups acting within or outside the agency of a state, they may not always have symmetrical military resources, equal access to wealth, similar forms of social hierarchy, or common cultural practices. Across such dissimilar characteristics, the interaction of groups should be analyzed. For example, we can analyze the relationship between the cultural characteristics of minority groups and their levels of conflict without assuming any culturally determined process. Or we can simply examine the relationship between the cultural differences and similarities of minority groups and their involvement in conflict and feuds.

In dealing with the culture of conflict and the conflict of culture among ethnic and minority groups in the Arab world, it is important to introduce another analytical factor: the sublimated ego-psychological-emotional tie (i.e., perception of a common quality shared by one individual with some other person or group). The mutual tie between group members is in the nature of their identification. It is based on an important emotional common quality, and this common quality lies in the nature of the tie with the leader. A good example of a common work and love bond is offered by the army and religious institutions, where perceived mutual love gives rise to the same illusion (i.e., the leader is regarded as an elder brother or father figure). Here, the similarity with the family is invoked as well as the possibility of a leading idea being substituted for the leader and upon the relations between the two.[40]

There exists a culture of fear within the Arab family that makes families feud. Members of the same family are afraid of harm. This creates a mass mind within the family that is transferred to the community or group. Arabs are united by their shared fears. Freud calls this "ego ideal," and it is commonly known as the "moral conscience."[41]

Freud explained the function of choosing and following ideas and ideals in relation to their embodiment in leaders, historical personalities, and group identities. This will pave the way for combining the forces of love, identification, and group identities into an integrated dynamic whole. In individual love relations, Freud says, everything that the object does and asks for is right and blameless. Conscience has no application to anything that is done for the sake of the object. In the blindness of love, cruelty is carried to the pitch of crime. The whole situation can be summarized in the following formula: The object, which is Freud's replacement for "person," has been put in the place of the ego ideal. In this sense the loved person has been put in the place of the conscience. This applies, of course, not only to lovers, a group formation with two members, but also to masses in relation to their leaders, where people put one and the same object in the place of their ego ideal and also identify themselves with one another in their ego.[42]

The manifestation of ego ideal as conscience and group identity results in the individual giving up his ego ideal and substituting the group ideal as embodied in the leader. Social psychology is rich with studies of how the minority group can somehow overpower or overwhelm the autonomous genetic self through a leader. If we are to apply such studies on the minority groups' reality in the Arab world, we observe clearly the de-individuation, risky shift, conformity, obedience, groupthink, social loafing, and diffusion of responsibility, socially responsive behavior as framed in opposition to individual behavior and construed as compromising individual behavior.

Are minority groups in the Arab world free to chart their own destiny, or are they slaves to their history, culture, and psychology? Perhaps the continued study of minority groups from a political psychology perspective will reveal how cultural and psychological frameworks powerfully structure diversified minority groups and keep them from dissolving in the larger political settings.

6

Religion

Appeasing Psychological Fear and Creating Political Instability

Although psychology is a methodical field dealing with the human mind and nature, when it comes to the study of religion it is completely ambiguous. If what we understand about the human mind and the power source of religion is limited, it would be impossible to supply information explaining the fundamentals necessary to achieve an understanding of religion and its command over the individual, society, and the state.

Being conscious of religion is a complex proposition between our senses, our thoughts, and our emotions. But our subconscious is vague in its output. Either it supplies a specific emotion to a specific thought, or it radiates the emotional hum of our basic instincts of fear and anxiety inherited at birth. If psychic fears exist, they lie within the subconscious and radiate as a basic instinct. One of these instincts is responsible for our ability to feel the emotions of another because we could relate to other people's fears. In these instances, fear becomes a combined social and psychological phenomenon. It does not leave the confines of the mind, for it remains a part of the whole. In many instances, fear generates energy that expands from the confines of the mind. This energy is manifested in human relations at all levels in family, religious solidarity, and social and political interactions.

Literature on the psychology of religion presents ten hypotheses as potential theoretical explanations, subdivided into three categories: origin hypotheses (i.e., neural factors, cognitive need, fear of death, superego projection, sexual motivation), maintenance hypotheses (i.e., social learning, deprivation, personality factors), and consequence hypotheses (i.e., personal integration and social integration).[1]

The concern of this chapter is to bridge these categories and specifically to highlight the concept of fear in their imperative relevance to the understanding of the religious phenomenon. I begin with the connection be-

tween fear and religion as a form of ideology, and from the outset I emphasize the irrational nature of separation and locate these two forces in social
or interpersonal relations. Fear and religion as ideology do not exist in
isolation. This discerning is derived from Freud's sociological essays. The
essays in question are *Totem and Taboo, Group Psychology and the
Analysis of the Ego, The Future of an Illusion,* and *Civilization and Its
Discontents.* Freud was much concerned in these essays with matters of
ideology, for he attacked religion as an institution. He claimed that religion distorted the picture of the real world in a delusional manner by
forcibly fixing people in a state of psychical infantilism and by drawing
them into a mass delusion.[2]

Freud was at first reserved about the dynamics of fear, and during the
middle phase of his creative years he was mainly interested in biological
urges, for libido as a form of energy seemed to provide a scientific para-
digm for psychoanalysis. He wrote little about fear, for like love, fear did
not fit into any of his theoretical models. Fear, not sex, was Freud's last
hidden concern. He reversed his denial of the real and causal role of fear
in relationships when he speculated on aggression, especially that which is
derived from fear, and fear as it manifests itself in the death instinct.

Fear is a pervasive reality in personal, social, legal, and political relations. Then again, fear that stems from pain is a necessary biological precondition for the preservation of the species. However, fear in the child
allows him to recognize parental power. It is fear of pain that makes the
child see his parents as not only powerful but omnipotent, and it also
creates the images of the good and the bad parent, for that power can be
used to heal and to hurt, to protect and to punish. Parental power can be
compassionate and empowering, but it can also be abusive and criminal.
Parents can overpower their children by enforced deprivation, indoctrination, physical torture, mutilation, and even murder.

In the religious realm, power and authority are derived from fear. Religious institutions, in any form, mean the wielding of power derived from
the fears of believers. Absolutism, or autocracy, the ancient form of religious rule in which power was vested in a religious figure or an institution,
could be either enlightened or tyrannical. In line with this and in the same
practice, the abuse of power in the family, a ruling-class group or party, or
the state creates the soil for the social and psychological creation of omnipotence claimed by the mighty on earth and attributed to the Almighty
in heaven. In many religions the central attribute of the deity is limitless
power called God Almighty, Allah-Akbar in Arabic, and omnipotence in
Latin. Individuals can be powerful in many ways, but their power has

limits. It is only God who is all-powerful, which brings us into the realm of religion and belief.

Arabs regardless of their confession believe that faith moves mountains and conquers enemies and that the word of God is mightier than the sword. Somehow next to the rude power of physical force there is the power of ideology and belief, the power of persuasion and indoctrination, of political propaganda, of image and opinion making, the power of demagogues and spiritualists that become the controllers of the masses. Religion is one thing, and its use is another. In the Arab world it is being shaped in the media and the meetings and in ways through which the Arab masses can be manipulated.

In the Arab family, religion sustains parental power: the various ways in which parents rationalize their power by an appeal to nature-given or God-given authority, sacred by custom and religion. Such beliefs are based on well-wishing. There is a tendency to represent the parents as God-like and God as the heavenly all-loving father. Arabs have traditionally believed that God's unquestionable attributes are his omnipresence, omnipotence, and omniscience. Freud attributed religious beliefs to a projection of mankind's inherent state of fear, helplessness, and dependency onto a God imagined as all-powerful.

As expressed by Sartre, an individual's basic project is to be similar to God. An Arab's desire to imitate God is acted out in collusion between the rulers and the ruled to result in mutually shared dreams, or delusions of omnipotence, contrary to reason and the limitations imposed by reality. The Arab rulers act the part of self-styled gods, and the ruled worship such man-made gods as portraits and facsimiles, to participate in the reflected glory of their declared omnipotence. The ruler and the ruled share a burden of responsibility for this collusion. But here is one social difference: The collusion between the Arab leaders and their subjects allows the former what is not allowed to the latter.

Kings and presidents in the Arab world have the power to act and speak like gods, and they are obeyed as gods; ordinary people saying they are gods are regarded as madmen and locked up in asylums, even when they are harmless. Do such explanations help us understand social and political phenomena in the Arab world, such as the rise of dictatorships and the ideology or the current trend of fundamentalism?

In many psychoanalytic texts, power is a descriptive, dynamic, and developmental concept. Descriptively, it frequently appears together with such social and political labels as grandiosity, supercontrol, self-importance, and terror. Dynamically, it is a mechanism of defense. Developmentally, it is assumed to be the most ancient mode of relating to oneself and others. Dialectically, with the widening of the scope of psychoanalytic theories, there has been a tendency to apply traditional psychopathological entities to ideas and feelings experienced in the course of ordinary life. Thus, power is now everyone's defense against fear.[3]

From this perspective, the quest for Islamic power is collectively appealing to Muslim fundamentalists, which some social scientists dismiss as irrelevant in the study of Islamists and insist on all side-distinctions between revivalist and fanatic or extremist fundamentalists. Such fundamentalists share the common objective of reestablishing the power of Islam as the basis of recovery and strength to overcome fear and anxiety derived from perceiving the other as superior. Their central theme of power relations and authority over a century has been given an explicit revolutionary logic by modern Muslim fundamentalists.

But history demonstrates that the logic derived from certain types of fear could produce other forms of fear, thus fundamentalist revolutionary violence did not win the day in the Arab world, i.e., as in Algeria, Sudan, Syria, and Jordan. In the contest of power, using its repressive arm, the state emerged triumphant over the fundamentalists. Indeed, throughout the Arab region, the militaries and security forces, under the tight control of the regimes, manipulated the common fears of people and acted as instruments of consolidation and repression to preserve the status quo. Thus, contrary to the perspective of social scientists that the Islamists could find the Sudanese example of military-fundamentalist alliance a guide for future strategy, the military-backed fundamentalist regime in Sudan remains an unsuccessful deviation in the Arab world.

In psychoanalysis, power and fear are a joint formation of the individual called the "Rat Man" and his parents. According to Freud, whenever the Rat Man is enraged at his father, he will succumb to the obsessional belief in the omnipotence of his wishes so that evils would be bound to come upon his father. This exemplifies the relationship between individuals and the state. Again, the individual comes to a shaky belief in the omnipotence of his thoughts and feelings, whether good or evil, and a doubt in the omnipotence of his love and his hatred that is independent of his parents, and thus the state is not to be blamed. Omnipotence as a concept does not stand by itself; it is an empty vessel that has to be filled with something, such as the belief in the omnipotence of thought or, as here, the omnipotence of love and hatred. On the other hand, Freud is inclined to assume that this idea of omnipotence is a delusion and to explain it as a historical object of the old megalomania of infancy. Freud was not positively sure that the attitude of omnipotence could have been a product of a specific power interaction between the Rat Man and his parents.[4]

The belief in religious omnipotence is probably a throwback to a stage of child development. It is characterized by the child's reluctance to act out of fear of consequences of his or her actions. Then again, the individual is never quite satisfied with this feeling of omnipotence. The source of this is due to the apparent delusion of omnipotence in the mother-child relationship. Originally, as indicated in psychology, omnipotence is a feeling that one has because it is what he desires. It is created by life in the womb and as such it is not an empty delusion. The problem arises unconsciously as the basis for subsequent repeated demands for the return of a state that once existed. The newborn spends all his life longing to regain this situation of being protected. The substitute is found in institutions like religious societies, political parties, or the state.[5]

Leaders of religious societies sometimes develop the personality of a good nurse, instilling a sense of belonging into the soul of the newborn. A person who abides by religious leaders' directives is like the infant who relies on the nurse to replicate the warmth and comfort he or she experiences with a mother. When such is unrewarding, the individual will realize it in the form of a wish-fulfilling hallucination, creating the feeling of a magical-hallucinatory omnipotence.

People need to be loved, to be the center of the universe. The disappointment in love that comes through punishments, threats, and a harsh tone of voice has a traumatic effect. Personality disorders occur. The individual has to adapt and thus he lingers in the hallucination: "Nothing has happened. I am still loved the same as before. God loves me and protects me and gives me power." This is a manifestation of hallucinatory omnipotence. All subsequent disappointments in one's love life may well regress to what Ferenczi called the wish-striving fulfillment.[6]

The individual is always in a group and is always fearful of the power of his wish to destroy his family, i.e., his group. He feels guilty, and thus he is convinced, Freud said, of the omnipotence of his love and his hatred. In many instances, his emotions are overpowering and he falls victim to his own obsessive thoughts.[7]

How does this work in the Arab world? Omnipotence at times needs to be defused in societies where fear exceeds the bonds of reality, when it is so overpowering or so self-oriented that it becomes irrational and delusional. But such an assessment of omnipotence, like any other thought or feeling, may be only in the eyes of the beholder, not the upholder of such feelings as fear and love. The upholder is convinced he is right; the beholder believes the other is wrong. It then becomes a question of who judges whom and who has the power to judge whom.

This analogy could be extended to religious behavior in the Arab world in the sense that Arab individuals are known for their momentous reverse. Not unlike the primitive man, against whose irrational beliefs Freud was inveighing, Arabs exchange the structural conditions of their minds into the external world, to life in society, suggesting an evolutionary sequence.[8] At the animistic stage, individuals ascribe omnipotence to themselves, and at the religious stage, they transfer it to the gods but do not seriously abandon it themselves, for they reserve the power of influencing the gods in various ways according to their wishes.

Arabs have the tendency to incorporate the power of the act to the power of the wish, especially the suitable wish. On the same theme, Freud roughly depicted politics and religion. That is why Freud realized the importance of power in the life of groups, masses, and the body politic and the dynamics of groups and their leaders. Religious leaders combine the dynamics of the power of the wish and the will to power. In doing that, they are faced with the nexus power of love, love of power. The need to love and to be loved in return is as powerful as the need for food and sex. Although only hunger and lust were classified by Freud as drives, nonetheless he has asserted that frustrated love seeks compensation in omnipotent self-love and in acts of aggression, violence, and destruction aimed at individuals and societies. Religion provides justifications for such emotions, and the normal human emotions of love, pity, and sympathy are destroyed in the process of dehumanizing the God-hated external enemy, turning him into a scapegoat and a target for chronic rage.

By looking at religion in the Arab world, much work in the last century has tried to deal with the subject as the prime integrator of society. These attempts have resulted in two sorts of dead ends. Either concrete religions provide unity for only a restricted segment of society, or the lack of a concrete integrating religion leads to functional conceptions of religion that make the argument circular. In simple terms, the implications here are that religion integrates societies and that whatever integrates societies is thereby religion or at least religious.

In this sense religion in the Arab world is regarded, like identity, as both individualistic and collective. A brief look at the Arab historical developments in this sphere can show why. The idea here is that religious expressions are a series of delimited, systematic, and comparable units that existed side by side in the Arab world.[9] Observers have regarded them as manifestations of some sort of basic or natural religion, an essence that might or might not be attainable. The latter notion was and still is critical because, like the concept of nation, it restyled religion as an abstract universal that could only appear as a plurality of particular identities.

And as with Arab states depicted as small nations, the distinction between formally equal religions gradually but never completely replaced other ways of understanding religious diversity, especially that between true and false religion, between effective and ineffective religion. Indeed, then as now, in the Arab world the idea of religion often ran parallel to or competed with nation and other collective self-descriptions.[10]

Moreover, and of equal importance, much as we still have difficulty separating the Arab nation from the Arab state, we move back and forth between seeing religions as descriptors of particular collectivities and regarding them as all the same instances of a type of systemic and instrumental communication. Phrased as a question, we seem to ask ourselves: Are religions an Arab subjectivity, or are they one of the things that they do?

The idea that religion is a functional domain that overrides other functional domains in the Arab world is a valid argument. For the Arabs, religion manifested itself as a totality. The institutionalization of these ways of seeing depended in large measure on cultural realities. Somewhat in contrast to the fate of the idea of nation, however, Arabs have accepted this development only to a limited degree. The carriers of Islam have rather consistently fought against separating religious functions from other social and political functions. Nonetheless, religion has very often become a collective identifier in Arab societies, a way of declaring collective actorship in contrast to other such actors. Perhaps the most visible way of accomplishing this has been through the politicization of religion, a strategy that brings us directly to the question of identity and character convergence under conditions presently prevailing in Arab states.

One of the most striking aspects of the various politicizations of religion in the Arab world is that they are, precisely, politicizations: They involve the modern state. They seek to harness the mechanisms of the state in order to enforce religious standards.[11] Insofar as religion today is a prime source of identity and character, the effective range of these attempts to bring about convergence in this regard has been, at best, only somewhat more successful than resorting to nationhood, precisely because both identifiers rely on the territorially delimited state. In this respect, Islam provides a unique case. And if politicization of religion has limits because it depends on the pluralistic state structures, then ultimately coalition on the basis of religion is extremely difficult. The question then becomes whether there are more effective ways to solve the enigma of competing factions among the Arab masses. The means for generating and maintaining diversified identities and consistent models of proper character seem hard to realize at least as they are at present. And I would venture to say that the social forces needed to push Arabs together into a single society have to be constructed.

On the other side of this coin are the tendencies and possibilities for individualization and hence privatization of religion. Thus, in spite of the relatively recent resurgence of religious politicizations in the Arab world, and the continued development and expansion of fundamental religious movements, in most parts of Arab societies religious fragmentation continues to occur. If certain Islamic countries in the Middle East, for instance, have been moderately successful in enforcing religious convergence, most Arab states, through semisecular nationalism, show little such tendency and in many cases more internal religious pluralism than in the past. Here again, the source of this direction lies essentially in the availability in progressive Arab states of a large number of very effective means to realize and deal with the various differences in religious identity and character.

However, just because most Arab states' systems with their technical leverages are so powerful, the realm of personal and collective identity remains a primary outlet for variation that responds to inevitable differences in the situations people find themselves in. To the extent that religions are resources for constructing those identities, and in spite of the fact that they generally provide holistic perspectives that emphasize human unity and community, religions seem more to fuel the perpetuation of diversity differentiation and conflict than to counter it.

Religion is a vital part of the social life of Arabs, and it is reflected in their beliefs, rituals, and institutions, which provide a guide to everyday life. Three key metaphors that commonly appear in sociological literature may be employed: the sacred shelter, the religious marketplace, and elective attachment.[12] These metaphors assist in revealing how Arabs interact with religion. For example, faith provides the Arab with a sacred shelter even in the everyday expressions of meaning. The word *Allah* is always in Arabs' conversation. Potential followers compete in the religious marketplace for who has a stronger faith. And elective attachment leads the faithful to match their particular interests with different doctrines of the same religions. These metaphors are limited in their ability to explain, and accordingly we need to support them with more formal theory.

By looking at religion from a sociological standpoint, we acknowledge, reflecting a postmodernist position, that sociology is only one means of understanding this complex phenomenon.[13] Psychology could be used to explain beliefs and attitudes, opinions and values of the faithful inasmuch as it could reveal behavioral patterns rooted in religious perspective of the individual. In this respect, modernism in the Arab world, which is associated with scientific thinking, technological adaptation, and increasingly changing culture that began with the expansion of the urban areas, confronted religion with the twin crises of psychological and scientific criticism and politically oriented cultural pluralism.

Early modernists and Marxists used scientific reasoning to attack religion, focusing on the authenticity of its assertion in holy texts of infallible revelation and exclusivist claim to be the sole possessor of truth. Modernists worked to introduce a secularized rational system of norms and values that they intended to replace the arbitrary authority and illusory thinking of religious institutions. However, religious pluralism posed additional problems, especially ones involving spheres of influence and legitimacy, as diverse faiths competed.

Suffice it to say that a breakdown of religious uniformity even in the same sect is becoming a mode in the Arab world. Various Sunni, Shi'ite, and Christian fundamentalist movements have emerged. These new religious factions have devised their own interpretations of the available theologies. Individualism, consumerism, civil obligations, and nationalism surfaced as new religions or quasi-religions. Modernist thinkers and modernism by itself did not squelch religion but rather made necessary its reformulation and ironically may have revitalized it.

Religious factionalism comes at a time when the Arab world is more interconnected than ever. This is due to increasing communication facilities, significantly so in the realm of religion. Conflict has increased with religious diversity, and the potential for even greater conflict is a reality. Every major religious faction offers a justification for the use of violence. Religion is presently used in Lebanon, Jordan, Egypt, Algeria, and elsewhere as a cosmic justification for violent ethnic, economic, and political struggles. A central issue involving religion in the future will be how to deal with conflict in constructive and creative ways.

The existing major religious traditions are in many respects already diverse, and one could assume that they promise both a common understanding and a diversity in social life that could result in common grounds in the Arab world—that is, if it does not destroy the rich fabric of human religious life or force people to participate in religious practice against their will. Religion can be very dangerous, especially in a culture that developed along lines of drastic fears. Yet during a relaxed state of affairs it carries a potentially positive force for dealing with conflict.

Religious fanaticism comes and goes, and religious conflicts fluctuate. Defying all expectations of globalization theory, the aftermath of the attacks of September 11, 2001, on the United States provoked a reawakening of religious ideas and social movements. This has been particularly true in the Middle East, which provides the setting for initiating new research on globalization but has demonstrated more recently that retaliation by the super powers is not necessarily associated with increased secularism. In the Islamic countries of the Middle East and in Israel, it is now more important than ever to devote attention to religion and religious movements when examining social and political terror.

Despite religion's increasing salience in the Middle East, a systematic and coherent understanding of the connections between the individual, group, religion, and politics remains elusive. First, studies are often highly descriptive, confined to particular cultural or sociopolitical settings and concerned with explaining the causes and consequences of specific events rather than contributing wide-ranging theoretical insights. Second, only rarely are studies concerned with fears of individuals and groups. There exists a vital gap that cannot be covered in this book for discovering systemic psychological variables that condition religious, social, and political relationships at the level of the individual. Third, and perhaps most important, there has been little research in which the cultural character is the unit of analysis.

I have to admit here that this book is an early stage of political psychology research. Notwithstanding, to contribute to an understanding of whether and how religion influences the way that ordinary men and women think about their society and polity, and at the same time to shed light on religious feuds in the Arab world, this book relies on the assumption that religion plays a critical role in shaping both the normative orientations of individuals and their understanding of the surrounding region. Religious beliefs provide answers in unpredictable surroundings and guide behavior through compelling ethical or moral prescriptions.[14] This is especially true among adherents and believers because, as anthropologists note, religion characterizes its answers as sacred, eternal, and implicated with the ultimate meaning of life.

Scholars have constructed diverse functions for religion in its association with political progression. One function is pastoral and holy. Another is a referee societal function.[15] In its pastoral function, religion is a force that provides government with backing and, in justifying state policies on the basis of a superior, transcendent morality. If a religious function is widely cultural, it contributes to common norms in support for the ruling elite and their policies.[16] In a referee function, by contrast, religious ideals provide criteria by which to judge the elite's authority and, more often, to criticize assessments or policies deemed inconsistent with godly principles. In this way, religion provides support for opponents of the status quo. Finally, as a referee function, religion offers shelter from excessive authority control and oppressive tendencies. By providing confidence in one's identity as primary commitment to God, and also through the economic support that usually is provided by religious institutions in the Arab world and thus reducing dependence on the state, religion generates a momentum of its own to parallel the political processes.

No scholar yet, and rightly so, has argued that religion has little or no influence on political orientations in the Arab world. The individual in the Arab world is always afraid and concerned with the different other in society. That is why open attempts at religious fulfillment in the perception of Arabs is associated with apprehension, and thus it cannot be detached from the daily functioning of political affairs. In this respect, religious norms are influential in matters that go beyond the personal ethics and morality. The utility of religious factors in explaining political attitudes and behavior in the Arab world always depend on the kinds of religious orientations that individuals hold and the broader societal and cultural context within which they reside.

Religion and politics as twin realities in the Arab world can be seen at several levels. At the foundational level, constitutions declare Islam to be the official state religion in almost all Arab countries, and so religious holidays are national holidays. At the educational and pedagogy level, religion is part of the curriculum in state-run schools, the government has responsibility for mosques and other Islamic institutions, and substantial segments of national legal codes are based on the holy scripts.

Within their inner circles, the religious sects assert that one of them has to assume leadership of the country. Most often the projection implies that only a religious leader can govern and that the main function of any government is to ensure obedience to God's law as explained in the holy scripts.[17] This strong and historically validated connection between religion and politics contrasts dramatically with the established patterns of secularism that, however imperfect, characterize most Western societies.

Most Arab leaders, in crisis, play the game well. For example, Saddam

Hussein of Iraq and other Arab leaders have used Islam to contribute significantly to their legitimacy, ideology, and institutional alignment. Accordingly, in exploiting religion, the government and opposition play themselves out in most Arab countries. Although there is some variation across political systems and also over time, it is common for governments to employ Islamic symbols in an attempt to shore up their legitimacy and to use government-appointed religious officials to justify the regime and its policies.

It is not only an association; it is an intimacy of mutual contribution between religion and politics in the Arab world, making it reasonable to expect that the influence of religion on the individual attitude will be stronger and more consistent than the ambiguous pattern of political-philosophical ideologies and doctrine. Religion is much simpler to understand and helps more in easing psychic fears.

Intellectually speaking, generalizations are always condemned. The impact of religion on politics in the Arab world should be associated with explanatory factors. As an example, perceived economic security by individuals and within the Arab states is a significant factor. Common to all factors is the concern that charismatic personalities do make a difference in their ability to crystallize dissent into mass movements. Social revolutions and transformations of culture and social structure appear to be led after all by unique personalities.

At times of political and sociocultural opportunities in the Middle East, charismatic fundamentalists galvanized previously untapped networks of discontent. By virtue of both the messenger and the message, fundamentalist discourse resonates with parts of the populace. The lasting success of these fundamentalist movements, however, depends on a successful personality with charisma. The successful personality with charisma entails the ability of its bearer to negotiate a narrow path, that is, to retain his mobilizing style and to avoid zealous excess. Failure to achieve the former may lead to fragmentation, whereas failure to do the latter may result in the overextension of ideological and organizational resources and the inability to respond to challenges to authority. Precisely in this way, Khomeini and other politico-religious leaders were successful. They were able to transform their fundamentalist discourse into secular structures, striking a sensible balance between other worldly orientations and worldly institutions to support those in the pursuit of these orientations. Inevitably, in all fundamentalist movements that outlasted their founding period and transcended the confines of local cultures, institutional longevity necessitated long-term planning and was predicated on a high degree of flexibility in the leadership's method and the accommodation of conditions imposed by national and cultural agencies and structures.

Given the wide span of religious movements and groups operating in the Arab world, this book is apt to neglect some of these important aspects. The analysis here is bound to be short on the political, cultural, economic, gendered, and ethnic contexts in which the leadership takes place. My basic objective is to utilize the psychological ramification to provide the basis for understanding why religion is the Arab's oldest and most important institution. On a parallel track, psychological limitation has always been the concern of religion.[18] Individuals have always feared failure and death, dreaded being alone, and been puzzled by the purpose of their existence. These limitations have been the domain of all organized intellectual endeavors, institution building along religious lines or philosophical and ideological in the form of political entities and nation-states. This reality makes scholars wonder whether literature, philosophy, and religion have failed to satisfy our curiosities and eradicate our fears.

The assertion among Arab religious groups is that religion demands faith and unconditional submission of the mind and the spirit to a belief system. This spiritual commitment helps the individual form a steadfast line of defense against his fear of the political and social reality. Freud believed that the individual's emotional commitment to the heavenly father lay in the need for protection from the fear of death. In Freud's history of society, *Civilization and Its Discontents,* fear of death attitudes in religious thought lay in the similarity between the minds of the children and the mental operations of primitive man. Freud defined religion as the aggregate projections of the child's emotional relationship to the father. Thus the mental exercise common to both primitive man and children could be traced in the history of religious practices.[19]

Most Arabs' concept of God is never clear. They accept the notion without understanding it. In newly established Arab states, people are short of fully understanding the exact roles of their political institutions. They act like children seeking protection. At the same time, because they do not understand these institutions, they fear them. Individuals tend to fear the unknown. God provides safety from danger, but He is feared, especially by those who do not understand the concept of God, because He could withhold his protection. Freud reasoned that the young child's physical survival is dependent upon the parents' protection. For an older child, their physical presence may not be necessary to ease fears. Internalized images or memories of the omnipotent parent of infancy or the good parent of childhood suffice when the child's own psychological security does not. To the degree that early dependency needs persist, one supposes that religious experience reinforces the adolescent or adult need for God as the parent, at the same time that it reduces anxiety about death.

To Freud and Freudian theoreticians, the relationship between religion and fears stemmed from an essential connection between early man's belief in God and unconscious feelings toward the father. By the same token, in the contemporary understanding of the concept of the state, there exist a relationship and exchanged roles between the authority, duties, and responsibilities of the father and that of the government.

In the old religious writings, believers collected various images of God's benevolent protection and disciplinary authority. Political ideologies have tried to create an image of the state that somehow could balance between protection and excessive use of authority. When ideologies prove to be utopian and cease to meet the people's goals at a time when the state is not trustworthy, people feel lost. They turn to God for protection.

It is within this general assumption, one could say, that the more dependent the person's unconscious attachment to childhood parental images, the clearer his fears become. Fear of the unknown is generally given ample room for disguise in the neurotic use of spirituality and religion. Religious prayer and worship have the potential to both perpetuate and alleviate the fear of the unknown. The processes of fear perpetuation and alleviation reinforce one another in a person, making him very much attached to his religion and ready to defend and fight for its values in society and in the political system and state. As Freud suggested, religion fosters denial of death fears by means of identification with God, the omnipotent father.

Besides, religious ceremonies can lower death fears via the person's identification with the religious community. In a society where the state lacks resources and readiness to provide for most of its population, a deprived individual focuses on personal spiritual fulfillment in the hope that his prayer or worship allows him to ask God for favors, blessings, or support. One could argue that such religious practices at this juncture of time in the Middle East are good manifestations of the failure of the state and mundane ideologies to provide security for people. They renew dependence upon the benevolent father, who is viewed as the source of human happiness or as the all-powerful protector. On the other hand, the Islamic and Christian ethical tradition of striving for a just moral life in the hope of reward in heaven provides more of a framework for the continuity of life.

One of Freud's contributions on the subject was to define religion as a logical outgrowth of the ancient family history of man and the attempt of later societies to overcome unconscious guilt feelings.[20] Man's full expressions of primal guilt were recorded in the foundations of all religious faith in the Middle East. The conception of guilt revival in religious worship evolved from the disobedience of the original parents. Freud believed that Moses and Christ assumed the guilt of the murdering crowd and that their deaths served as a communal atonement for the guilt. Inherent in all of these formulations was a central notion that religion demonstrated a collective neurosis based on the guilt and fear complex. The Shi'ite Muslims still mourn the assassination of al-Hassan and al-Hussein in an assumption of guilt inherited from their ancestors, who did not do enough to save them.

In their dogmas and beliefs about the nature of reality of man, most religions emphasize that the individual could not overcome his fears alone. The illusion lay in the wish for protection in the face of the cruel trials of life in the modern world and the wickedness of human nature. Primitive man, according to psychologists, ingeniously devised this psychic protection to counteract his helplessness in a perplexing and terrifying world. Mankind projects the infantile relationship with the father onto God to sustain the attention of a powerful, watchful, and glorious protector. The more intellectually primitive and ignorant early man was, the greater his experience of helplessness. At this point, one could emphasize the role of the father in protection against the ultimate fear of death. The young child's death fears persist and vary in degree with the extent of his or her sophistication and maturing capacity for defense under emotional and environmental stress.

I am not revealing a secret in saying that most psychological theories about religion and especially those of Freud are based on the revolutionary work of Charles Darwin. In this sense, religion satisfies psychological needs but does not provide scientific answers. Freud utilized his own psychological methodology in analyzing culture and religion. He reasoned that murderous impulses lie in modern man's unconscious, thinly veiled by the trappings of civilization and easily stirred by war and combat. In simple terms, individuals have put in God's will what is in their interest to protect themselves from one another.

Freud's assessment of religious men's attitude toward the devil is based on man's fear of a demonic father figure who is as powerful as God. He likened evil spirits with the projected derivatives of repressed evil wishes. Freud speculated on the notion that the devil represents the child's projections of negative aspects of the father's personality. Most men's anger and fear result from a mixture of hateful and loving feelings toward their fathers. In a way Freud was close to linking depression and separation anxiety with neurotic death anxiety. In Freud's theory, the fear of God and the devil found its clearest rationale in the fear of castration, whereas in the present view, the fear of God and the devil is composed mainly of the fear of helplessness in the face of death anxiety and the uncertainty of the human will.

Freud drew many analogies between religious practices and the symptoms of obsessional neurosis in his earliest papers on religion. He defined obsessional neurosis as a kind of private religion. Religion approached the status of a universal obsessional neurosis that obviated the individual's need for a private, more personal one. The religious practices left intact the observer's psychological armor against the expression of some unacceptable unconscious impulse. From a contemporary psychoanalytic viewpoint, unconscious sexual or aggressive energies simply do not account for the complexity of characterological strategies in this defensive process. Depression and the unconscious fear of separation seem to provide a more richly appointed context for the individual's fears of life and death.[21] In *The Future of an Illusion,* Freud remarkably associated man's continuous longing for a father's protection with the need to combat helplessness and the memory of the helplessness of childhood.[22]

The transformation of the forces of nature into gods by the ancients was described parallel to the later repression of civilization. This change yielded further safety from the fear of death. Freud traced the development of monotheism and explained its relationship also by the need to reexperience the child's feelings of intimacy with the father. Belief in some form of life after death continued the promise of compensation beyond what was humanly possible because of the cruelties of civilization and fate. In this conceptual framework, it followed that Christianity and other religious systems arose from the ancient need for self-defense against the forces of nature. Religious beliefs realized particular manifestations of this view.

There are instances when individuals replace their need for a father with a political or religious outstanding figure instead of replacing this need with God. The individual stays religious, especially if the outstanding figure is religious. This political or religious outstanding figure rises to assume the role of father for his followers. He is to be obeyed, and he is the protector and provider, both materially and psychologically. This scenario is dangerous, however, especially in the Middle East because of the repercussion that it may have in the disintegrating society or in shifting society on a dramatic path.

Freud based most of his theories and views of religion on a composite of mankind's wishes to be ruled and controlled. This way, individuals could blame the other (outside entity) if things went wrong. Freud suggested that religion arose as the universal neurosis due to ubiquitous Oedipal conflicts. The origin of formal religions coincided with mankind's passage through a developmental stage that resembled obsessional neurosis. The positive aspects of religion were overshadowed in this theory by the emphasis on its role in avoiding punishment for Oedipal strivings.[23]

Religious beliefs and ceremonies were said to fend off the hostile feelings toward God and to promise his protection from Oedipal punishment and the violence of nature. Freud conceptualized primitive man's creation of the gods because of the deeply felt need for them to exist. Modern man's creation of religion was characterized as an attempted resolution of his longing for the father and his archaic feelings of helplessness.

Again, social scientists and psychologists have repeatedly expressed dissimilar views with regard to religion in the Arab world. A wide-ranging analysis exists on the subject of religious experience. Some asserted that the essential elements of religion were obvious in the extreme; most exaggerated instances of religious experience. The importance of this category could not be dismissed even if it were contaminated by visions, hallucinations, melancholia, or pathological obsession. The implication here is that religion in the Middle East approached the totality of the individual's actions, feelings, and experiences with a religious happiness unparalleled in the possibilities of human experience. The religious life of Arabs is based on three characteristic beliefs.

First, the significance of the world lies in its appreciation in a spiritual universe. Second, man's true purpose is envisioned in the harmonious union with the spirit, or God. Third, prayer lingers as an open-ended process of communication and energy flow from God; it vitalizes and changes phenomenological experience. Spiritual happiness necessitated surrender of one's will to the divine. A life of sacrifice for an Arab gives the firm impression of a renewed sense of power and freedom from tension, dejection, and loneliness. The ultimate religious happiness combines an absolute transcendence of human fear with grateful moments of joyful self-abandonment.

In this respect, again, we go back to the dimensions of death anxiety. The inherent relationship between the depression, the fear of death, and separation anxiety is depicted in the dilemma of the "divided soul."[24] Religious conversion and second birth might ensure a means for deliverance from fear of death. It is an Arab cultural belief that the sick soul runs parallel to the depressed, anxious suffering of the neurotic who is overwhelmed by the fear of death. In fact, psychologically speaking, the terrors of the panic seem rooted in the ultimate fear. The emotional experience of religious depression seems equivalent to the neurotic's depression and death anxiety stated in religious or philosophical terms.

An Arab who becomes overly depressed about the evils of the world and metaphysical irregularity may protest exceedingly against the other, the nonself. In addition, individuals with a more personal and neurotic level of insecurity and despair may express themselves by magnifying religious issues. It has been known since Freud's initial efforts that religion can be the matrix for the expression of a host of neurotic, embarrassing situations. By the same token, intense, tortured involvement in religion can be a symptom of unrecognized and unresolved entrapment in the fear of death, depression, and separation anxiety.

Again, one supposes that religions emphasizing a centrality of guilt, obsessional ritualistic practices, and codified prohibitions can function smoothly as media for neurotic fears. In simple terms, religion offers ample opportunity for solutions to the fear of death of those whose character problems combine a religious upbringing with pressing neurotic needs. Unconsciously for Arabs, embracing religious practices, separation, death anxiety, and depression can be put off as psychological realities through any neurotic attachment that symbolizes symbiotic union. Thus, blind adherence to religious teachings and to imposed codes of moral values might reflect neurotic defensiveness. To the extent that these attitudes keep the worshiper, as the child, in the subservient dependent relationship with God and the religious figure, they can mask anxiety about autonomy.

Religion psychologists argue that the more authoritarian and rigid a religion, the greater the potential conflicts unveiled in the adult's blind obedience to it.[25] We could also assume that the more neurotic one's religious commitment is, the more the involvement counters death anxiety and threats to the self.

When reading Arabic poetry and lyrics, the most striking impressions one gets are complaints about social doubts or brooding about philosophical issues as an echo to the influence of depression. Depression and the individual's characteristic defenses can be beneath what may be a legitimate concern. Absorption in countering death anxiety brings theological pursuits to the brink of neurotic self-deception.

The characterization of anxiety and Arab helplessness as an essential aspect of individual neurosis in psychoanalysis and religion takes us to a related issue stemming from the neurotic's choice between what political scientists termed authoritarian and nonauthoritarian religions. In authoritarian religions, man escapes isolation by surrendering to a powerful transcending figure; this provides the illusion of protection in exchange for obedience. Authoritarian religions command obedience and submission whether they are holistic, like Islam, or secular like fascism. In humanistic religious experience, the identity of man and God is affirmed out of love—but love that is associated with power. Here God could be understood as a symbol of man's higher self, power, and capacity for self-realization.

Gordon Allport distinguishes between people who have intrinsic religious values, mainly, those who are integrated and have comprehensive ends in themselves, and those with extrinsic religious values, those who are escapist and ethnocentric.[26] Allport was first intrigued by the meaning of religious outlooks as a result of the finding that high religiosity was prevalent among very prejudiced people. If this is true, then Arab religious prejudice and group-centrism are linked to the extrinsic religious outlook in which house of worship membership was based on allegiance to a powerful, socially approved in-group.

Arabs believe in the religious ideals of their house of worship, and they tend to be prejudiced against other groups. The question is to what extent we could assume that the extrinsically motivated person uses religion to provide security, status, self-justification, and social approval. Studies have shown that it seems even more likely that extrinsic religious affiliation captured the defensiveness, depression, and separation anxiety inherent in the neurotic fear of death. Research suggested that there are many deep-seated positive and negative reasons for the involvement in religion.

The mystery of death compels Arabs of all faiths, even if life is seen as eternal and an afterlife is believed to be certain. The human mixture of body and soul raises questions about the meaning of salvation and the terror of death. Since the prehistorical group-symbols worship among Arabs, religious rituals have provided a definite medium for dismissing threats to the self. If death is grasped as nothingness or ceasing to exist, then its terror for the modern Arab may not be mitigated even by the most sincere religious beliefs or commitment to humanistic religious practices. When religious experience fails to provide a person with a solution to the fear of death, depression and conscious fear of death may result. Religious commitment thus adds a new level of meaning to the child's fear of the world and the neurotic's fear of the loss of the self.

It is worth noting here that the relationship between depression and unconscious ambivalence about death stands out among individuals who have high death anxiety, and the degree of death anxiety can often be attributed to the influence of separation conflicts, that is, wishes for separation-individuation, fears of abandonment, and corollary wishes or fears of psychic merger and fusion. The fear of death as a central construct in personality functioning could be explored in its relation to philosophical, social, and religious issues as well as the difficulties inherent in depression and neurotic living. The notion of the fear of freedom provides a focal point and clarity to the diverse expression in social and political choices and practices.

Many people believe that fear was manufactured by religion and that both religion and fear will eventually disappear. But it would make more sense to realize that religion was created to relieve an overwhelming feeling of fear that was already there.

Religion and political ideologies in the Arab world are like one parallel set of springboards. Arabs bounce between the two, and it can be no accident that a decline in religion is accompanied by a rectification of political ideologies. The competition between religious and political ideologies has always been in addressing Arab fears and problems and extending promises for a better Arab world. Arabs have no choice but to take these promises at face value. But those who believe in these promises often feel that, if they were not true, there would be nothing left to live for. Fear prevails, making the situation potentially so dangerous.

Arab leaders without exception have employed a variety of political strategies with the objective of preserving their powers and safeguarding the semisecular nature of their governments. Despite the apparent differences, they all have been advocating a tolerant stance toward religion, which has guaranteed freedom of conscience, yet prohibited religious extremism. As such, the establishment of Islamic states, as the ultimate manifestation of extremism, has been vehemently opposed. The fear of fundamentalist takeover has become the subject of frequent commentaries by the leaders of Egypt, Algeria, Tunisia, Jordan, and others. Covertly, Arab states have gone so far as to propose a collective security pact to avert Islamic fundamentalism.[27]

Fear has enticed the incumbent Arab elite to strike hard at some Islamic fundamentalist parties, driving their supporters underground. But repression has not been the only method of combating fundamentalism. They are subjected to propaganda skirmishing by being viewed as terrorists trying to destroy the spirit of Islamic civilization and in the process serving the interests of the enemies of Arabs.

Each of these terms, Islam in the sense of a religion and Islam in the sense of a civilization, is itself subject to many variations. If we talk about Islam as a historical phenomenon, we are speaking of a community that now numbers more than a billion people, most of whom are spread along a vast arch stretching almost ten thousand miles from Morocco to Mindanao. This has a 1,400-year history and is the defining characteristic of the fifty-three sovereign states that currently belong to the Organization of the Islamic Conference (OIC). For obvious reasons, it is extremely difficult (though not impossible) to make any kind of valid generalization about a reality of such age, size, and complexity.

Even if we confine ourselves to speaking of Islam as a religion, significant distinctions must be drawn. First, there is what Muslims themselves would call the original, pristine, pure Islam of the Koran and the Hadith, i.e., the traditions of the Prophet Mohammed before they became corrupted by the backsliding of later generations. Second, there is the Islam of the doctors of the holy law, of the magnificent intellectual structure of classical Islamic jurisprudence and theology. Most recently, there is the neo-Islam of the so-called fundamentalists who introduce ideas mysteriously combined with a power-seeking tendency that sometimes is alien to the Koran, the Hadith, or the classical doctrines of the faith.

A first look at the present situation of the political systems in the Arab world, as a result of rising movements of religious fundamentalism, is not encouraging. Presumably many Arabs do not comprehend the concept of God, thus Thou power is never clear. They accept the notion of power without understanding it. By the same token, most Arabs do not fully understand the exact roles of their political elite. They try to trust these elite and to seek security from them. If they can provide security, then, the elite are perceived as powerful and deserve to be feared. Arabs tend to fear the power. Inasmuch as God provides safety from danger, Thou himself is feared because of this power. Religious beliefs reinforce the individuals' need for God as the parent at the same time that it reduces anxiety about death. This tendency usually allows people to tolerate authority even if it is dictatorial.

Arab people have thus far shown very little objection to authoritarian rule and thus enjoy few functioning democracies. One can find democratic movements and in some cases even promising democratic developments, but one cannot really say that they are democracies even to the extent that the Lebanese Republic is a democracy at the present time.

Throughout history, the most common type of regime in the Arab world has been autocracy. The dominant political tradition has long been that of command and obedience, and far from weakening it, modern times have actually witnessed its intensification. With traditional restraints on autocracy attenuated, and with new means of surveillance, repression, and wealth-extraction made available to rulers by modern technologies and methods, governments have become less dependent than ever on popular goodwill. This is particularly true of those governments which are enriched by oil revenues. With no need for taxation, there is no pressure for representation. In a system of no representation, the ruling elite feels no need for political transparency.

Another noteworthy historical and cultural fact in the religious, political, and linguistic stamina of Arabs is the absence of the term *citizen*. There has never been a reason to construct such a term. Arabs are the children of God, not his citizens. The word is absent in Arabic for a reason: The citizen is a participant in political decision making, and citizenship means participation, something that is not allowed in relation to God or in relation to the mighty father in the Arab culture.

At the same time, however, we can discern elements in Islamic law and tradition that could assist the development of one or another form of democracy. Islam boasts a rich political literature. From the earliest times, doctors of the holy law, philosophers, jurists, and others have reflected carefully on the nature of political power, the ways in which political power ought to be acquired and used and may be forfeited, and the duties and responsibilities as well as the rights and privileges of those who hold it.

Islamic tradition strongly disapproves of arbitrary rule, but this does not mean sharing. The Sunni jurists, to have contractual and consensual features that distinguish caliphs from despots, define the central institution of sovereignty in the traditional Islamic world that is the caliphate. The exercise of political power is conceived and presented as a contract, creating bonds of mutual obligation between the ruler and the ruled. Subjects are duty-bound to obey the ruler and carry out his orders, but the ruler also has duties toward the subject, similar to the relaxing relationship between God and people. The only difference is that the contract can be dissolved if the ruler fails to fulfill or ceases to be capable of fulfilling his obligations. Although rare, there have been instances when such dissolutions took place. There is, therefore, also an element of consent in the traditional Islamic view of government.

The complexity of this analogy here is that obedience is an obligation of a subject, but some indicate exceptions. One says, "Do not obey a creature against his creator." In other words, do not obey a human command to violate divine law. Another says, "There is no duty of obedience in sin." If the sovereign commands something that is sinful, the duty of obedience lapses. It is worth noting that Prophetic utterances like these point not merely to a right of disobedience, such as would be familiar from Western political thought, but also to a divinely ordained duty of disobedience.

When we descend from the level of psychological analysis to the realm of what actually is possible, the story is of course intricate. Still, the central point remains: There are elements in Islamic culture that could favor the development of stable and transparent political institutions in the Arab world.

One of the sayings traditionally ascribed to the Prophet is this: "Difference of opinion within my community is a sign of God's mercy." In other words, diversity is something to be welcomed, not something to be suppressed. This attitude is typified by the acceptance by Sunni Muslims, even today, of four schools of Islamic jurisprudence. Muslims believe the holy law to be divinely inspired and guided, yet there are four significantly different schools of thought regarding this law. The idea that it is possible to be orthodox even while differing creates a principle of the acceptance of diversity and of mutual tolerance of differences of opinion that surely cannot be bad for the diversified groups in the Arab world at the level of the existing state and region.[28]

The final point worth mentioning in this inventory is that the psychological emphasis on the twin nature of fear and power shows that subjects have a personal stake in religion. Religion has been a refuge for Arabs. By Ottoman custom, when the sultan received the chief dignitaries of the state on holy days, he stood up to receive them as a sign of his respect for the law. When a new sultan was enthroned, Arabs greeted him with cries of "Sultan, be not proud. God is greater than you."

Religious groups in the Arab world have their own interpretation of the term *freedom* as a political concept. The idea of freedom, meaning the ability to participate in the formation, the conduct, and even the lawful removal and replacement of government, is still unfamiliar. This notion, which belongs to the inner logic of constitutionalism and parliamentarian practices, is obviously not a product of the developing forces in the Arab culture and psychology.

Another psychological complication contiguous to the concept of freedom is the Western influence on Arab politics especially during colonial periods. When the West ruled much of the Arab world, freedom came also, or even primarily, to mean communal or national independence, with no reference to the individual's status within the body politic. The Arab world today is free from external domination, but Arabs are not free domestically. They are prisoners of their psychic, social, and political fears and anxieties. They seek protection from the state and religion but do not enjoy transparency. This shared deprivation, however, does not preclude the existence of very great differences among them.

7

Fear, the Self, and Arab Culture

In defining culture as a primary human foundation, one cannot avoid the evolution of its supplementary part, the institution of self. Most anthropologists speak of human culture as having originated in a natural context, the relationship between man as an individual and animal in a beast society. With the destruction of the animal order, issues of fear, insecurity, and guilt increased, laying the foundation for feelings of original anxiety. In this context, human identity was made possible through the group, which minimized this experience of being powerless.[1]

Culture in the reasoning of political psychology is somehow derived from Freud's metapsychology. Even if one concludes that metapsychological notions (libido, conservation of psychical energy, levels of excitation, etc.) are actually metaphors disguised as concepts, surely they suggest that Freud intended to ground the interpretation of these concepts in the dimension of culture. In simple terms, Freud described the psyche's energy processes in ways to conform to the fundamentals of culture[2] but which do make sense to societies' economic competition as strategies of conflict. Their significance as social concepts is precisely the mark of their success as cultural metaphors.

Again in the realm of culture, Hegel's philosophies are significant for motivating the emergence of disciplines of the social sciences, introducing the concepts of culture, ethnicity, nationalism, and self to the philosophical forefront. The philosophies of Hegel and Freud accounted for the theoretical contributions of the self in relation to culture.[3]

Recent studies in culture are characterized as having been dominated by empirical surveys, primarily in the form of psychological inquiry, survey politics, and linguistics. This book perhaps could serve to establish important interaction between the study of fear, the self, and culture on the one hand and political psychology on the other. This trend originated in the work of Freud. Freud's notion of the self-image was an internal substitute for God, and he believed that the larger cultural relativity of the psyche and moral values were alike, in that it postulates that man is the result of alienated desire and culture.[4]

What we seem to be addressing here is that culture and self are dynamic processes, constantly being defined and redefined as humans evolve. Many contemporary theorists focus on language and the production of meaning, thus analyzing processes of symbolization and representation in the field of culture in an attempt to develop a better understanding of subjectivity, the psyche, and the self.[5]

In assessing Arab culture, one of the central problems is the challenge that individual and group identities pose to concepts of national citizenship and attempts at civil state building. The role of individuals in the different Arab social groups and the society at large in cultural politics is at once a question about fear, anxieties, institutions, and identity.

Social fear as a theory operating within cultural studies, society, and politics begins by acknowledging the existence of multiple groups within society. It asserts the group as a central unit of the social order and is concerned with individuals in the context of their group memberships. Until recently, the dominant account of fear in psychology and political science was the one associated with mid-twentieth-century theorists of war and violence. Theorists of fear and violence see group membership as a central part of the individual's political character, since competition, bargaining, and hatred among opposing groups determine fear and anxiety.[6] This understanding of politics has been much criticized, particularly by democratic theorists interested in developing a normative concept of citizenship that challenges the notion of politics as a wholly self-interested realm.

Both trends, the one that centers culture on the relations between worried groups and the one that describes a politics which transcends groups, have been challenged by theorists concerned with fear as a result of continued inequality, systematically privileging some groups at the expense of others.[7]

The topic of conflict and fear in the Arab culture has never moved to center stage in the field of Arab politics. It should be given more attention by drawing interdisciplinary work, from sociology, anthropology, psychology, and political science, into a common enterprise. There is an enduring and widespread perception that group conflict in the Arab world is increasing. Recent studies suggest that states are more inclined to negotiate with aggrieved minority groups. At the same time, many minority movements are increasingly inclined to seek violent means for achieving their aims. Arab states appear to be more movable, malleable, and contestable than ever. Arab states consist of a set of institutions that are oppressive only because other sets of social institutions recognize and accept them as such. The relationships among Arab individuals and groups within the state, and the relationships between states and the people on whose behalf they claim to act authoritatively, remain problematic, conflictual, and unstable.

The most problematic tension between governments and those over whom or on whose behalf they assert authority run the gamut from deprivation of the basic necessities of life to widespread and routine abuses of human rights, not to mention brutality, including the wholesale destruction of communities in Kurdistan, Syria, South Sudan, South Lebanon, and Algeria. State boundaries are not always concurrent with the boundaries of culture, and they almost never coincide with minority homogeneous populations.

Constitutional and institutional frameworks within the states of the Arab world are not compatible with the religious and political elite mobilization of the masses. This is reflected through hate speech, the militant rebirth of Islamic fundamentalism, the historical complex structure of minority relations, and the uneasy balance of minority power among relatively substantial ethnic pluralities.[8] Such a reality poses essential questions: Why are ordinary people unable to deal with fear? How is it that individuals are persuaded to abandon one political tendency in favor of another? Why were elites able to mobilize people to undertake acts of barbarity on the basis of appeals to identity? And why did some people resist the antagonistic and war-making rhetoric and remain decisively opposed to the war? To understand how and why identity can be manipulated within culture, and how and why threats to identity can evoke the most virulent and violent defenses of the self, we must examine the links between individual psychological constructions of the self and identity and the intervening forces of culture.[9]

The self, out of fear of not having enough space to survive is always concerned with the issue of material and social space. Nagel and Olzak note that cultural identity is most closely associated with the issue of boundaries, and they ask, "What are the processes that motivate ethnic boundary construction?"[10] Object relations theory offers one way of answering this question. Boundary construction is the process through which the *self* becomes self-conscious and thus conscious of the twinborn *other*. Threats to the destruction of self-boundaries may, however, evoke the most primal insecurities, since it is not only the boundaries but also the self that is at risk of being annihilated or assimilated into the *other*. Identity within any given culture, in this sense, is the perception of defined space that the bounded self occupies individually and through others. Thus boundaries are also the answer to the question "Who are we?" Identity is the mechanism through which we locate ourselves in culture and in relation to the outside world. Identity links the self with its social context in a self-defined culture.[11]

In *Melanie Klein and Critical Social Theory*, Alford has theorized about the applicability of psychological theories regarding the construction of the self to be able to deal with the problems of cultural conflict and the ability to form and sustain a social contract between the self and the government and thus a polity. In the Arab world, object relations (the other is an object to be used) focus on the self's growing awareness of the other. Then again and eventually, perceiving of the other as both a good object capable of meeting one's needs as a dependent and developing infant, and a bad object, to which one attributes the frustration of unmet needs, including the need to relieve pain or satisfy aspirations. The self and the other are thus truly twinborn. Self-boundaries immediately bring into cognitive existence recognition that the other is not a part of the self but is, like the self, constituted as an independent agent. From the perspective of infantile development, this awareness is accompanied by strong emotions: affection or love when needs are gratified, and frustration or rage when they are not.

The primary task for the self is to acknowledge the coexistence of the other's capability to satisfy or frustrate needs and therefore to evoke emotions of love and hate in the infantile self. In this way, the self can also come to terms with the coexistence of its own capacities to feel both affection and rage. This is critical to the development of a mature and integrated adult self who acknowledges his/her own capacity to care about others as well as to cause harm.

Arabs' acceptance of their dual capacity for caring and harming has always been crucial to the development of their culture. Hospitality, for which the Arabs are famous, is a manifestation of their capacity to care. This has provided the basis for developing and sustaining obligatory connections with other citizens. However, their fear of losing themselves and the insecurities stemming from harsh historical experiences fuel their capacity for doing harm to those that they have treated well. Thus doing harm is acknowledged as one's own capacity, rather than projected onto others, whether the other is construed as those who are different in terms of ethnicity, religion, class, and so on or as others external to a culture in which multiple identities otherwise peacefully coexist. The capacity to do harm is also held in check by an obligation to care, and so individuals refrain from harming others.

Alford further argues in *Melanie Klein* that the guilt that arises through acknowledging our own capacity to do or wish harm to others, when integrated into the self rather than projected onto others, becomes a motivating force for entering into restorative relations with others. In political terms, this restorative relation allows the individual to enter into a social contract and to construct a civil society.

Reparative emotions are a prerequisite to negotiating peaceful relations, whether in interpersonal relations or with other societies in the form of a comprehensive nation. A key issue is the extent to which and whether or not the maintenance of self-boundaries depends on the maintenance of negative images of otherness.[12] It is my belief that the process of becoming and maintaining psychic integration is a lifelong process, vulnerable to episodes of disintegration brought on by trauma. The integrated self, in the face of trauma, may revert to the more Manichean and infantile cognitive position as a psychic defense against the trauma. Social and cultural forces mediate the self's continuing effort to achieve or maintain integration, which in turn is subject to relative degrees of disintegration when confronted with needs, frustration, and stress.[13]

In cases like the Jordanian-Palestinian showdown, ʿAlawites and Muslim brotherhood bloodshed, Lebanese strife, the Algerian quandary, Iraqi-Kuwait crises, Maroco-Moritanian conflict, and Yemen's bloody unification, the state was unable to generate the civic, rather than ethnonationalist, identity sufficient to maintain itself as a satisfactory mechanism through which individuals could fulfill the need to be a part of a project larger than the self, either ideologically or in communitarian terms. This contributed to the instability of identity on which elites then preyed with nationalist rhetoric. Ironically, the rise of religious identity and practice became stronger during all of these conflicts and especially because of the inability of Arab secular governments to regain the space of societal terrain taken by Israel. This terrain is needed for the fulfillment of self-transcendent expectations in the Arab culture. As stresses increased, associated with the fragmentation and failure of the Arab states and economy, it should not be surprising that an interest in (religious) ethnic identity and participation began to regain lost ground. Nor should it be surprising that Arab Muslims, the majority of whom do not claim to be fundamentalists, are currently supporting Islamic political inclinations.

Culture and history are the substance of communities. They are also the basic materials used to construct communal meaning. Culture and history are often intertwined in communal construction.[14] Hobsbawm identifies three functions of traditions: (1) to symbolize group cohesion and membership, (2) to legitimize institutions and authority relations, and (3) to socialize or teach beliefs, values, or behaviors.[15]

Arab history and political culture intersect at the three points mentioned above. The shared experiences of one generation is passed on through the interpretation of ordinary people to the next generation or two as part of the national educational curriculum as appropriated by the different political elite. This is done to mobilize people for their political support of a particular regime and/or to express that support in service to minority interests.

The elements of psychoanalytical theory relevant to an examination of these intersections between history and political culture play a major role in the construction of collective identity in both positive (who we are) and negative (who we are not). Such terms provide potential for individuals to move to what Alford calls the paranoid-schizoid position of splitting and projecting one's self onto good (heroes) and bad (enemies). People have a need for identity and for locating themselves in the larger scheme of things, to be able to transcend the self by identification with an entity larger than the self.

Historical narratives, in a conflicting and divergent environment, provide a framework for locating the self within the contrasted and particular interpretation of larger social processes. Arabs learn history not only through educational institutions but also through the telling and interpreting of historical narratives within the family. The most immediate historical experience bears on the q-memory of the recent Arab-Arab conflict, passed on by ordinary people to their children.

The cultural background of the Arabs is, in psychoanalytic terms, a complex whole of mirrors in which positive and negative identification with others has confounded the group boundaries constituting a constellation of identities. Islamic identity has long been intermingled positively with the notion of being Arab but not necessarily an Arab nationalist. For most of its modern history, Arab territories constituted potentially the most vulnerable borders of the Middle East region. Quite a few minorities in the Middle East under the rule of the Ottomans enjoyed a high degree of autonomy. Minority and confessional identity was strengthened during that period, and this led to resisting imperial non-Arab Sunni governors. The clash of Western and Islamic civilizations left its most permanent boundaries between the divergent minorities and its most convoluted boundaries along with those of the Ottoman Empire. To make matters worse, the French and British employed minorities as a military force during their mandate rule after World War II.

Although all minorities share the same Arabic language, ethnic and colloquial languages have taken on great significance as cultural markers. Language is not just a means of communication. The language preserves the nation's history and culture. The language is the womb.[16]

Reviewing stories published by minorities during the civil strife in Lebanon, one finds the most common theme regarding minority identity to be that of victims of hostile outsiders. One concludes, at least in the case of Lebanon, that overemphasis on confronting external enemies from the same region creates not only a fixation on enemies but the impression that the segregated communities within the same state are in agreement. This is a psychological escape for all concerned minorities in Lebanon to preserve the state that is already reduced only to the borders that define its sovereignty and identity.

Arab literary histories are rich with battle and warfare stories that serve to treat real history in an emotional manner and thus preserve it as an active part of Arab consciousness. It is ironic that organizations calling for Arab unity of a pluralist Arab world along nationalist lines created the structural context in which the nationalism that destroyed cultural cohesiveness turned venomous. When Nasser died, Arab unity died with him.

Drawing on the case of Lebanon, it is not simple to explain why many Arab minority groups were alarmed and outraged by appeals for nationalism. Nationalism had only limited appeal, as suggested by the rejection of Islamist downplaying of nationalism in the Algerian, Sudanese, and Jordanian elections during the 1990s in the aftermath of anti-regime demonstrations.

One of the problems with defining the Arab culture as not fit for nationalism (that is, purely in terms of minority conflicts) is that it turns individuals into members of a group that is then portrayed and discussed in monolithic vs. universalistic terms. What I am interested in is the fear that drives individuals to behave brutally and how the political culture, both preexisting and transformed during recent confrontations, contributed to this paradoxical culture that is unfitting for Arab nationalism and Arab unity.

Psychoanalytic theory suggests that Arabs are political hostages to their group identity. Identity consists of knowledge of the self as well as of the nonself. Gender identity, in particular, provides some insight: Masculine identity is constituted both by positive identification with maleness and by negative identification with femaleness. What is the relationship between these two sources of identity? If the self is well grounded in positive images, it might rely less on sustaining a negative other. What is the role of cultural orientations toward leadership, for instance, if leaders are cast as heroes, philosopher kings, monarchs possessed of divine right, or revolutionary messiahs? Is this as problematic as a national identity sustained through the demonization of enemies? There are many examples of collective identification developing a split and projected collective self: the demonization and therefore rationalized destruction of *others,* however they are defined, and glorification of members of the group carrying out such projects.[17] Alternatively, culture implies that we regard leaders as fathers, indirectly implying that the leader is a provider. But are expectations alone sufficient, or will they lapse into authoritarianism if not supported by a strong unified culture? These are some of the questions raised by a psychoanalytic interpretation of the civil society in the Arab world.

In the Arab world and as perceived by Arabs, Westerners as the *other* were the mirror image of the Arab individual *self.* This mirror image played itself out in the form of opposition to all political movements, communists, Arab nationalists, Islamists, and so on. Thus, Arab nationalists and Arab communists presupposed they were fighting a common enemy during the cold war, and they even formed a brief alliance. Additionally, the enemy was internal, since fighting for an ideology in the Arab culture meant Arabs fighting one another. The Western world consolidated its own identity in antifascist and anticommunist terms, while in the Arab world this presented a dilemma for a unified national identity.

There appears to be evidence that Arabs rely on the negative identification of enemies as a source of national identity. Arab newspapers and state propaganda rely on this notion. Victimization has long been an important, though not a desirable, component of Arab national identity. Arabs tend to demonize the Ottomans and Western colonizers in their historical experience in Arabic literature and folk culture. They used the Ottomans' policy during World War II as an intergenerational experience that was powerful enough to boost Arab identity. Hate for the Ottomans has provided a continuous sense of unified identity among Arabs but not among Islamists. The latter are depicted as traitors of the nation left behind by the Ottomans in the form of political Islam. In the process of constructing fantasies of demonized Ottomans and Westerners, Arab nationalists just tell the stories of their own victimization.

A number of factors contributed to the societal stress of Arabs, which was a critical factor in their vulnerability to psychic disintegration or, in psychological terms, to digress to the paranoid-schizoid position. In this infantile cognitive position, the world is polarized between good and bad. It consists entirely of decent and awful objects whose splitting and projection produce scapegoating of others and idealizing of the self. Suffice it to mention that the idealized self is also often manifested in idealized leaders and heroes. The good always provide positively, and the bad bring about deprivation. This polarization stems from the combination of extreme economic and political destabilization. It is under such conditions, I believe, that the failure to address past injuries of one group from another in an unreconciled society creates the greatest vulnerability to collective deterioration and even depression.

A cultural reconciliation process never took place in the Arab world. Anticolonialism and decolonialism movements during World War II aimed at creating a culturally pure Arab nation by converting the different confessional groups to Sunni-oriented understanding of Islam and convincing the other ethnic groups that they are Arabs. The need for cultural reconciliation in areas where past injurious conflicts remain unforgotten are not adequately addressed. In varying degrees, such processes would be required in Iraq when it comes to reconciliation with Kurds, south Sudan when it comes to reconciliation with African tribalism, Mauritania, Morocco, and the Polizario, when it comes to reconciliation with Berbers in all of the western part of the Arab world. All of these factions entertain the idea that only by addressing the past and by assigning guilt could future generations prevent a recurrence of the digression into uncivil society.

The study of minority conflicts often misses the complexities of the relationship between individual psychological, cultural, and sociological variables. As Markus and Kitayama have demonstrated, political culture matters when we are trying to account for collective and publicly rationalized descent into inhuman behavior.[18]

What could be done to diminish the likelihood that psychologically vulnerable individuals and groups will be aroused by the emotionally charged appeals of nationalist politicians to carry out the brutalities of war? What conditions would have enabled them to resist the hatemongering that, as one Lebanese journalist said, made the civil war inevitable in Lebanon, in Iraq, and among Algerians before the first shot was even fired.

The last point necessitates a confrontation with, rather than denial of, the truth about one's history, including harm, injury, or injustice perpetrated by one's own society. In this way, the cultural self is identified as a whole and integrated self, acknowledging one's own capacity to do harm, and thus less prone to splitting, projecting, and scapegoating others.

The Middle East political quandary, with its clash of group ideologies, does create unique opportunities for research by political psychologists. Arab military psychologists' ability to rally popular support during wars in the region, as is the case of the Arab-Israeli wars or Iraqi wars, emphasize the cultural context. We could also note fear emanating from the increasing isolation of the nuclear family, apart from traditional communities and extended families, and the growing dehumanization of the workplace is creating a new purpose for political psychology.

Psychologists believe that the anthropological concept of culture has long been indebted to two principles that are fundamentally at odds with each other: relativism and psychic unity. The principle of relativism allowed anthropologists to treat all cultures as unique historical developments and to free anthropology from simplistic evolutionary designs that would privilege some civilizations in contrast to others. In studying Arab culture, it is fruitless to arrange it along with all other cultures moving on an evolutionary trail leading to Western civilization. This is not to deny that some anthropologists were in an excellent position to study Arab cultures empirically, without the constraints of social evolutionist frameworks.

Paradoxically, however, the principle of cultural relativism is still short of patching up what psychologists consider to be Arab psychic unity. If all Arab individuals are equipped with the same neural hardware, then the variability of their human behavior and of cultural forms generally can be constrained.[19]

Psychic unity as a concept is limited.[20] Psychology is still a long way from understanding how humans construct, hold onto, and abandon meaningful concepts, as is the case in the Arab world. Anthropologists, nonetheless, have been suffering from a cognitively impoverished notion of culture, especially with a handful like the Arab cultures. To them the culture concept is located exclusively in spoken language or in material power relations. Arabs present a unique amalgamation of cultures that could not be assessed by a disorderly cognitive system consisting of limited selection of models.

Cultural models should deal with the minds of the Arabs and their social institutions, human behavior, and linguistic utterances. They should also include rules for appropriate physical manner in various social settings: Whether Arabs shake someone's hand or bow deeply when being introduced is part of the culturally constructed models of physical space. In analyzing a particular kind of simple model, sport games, one could find fascinating resemblance between the organizational principles of the game and fundamental principles of Arab culture. The pattern of behavior among individuals that fluctuates between individualistic and communitarian values is clearly evident. The Arab sportsman's selfish assault in attempting to score for himself and not for the team is very much related to the structure of his society. What is important here is that the origins and development of Arab selfishness could be traced to a manifestation of fear and anxiety.

Structural components of Arab culture have been changing. Some changes have broad ramifications, underlying everything from trading personal effects to individually tailored educational programs. Shopping malls, mass production, and synthetic commodities are all becoming accepted features in the Arab world. Again, excessive television viewing makes people think that pushing a button could simulate reality and that computer technology allows its users to create their own illusions of space and place. Even "random violence" is an underlying component of Arab culture. The victim's identity does not matter, because all people are interchangeable.[21]

Many of the Arab world's cultures have embraced, imitated, and strived toward modernization at an unbelievable pace. This tendency is somehow rooted in their culture of trade, which is part of their social and economic progress. The atomism of trade culture that suggests ideas of interchangeability and substitutability is congenial with ideals of tribal-social equality but not necessarily with individual equality.

In considering that Arab cultures manifest themselves in theories of language and traditions, their limitations must be grasped. The principle of randomness that is fundamental to structural anthropology, therefore, falls short of meeting the requirements of Arab cultural studies. The structural principle of arbitrariness has greatly undermined anthropologists' attempts to understand the complexity of fear and anxiety, not to mention cultural symbols and thought processes. All people everywhere employ a number of cognitive modalities that have various kinds of culturally specific legitimation and status. The early anthropological debates about totemic, mystic participation and primitive thought assumed an overarching rationalism and classificatory logic, which seriously misrepresented the multiplex dimensions of fear and anxiety as engines. Furthermore, it is important to remember that principles such as belief in groups' symbolic bonds and participation are not restricted to nonmodernized societies.

To draw attention to the multiplex dimensions of Arab cultural fears, that is, fear of starvation, it is important to analyze myths and rituals of desert Arabs. Bedouin Arabs have had to make their living from animal stocks they developed, a kind of contract between them and these stocks. Animals sacrifice themselves as food for Arabs, and Arabs conduct rituals to ensure that the sacrifice does not go in vain. To characterize how Bedouins see themselves in relation to other species, one has to categorize the concept of psychogenic motivation, a term which shifts attention from the logical qualities of the symbol to the psychological motivations of the symbol user.

In analyzing the desert Arabs' myth and ritual, one realizes the outstanding use of epistemogenesis, a process by which one's knowledge of the world becomes consciously available through language. Urban Arabs, mainly traders and businessmen, have a different use of the language, and this is obvious in their myths. This language is associated with middle and high levels of thought, stressing the importance of analogical reasoning and analogy formation. In other words (and I do not mean this as an insult), Arabs tend to use language the way a drunk uses a lamppost—for support rather than for light.

Arabs assume, often in the face of considerable contrary evidence, a necessary relationship between words, self-interest, and magical solutions. While such behavior might make sense during unending conflicts as in the Middle East, such an attitude has been a warmup for nothing less than restructuring the Arab culture.

Modern Arab cultures are witnessing other limitations. Individuals retain consistent past/present viewpoints. They are constantly torn between the conflicting goals of self-interest, social reform, and patriotic duty. In fact, many individuals, reflecting these split loyalties, contradict themselves continually. The premise here is that religion is the manner in which Arabs express their need for ultimate order and existential meaning. Given their heterogeneous society, Arab cultures have been shaped by diversity, by the awareness that there are others besides us and besides our own communities.[22] However, Arabs have come to realize that, if they are to achieve stability and mutual respect, it is imperative that they identify with others who are not part of their community. In the context of diversity, Arabs try to live together peacefully in a common culture. However, diversity inevitably raises the difficult issues of power, loyalty, and identity. The problem of identity, which has to do with knowing to whom or to which people each Arab belongs, is always a religious matter because it involves the individual's ultimate placement in a meaningful and ordered world.

Since it is not easy for Arabs to accept non-Arabs in the fear that this profoundly threatens their identity, stability is difficult to achieve. In fact, the typical human response to diversity has been either to conquer or to convert the other. However, Arabs have long recognized their diversity and have aimed for stability.

The institution of value, with its roots in Arab culture, functions both as a response of diversity and a facilitator of it. Value holders attempt to find a workable consensus, an alliance in the midst of dissent and differentiation. By the end of the 1980s, for example, an ideological coherence of a sort was temporarily achieved among Arabs by assuming that certain religious foundational principles suffused all Arab values. However, as the number of minority conflicts increased in the Arab world, the relaxations of yesterday have become highly exclusionist in the midst of diversity, since, among other things, they have failed to embrace the notion of foundational principles. Religious diversity, organized in terms of sociopolitical groups, ideological tendencies, and ethnicity, increased dramatically during the 1980s and 1990s because it was a time of turning away from the status quo, the great Arab nationalism flood that bleaches everything in its path. During the prime time of Arab nationalism, individuals with sensitivity to the issues of sectarian differences, language differences, and ethnicity have attempted to include diverse others in the hypothetical culture of Arab nationalism.

One major factor involved in Arab diversity is the process of secularization projected by Arab nationalists as a component of Arab culture. Ironically, though, whenever cultural life is managed as if religion did not exist, religious tendencies begin to proliferate. The secularists themselves thus compound religious diversity when they attempt to demystify religion in the Arab world. Demystification breeds reaction, perhaps because mystery cannot be denied. And so people turn to new religions, or probe the old ones, for some satisfaction. Religious resurgence abounds, and the diversity increases.

Thus what characterizes a nominally Arab culture is not mere diversity but, rather, multiplicity and unequal group differences whose general picture is historically produced, mediated, and sustained by oppressive power relations. Inspired by recent social movements that have made concerns about inequality and difference a focal point of political debate, and in the fear of the rising power of fanatic Islamic fundamentalism, Arab minorities have begun to consider the political potential of giving a facelift to Arab nationalism.

There are two perspectives on the meaning of set-free politics that have been imagined and enacted in response to these understandings of power as productive of group identity. The first perspective, suggested and pursued by a variety of social movements, is to redefine the meaning and value of group identity.[23] This is controversial, of course; both theorists and activists have argued that such strategies either perpetuate the category that should be challenged or obscure its constructed nature. Thus the second perspective is to resist the very notion of categorization. This can be undertaken in a modern individualist mode (refusing to treat group difference as significant) or with a postmodern sensibility (refusing to speak in terms of fixed groups and enacting multiple and fluid identities). Critics of the modern individualist mode argue that we live in a world in which difference does indeed matter and that ignoring its effects perpetuates inequality. Critics of the poststructuralist mode are concerned that it emphasizes fluidity and diversity at the expense of being able to make generalizations about social structures.[24]

In studying Arab culture, these debates about groups and group identity determine how Arabs think cultural practices and thus old and new institutions are shaped and will shape the individual's psyche to emphasize, produce, and preclude various versions of *I* and *us*. Attempts to democratize the Arab world in its existing cultures have contestable conceptual sorting of collectives to rely on. Any attempt will be an act of power, which is to say, in agreement with the analysis of power as productive, that it will materialize in the world new group identities and meanings. But because institutional power is productive in this way, democratization requires pursuing the normative question: What should be represented? What should be materialized and made possible through reforming representative institutions?

Given the role of culture in a context of inequality, democrats need to consider ways to pursue the structural interests of social groups. But given the absence of truth about such interests in the Arab world, how can we consider basing representation on anything but the conscious purposes of those in the group?

To answer these questions, two proposals are drawn, and they may seem opposed to one another, since they deal with a given social identity, yet there is a rejection of the notion that one's membership in a religious or social group is a simple proxy for political interests or purposes.

Arab politics have always faced problems of cultural equality and fair representation. However, some groups stress that the majority should enjoy most of the power, and this comes as a justification for changing the political reality in Iraq, Lebanon, Syria, and some Arab Gulf states. But in a fair system, a permanent majority should not exercise all the power, and a permanent minority should not always lose.[25] In other words, each group has a right to have its interests satisfied much of the time.[26] Minorities have long been associated with social, political, and economic shortcomings.

At the core of Arab culture lies a deep concern for politics and principle. These two concepts are dynamic in their interaction, for both a principled concept of politics and a political concept of principle are a matter of Arab peculiarity. Many Arab nationalists profess to reject the opposition between the particulars of democratic politics and Arab cultural principles. In this context, the intention here is to explore a cultural reality, whether acceptable or not, far from being philosophical, and to touch on the morality as it is considered necessary. Sociologists are well known for their claim that values are relative to social and political meaning.

The crux of the matter here is that minorities in the Arab world each have a particular political culture and social moral values. There is a "thin" and universal morality across the Arab world. Thick and thin political moralities are different, but they are nonetheless interrelated forms of social and cultural conflict. One could detect the difference by observing how members of minorities adopt a way of talking within their inner circles, and a way of talking to people across their immediate group.

I pursue this query not in the interest of upsetting the particular but in an effort to do justice to it. I will focus on thick and thin because I find it more significant, persuasive, and complex than dealing with Arab culture as if it were either homogeneous or variable. The analysis here belies a presumption that who we are or who they are is singular and uniform; there seems a preference, even nostalgia, for such clear-cut identity.

Again, there is the issue of group inner-circle and across-circle toleration that touches on the peaceful coexistence of Arab groups characterized by different local histories, cultures, and identities. The assumption here is that toleration makes coexistence within difference possible and that difference makes toleration necessary. To understand how toleration works and what periodically sustains it in the Arab world, I explore five regimes of toleration prevailing in the Arab world: multinational coexistence, multiracial society, multiconfessional consociations, Arab nationalism vs. states, and immigrant societies. However, given that the concept of toleration is based on group identity, it seems that, as pure groups dissolve in statehood, toleration changes, perhaps even losing its meaning. However, when the common sense of group identity is unsettled or even surpassed, toleration does not lose its meaning but finds, as it were, its true self. The latter is at least a possibility I want to explore.

To be more concrete, one has to understand the political relationships and moral arguments both presupposed and opened by the fact that when watching television news of minorities marching in the streets of Arab capitals with signs proclaiming honesty and justice. Do we really know immediately what they mean? It is not easy to comprehend the full magnitude of such demonstrations. At best, the media recognizes partial commonality and not the full moral significance of other group cultures.[28] But what political scientists understand is extremely important because such protests cut close to the bone even as it is culturally thin. The perception here probably has as much to do with what the marchers did not mean as with what they did mean. The marchers were not holding out a substantive account of distributive justice or advancing an epistemological theory. The marchers wanted to hear true statements from their political leaders; they wanted an end to arbitrary arrests; they wanted equal and impartial law enforcement.

Research should be bound to the marchers and other minority political manifestations by a basic understanding of moral terms about which authorities have distinct interpretations. These shared minority activities, though sufficiently elementary, express moral meanings that are embedded in thick, cultural understandings and their historical, cultural, religious, and political idioms. That is to say, the Arab culture is thick right from the beginning, morally integrated, fully echoing, and it reveals itself thinly only on special occasions that could be dangerous if manipulated to specific political purposes. On such occasions, moral argument reaches beyond the local context and travels abroad. However, moral meanings that are light enough to travel are not substantively minor or emotionally shallow. Rather, they evoke and provoke intense reactions. It is a common notion that there isn't much that is more important than honesty and justice.

Paradoxically, with moral understandings come qualification, compromise, complexity, and disagreement. For instance, although Arabs may agree in principle to oppose political tyranny, this does not necessarily yield agreement about the distribution of social goods within their political culture, let alone across minority groups. Argument for moral understanding of thick and thin, relative and universal, builds upon what one perceives in the Arab culture as a dualism intrinsic to their society. It is universal because it is human, particularly because it is a society. Living in a particular place is morally significant because minority groups live in societies that are necessarily particular and have personalities and memories. The individual in such societies has memories not only of his own experiences but also of the experiences of other individuals in his group. The thick Arab culture, by contrast, has members but no specific memory, and so it has no particular historical account and no specific morality, no common customary practices, no explicit familiar lifeways, no festivals that are common to all Arabs, no shared understandings of social goods.

Debates about relativism and universalism in the Arab world are best understood as arguments about the extent and legitimacy of the translations and resonant meanings of moral understandings between Arab societies, say, Morocco and Lebanon, or Tunisia and Saudi Arabia. Any actual assessment of cultural distribution of morality among such societies will be highly circumstantial, because they are historically dependent on the particularities of the region and factually detailed, and because the basic principles and procedures of their thin culture have been worked out over a long period through complex social interactions.[29]

The reflections presented above on the moral significance of the Arab minorities' particular social cultures are an important consideration to articulations of an Arab political culture. This is not to underestimate the necessity of transformative translation between thickly particular moral understandings. These transformative translations are crucial to the appearance of the Arab culture, which we see in only single, eventful moments. That is to say, the impulse of Arabs to think together is sometimes thin and thick morality. However, we should retain a concept of individual and group identity that unduly circumscribes this projection. Efforts to appreciate the diversity of humanity and the complexity of Arabs would benefit from attention to the concept of alterity, that is, a sense that self and other, internal and external, are always inside one another.

Is it possible for the thin culture of minority groups to survive within the thick Arab culture? Do we see a return of the tribes in assertions of particular ethnic, religious, and national identities in the Arab world? How should we evaluate and respond to these questions? If we are to evaluate the protests and provocations of thick political cultures, it is most likely that this is done for thin or minimalist reasons. The plight of minority groups when they resist oppression, torture, and treachery constitutes not a transcendent totality of culture but a reality of their own. Indeed, they seem increasingly to press upon others as tribes that have become ever more culturally entwined.

There are limits to the possibilities of translation between thick political moral cultures. But this does not mean that we must treat these limits as given rather than as practically delimited. The result may be ways of tolerating difference that actually refuse to know others, especially as they might transform what Arabs know about themselves. The concept of identity is at the root of what amounts to a toleration of others. In addition, one could say that the special nature of toleration fortifies the impulses of cultural groups and individuals to remain the same. Remaining the same in the Arab world means a plight by minority groups for relative self-determination.

The recognition of relative self-determination among the minority groups in the Arab world is at stake in the value of the historical, cultural, and religious communities and the political liberty of its members. This value has not yet been compromised by the modern affiliation to the state. The claims of minority groups are no less real or authentic for their members as they recognize their adherence and sometime loyalty to their states. Minority groups in the Arab world more often assert in their inner circles that no matter how they as a community have come into being, they ought to be allowed to have relative autonomy or relative self-determination. The group assimilation tendencies and the reconstruction of group identity as it is taking place in the Arab world have not been effective in decreasing the importance of minority identity. Indeed, in many cases, these efforts seem to inflame the desire for exclusivity of identity. Assertion of authentic identity seems a prevalent response to actual threats to identity, even if such assertion often provides further fuel for conflict, which is not to say it is a legitimate reason for aggression.

Such a dynamic reality of thin and thick cultures and resisting assimilations seems to me at least part of what energizes identity politics, within the Arab state and across the Arab world. Pointing out the historical and contingent character of identities in itself will not alleviate conflict. It is the case, however, that once we recognize the intercultural character of groups and interdependence of individuals, we may come to see that claims to self-governance always contain an element of fear. The fear among individuals and groups is the perception of danger to their pure identity. Arab nationalists overlook this fear because they misconstrue the political implications of the claim that all groups are mutually, not sovereignly, self-constituting.

The point is that group identity does matter. Claims to sovereign self or collective rule in the name of difference can trigger politically aggressive acts because they either deny the connections that do exist with others or endeavor to master those connections in a forceful manner. Usually claims to sovereignty hurt some in the course of making others more secure. Sometimes, though, minority groups seem willing to tolerate more aggression than is humanly acceptable. At other times, minorities are not comfortable with mild aggression. This is all related, I believe, to the failure to recognize boundaries between the self and others in group relations. This lack of recognition is contentious in its asymmetrical relations, and it is merely matters of cultural difference within or between thick cultures. This acknowledges the complexity of group and individual identity, especially that group loyalties ordinarily are divided. Often when a group's sense of a particular history, culture, and identity is threatened, it becomes narrow-minded. Under conditions of security, minority groups acquire more complex identities. When identities are multiplied, passions are divided and, as a consequence, disciplined.[30] Under what conditions does an individual's security lead to multiple loyalties? And under what conditions are a group's different history, culture, and identity tolerated by other groups?

It seems that intolerance ultimately is bred by the perceived threat that others pose to minority groups' distinctive identities. Minorities always see difference as otherness, but the insecurity difference provoked only becomes intolerable when minorities feel threatened. The problem to which toleration is a response is not so much difference itself but the desire for unmixed difference, the desire for a purity that, because it does not usually exist in the modern Arab world, can only be forcefully pursued and insecurely achieved. Group identity is never clear, and neither is individual identity in the Arab culture. Groups and individuals are actually mixed with what appears to be outside them. They maintain the delusion of their purity only by denying that fact of mixture and by displacing what is other within them onto those outside. This is not to say that this is a conscious or intentional move. Indeed, it is often unconscious. But even so it is not without political consequences.

If we are to characterize Lebanon and Tunisia as having a higher culture of toleration by contrast to the relatively tribal society of Saudi Arabia, then each of these cultures can appear exceptional when compared to one another. However, all have had a culture of violence that is different in nature. In all cases whether the culture is confessional, feudal, or tribal, when a minority group is sufficiently threatened, it deems sovereignty a necessary protection.[31] But when group identity drives minorities toward sovereignty, inspired by a felt need to maintain an unmixed difference, the perception and the actuality of threat are heightened. Even if the effort to achieve sovereign security and a state of pure difference is ostensibly successful, it is only a matter of time before minority groups find the difference within themselves, which they had thought was only outside. Isn't this what is at issue in current civil hostilities and unrest within the Arab world over the definition of "Who am I truly"?

Significant differences do exist among the different minorities in the Arab world. They matter, and something of universal moral value rests within them. The neo-Kantian or Pauline universality that would make difference disappear by erasing it in the course of tolerating it is not really a plausible forecast in the Arab world. To affirm difference is to recognize that difference is never pure. Actual difference is never the same as the self it would imagine as opposed to others. Nor is difference ever the self-same: Difference always has others within as well as outside. Differences matter even as, and indeed because, they are mixed with that which we would mistake for purely different.

Notwithstanding, sometimes minority groups and individuals in the Arab world need to fight for self-determination and for their lives, no more so than when they are so powerless as to verge on being hopeless or socially and politically dead. This is very much the case for the Kurds in Iraq, Christians in southern Sudan, Shi'ites in Iraq, and Christians in Lebanon. However, politically speaking, the end result for minorities pursuing or exercising sovereignty in the name of unmixed difference usually brings harm to others and risks self-destruction.

What then is the universal Arab value within particular political moral cultures? Arab minority groups find themselves tending more to their particular moral political practices. Following from this perception, an individual from one group who finds his same values in his group confirms his given perceptions of apparently pure difference to others in other groups. Once minority groups perceive themselves as constituting distinctive cultures and can transform those cultures into action, then, free actions that constitute and alter differences are a sign thereby of the universal within particular political cultures and of those cultures' necessary and ceaseless mixing and transformation. Thus, what is principled and culturally valuable in Arab societies is intimately related to the fact that they are, at times, modified but relatively undiluted.

Notes

Chapter 1. Fear and Anxiety as Concepts Linking Psychology and Political Studies

1. Wituski, "Bridging a Disciplinary Divide," 1–2.

2. Hermann, *An Interdisciplinary Adventure*, 4–5.

3. Greenstein, "Political Psychology: A Pluralistic Universe," 457.

4. S. Freud, *Group Psychology and the Analysis of the Ego*, 66–67.

5. Bettelheim, "Individual and Mass Behavior," 422–24.

6. Alford, *Melanie Klein*, 21–23. On this subject see Benjamin, *The Bonds of Love*; Bion, *Experiences in Groups*; Chodorow, *The Reproduction of Mothering*; Deleuze and Guattari, *Anti-Oedipus*; Dinnerstein, *The Mermaid and the Minotaur*; Flax, *Thinking Fragments*; Foucault, *Madness and Civilization*.

7. Laing, *The Politics of Experience*, 1–6; Lichtman, *The Production of Desire*, 3–7; Loewald, *Sublimation*, 2–4.

8. Fast, "Object Relations," 186–99.

9. Ajami, *The Vanished Imam*, 54–57.

10. Balay and Shevrin, "The Subliminal Psychodynamic Activation Method," 163–68.

11. Davis, "Repression and the Inaccessibility of Affective Memories," 155–62; Pipes, *The Hidden Hand*, 2–5.

12. Ihilevich and Gleser, *Defenses in Psychotherapy*, 16–18.

13. Strentz, "The Stockholm Syndrome," 312–19.

14. Kristeva, *Powers of Horror*, 11–12.

15. Vaillant, *Ego Mechanisms of Defense*, 3–4.

16. Brunner, *Freud and the Politics of Psychoanalysis*, 2–5.

17. Roth and Wittich, *Economy and Society*, 13–15.

18. Hechter, "Nationalism as Group Solidarity," 415–17. See also Horowitz, *Ethnic Groups in Conflict*; Jalali and Lipset, "Racial and Ethnic Conflicts," 589–92; Koopmans, *Democracy from Below*; Kriesi, "The Political Opportunity Structure of New Social Movements," 167–69.

Chapter 2. The Hidden Drives of Arab Politics

1. Vinacke, *Foundation of Psychology,* 454–59, 540.

2. Kristeva, *Powers of Horror,* 4–8.

3. Brenner, *The Mind in Conflict,* 3–5; Breznitz, *The Denial of Stress,* 1–3; Connor, "Measurement of Denial in the Terminally Ill," 53–56.

4. Juni, Katz, and Hamburger, "Identification with Aggression vs. Turning against the Self," 313–15.

5. Ibid., 318–19.

6. Benjamin, *The Bonds of Love,* 2–3.

7. Hilgard, "Human Motives and the Concept of the Self," 378–80.

8. Glass, *Delusion,* 1–3.

9. Grunbaum, *The Foundations of Psychoanalysis,* 39–41.

10. Reiff, *Freud: The Mind of the Moralist,* 4–5.

11. Reich, *The Mass Psychology of Fascism,* 2–4.

12. Beran, "In Defense of the Consent Theory," 261–62.

13. Poliakov, *The Aryan Myth,* 16–17.

14. On this subject see S. Freud, *The Ego and the Id; The Future of an Illusion; Civilization and Its Discontents; Why War?* 205–9.

15. Beck, Emery, and Greenberg, *Anxiety Disorders and Phobias,* 4–8.

16. Stein, Vidich, and White, *Identity and Anxiety,* 391.

17. Alford, *Melanie Klein,* 34–35.

18. S. Freud, *Group Psychology and the Analysis of the Ego,* 67; Fromm, *Escape from Freedom,* 23–25.

19. Flax, *Thinking Fragments,* 36–37.

20. Bion, *Experiences in Groups,* 46–48.

21. Fenichel, "Critique of Death Instinct," 460–62; Fenichel, "Neurotic Acting Out," 201–3.

22. Fenichel, "Critique of Death Instinct," 463; Fenichel, "Neurotic Acting Out," 205.

23. Juni, "The Role of the Object," 429–30.

24. Markus and Kitayama, "Culture and the Self," 224–25; Markus and Kitayama, "A Collective Fear of the Collective," 571–72.

25. Reich, *The Mass Psychology of Fascism,* 23–24.

26. Fast, "Object Relations," 186–89.

27. Hudson, *Arab Politics,* 21–24.

28. Miller, "Theoretical Issues in Cultural Psychology"; Berry, Poortinga, and Pandey, *Handbook of Cross-Cultural Psychology,* 86–88.

29. On this subject see Pennebaker, Paez, and Rime, *Collective Memory of Political Events.*

30. Allport, *The Individual and His Religion,* 28–29.

31. Money-Kyrle, *Psychoanalysis and Politics,* 2–3.

32. Fairbairn, "Synopsis of an Object Relations Theory of Personality," 224–25.

33. Pettit, *The Common Mind,* 3–4.

34. Cramer, "The Defense Mechanisms Inventory," 143–44.

35. Ibid., 145–46.

36. Donahue, "Intrinsic and Extrinsic Religiousness," 402–3.

37. Vaillant, *Ego Mechanisms of Defense,* 12–13.

38. A. Freud, *The Ego and the Mechanisms of Defense,* 8–9.

39. Loewald, *Sublimation,* 16–18.

40. Balay and Shevrin, "The Subliminal Psychodynamic Activation Method," 162–65; Bettelheim, "Individual and Mass Behavior," 418–19.

41. Lewis, *Shame and Guilt in Neurosis,* 6–8; Lewis, "The Role of Shame in Depression," 30–35; Lindsay-Hartz, "Contrasting Experiences of Shame and Guilt," 689–704; Lutz and White, "The Anthropology of Emotions," 413–15.

42. Markus and Kitayama, "Culture and the Self," 226–28; Markus and Kitayama, "The Cultural Construction of Self and Emotion," 99–102; Scheff and Retzinger, *Emotions and Violence,* 3–5.

43. Reich, *Power,* 2–3.

44. Ibid., 4.

45. Lecher, "Social Structure and Political Stability," 157; Anderson, "Liberalism, Islam, and the Arab State," 441; Perthes, "The Private Sector," 265.

46. Hermann, *Political Psychology;* Elster, *Political Psychology;* Kressel, *Political Psychology,* 8–9.

47. Tunick, *Practices and Principles,* 2–3; Bentham, "Fragment on Government," chap. 1, sec. 43; Klosko, "Presumptive Benefit," 242–44; Hart, "Are There Any Natural Rights?" 180–84; Rawls, "Legal Obligation and the Duty of Fair Play," 9–10; Walker, *Political Obligation,* 192, 205, 207.

48. Meissner, "Theories of Personality and Psychopathology," 632–35; Modell, "A Narcissistic Defense against Affects and the Illusion of Self-Sufficiency," 276–78; Ramachandran, "Anosognosia in Parietal Lobe Syndrome," 26–28; Schafer, "The Mechanisms of Defense," 51, 53.

49. Fenichel, "Neurotic Acting Out," 198–202; S. Freud, *The Psychoneuroses of Defense,* 48–50; Hilgard, "Human Motives and the Concept of the Self," 379–81; Juni, "Remorse as a Derivative Psychoanalytic Construct," 76–78.

Chapter 3. Arab Political Identity in Crisis

1. W. Brown, *States of Injury,* introduction. See also Butler, *Gender Trouble* and *Bodies That Matter;* Calhoun, "Social Theory and the Politics of Identity"; D. Cooper, *Power in Struggle;* Dahl, *A Preface to Democratic Theory;* Danielson and Engle, *After Identity.*

2. Khashan, *Arabs at the Crossroads,* conclusion; Najjar, "The Debates on Islam," 19–21; Hudson, *Arab Politics,* 21; Hopwood, *Egypt: Politics and Society,* 97.

3. Dryzek, "Political Inclusion and the Dynamics of Democratization," 480–82; Eisenberg, *Reconstructing Political Pluralism,* 2–3. See also Guinier, *The Tyr-*

anny of the Majority; Hirst, *Associative Democracy*; Kymlicka, *Liberalism, Community, and Culture.*

4. Casey, *Remembering*, 2–3; Dennett, *Consciousness Explained*, 6–8; Erxleben and Cates, "Systemic Treatment of Multiple Personality," 271–73; Gillett, "Multiple Personality and Irrationality," 112–14; Glover, *The Philosophy and Psychology of Personal Identity*, 34–36; Hacking, "Two Souls in One Body," 838–41.

5. Parfit, "Personal Identity," 4–6, and *Reasons and Persons*, 12–13; Schechtman, "Personhood and Personal Identity," 72–74, and "The Same and the Same," 201–3.

6. Fenichel, "Critique of Death Instinct," 458–60, and "Neurotic Acting Out," 197–99.

7. Cooper, "The Empirical Study of Defensive Process," 328–30.

8. Ibid., 332–34.

9. Brenner, *The Mind in Conflict*, 3–5.

10. Cooper, "The Empirical Study of Defensive Process," 330.

11. S. Freud, *Group Psychology and the Analysis of the Ego*, 68–69.

12. Schafer, "The Mechanisms of Defense," 52–55.

13. Weber, *The Protestant Ethic*, introduction.

14. On this subject see Taylor, "The Politics of Recognition"; Rorty, "The Hidden Politics of Cultural Identification," 158–59; Woolf, *A Room of One's Own*, 36; Holmes, *Passions and Constraint*, 13; Kukathas, "Are There Any Cultural Rights?" 106–8.

15. Lecher, "Social Structure and Political Stability," 157; Anderson, "Liberalism, Islam, and the Arab State," 441; Perthes, "The Private Sector," 265.

16. Barakat, *The Arab World*, 2–5.

17. On this subject see Gelvin, "Popular Mobilization and the Foundations of Mass Politics in Syria, 1918–1920"; Swedenburg, "The Role of the Palestinian Peasantry," 169–71; Johnson, *Islam and the Politics of Meaning in Palestinian Nationalism*, 31; Hurewitz, *The Middle East and North Africa in World Politics*, 179; Fromkin, *A Peace to End All Peace*, 21–23; Yapp, *The Near East since the First World War*, 6–8.

18. On this subject see Salem, *Bitter Legacy*; Heelas, Lash, and Morris, *Detraditionalization*; Hobsbawm and Ranger, *The Invention of Tradition*; Parsons, *The System of Modern Societies*; Smith, *The Ethnic Origins of Nations*; Thomas, Meyer, Ramirez, and Boli, *Institutional Structure*; Wallerstein, *The Capitalist Economy*; Weber, *Economy and Society*; Kittrie, *The War against Authority*; Kaldor, "Cosmopolitanism vs. Nationalism," 42–58; Gellner, *Nations and Nationalism.*

19. Zamir, *The Formation of Modern Lebanon*, 8–12; Batatu, *The Egyptian, Syrian, and Iraqi Revolutions*, 38–40; Anderson, *Imagined Communities*, 53–61, 113–40.

20. Parfit, "Personal Identity," 4–5, and *Reasons and Persons*, 2–4.

21. Schechtman, "The Truth about Memory," 5–8; Shoemaker, *Persons and Their Pasts*, 282–84.

22. Hughes, "Personal Identity," 180–84; Kluft, "The Postunification Treatment," 212–15; Korsgaard, "Personal Identity," 103–5; Locke, *An Essay Concerning Human Understanding*, 5–8.

23. Hattie, *Self-Concept*, 9–11; Hofstede, *Culture's Consequences*, 16–19; Kuhn and McPartland, "An Empirical Investigation of Self-Attitudes," 19, 68–76; Markus and Kitayama, "Culture and the Self," 98, 224–53.

24. McClure, "On the Subject of Rights," 11–14; McGowan, *Postmodernism and Its Critics*, 23–26; Minow, "Justice Engendered," 11–14, 91–94. See also Phillips, *Democracy and Difference* and *The Politics of Presence*; Skocpol, "Bringing the State Back In"; Young, *Justice and the Politics of Difference*.

25. Sampson, "The Debate on Individualism," 15–22; Shweder and Bourne, "Does the Concept of the Person Vary Cross-Culturally?" 161–65; Triandis, Bontempo, and Villareal, "Individualism and Collectivism," 323–24; Berry et al., "Comparative Studies of Acculturative Stress," 491–93, and "Acculturation Attitudes in Plural Societies," 185–88.

26. Swanton, *Freedom*, 12; Thagard, "Explanatory Coherence," 462–64, and *Conceptual Revolutions*, 4–5. See also Thagard, *Mind: Introduction to Cognitive Science*; Thagard et al., "Knowledge and Coherence," 6–8.

27. Erxleben and Cates, "Systemic Treatment of Multiple Personality," 271–73; Gillett, "Multiple Personality and Irrationality," 115–17; Glover, *The Philosophy and Psychology of Personal Identity*; Hacking, "Two Souls in One Body," 862–67, and *Rewriting the Soul*, 5–8; Hughes, "Personal Identity," 181–85; Kluft, "The Postunification Treatment," 216–18.

28. Hacking, "Two Souls in One Body," 839–41.

29. Schechtman, "Personhood and Personal Identity," 71–90; "The Same and the Same," 201–3; and "The Truth about Memory," 5–8.

30. Greenfield, "Independence and Interdependence," 3–9; Guisinger and Blatt, "Individuality and Relatedness," 105–9; Hallowell, *Culture and Experience*, 12–15; Heider, *The Psychology of Interpersonal Relationships*, 14–17; Heine and Lehman, "Cultural Variation in Unrealistic Optimism," 598–601.

31. Greenfield, "Independence and Interdependence," 32–35.

32. Triandis, Bontempo, and Villareal, "Individualism and Collectivism," 324–26; Berry et al., "Comparative Studies of Acculturative Stress," 492–501, and "Acculturation Attitudes in Plural Societies," 204–6.

33. Triandis, Bontempo, and Villareal, "Individualism and Collectivism," 336–38.

34. Schechtman, "Personhood and Personal Identity," 89–92; "The Same and the Same," 201–4; and "The Truth about Memory," 4–6.

35. Breznitz, *The Denial of Stress*, 4–8; Connor, "Measurement of Denial in the Terminally Ill," 52–54; Cooper, "The Empirical Study of Defensive Process," 327–31; Cousins, "Denial," 210–12.

36. S. Freud, *The Infantile Genital Organization,* 141–48.

37. On this subject see S. Freud, *Group Psychology and the Analysis of the Ego; The Ego and the Id; The Future of an Illusion.*

38. Hilgard, "Human Motives and the Concept of the Self," 375–78; Cramer, "The Defense Mechanisms Inventory," 146.

39. Ihilevich and Gleser, *Defenses in Psychotherapy,* 14–16, 18.

40. A. Freud, *The Ego and the Mechanisms of Defense,* 16–19.

41. Ihilevich and Gleser, *Defenses in Psychotherapy,* 12–15.

42. Juni, Katz, and Hamburger, "Identification with Aggression," 316–21.

Chapter 4. Nationalism: From the Power of Fear to the Fear of Power

1. Kaldor, "Cosmopolitanism vs. Nationalism," 42–58; Gellner, *Nations and Nationalism,* 21–23; Gutmann, "The Subjective Politics of Power," 571–74.

2. Alford, *Group Psychology,* introduction; Brunner, *Freud and the Politics of Psychoanalysis,* 18–22; Glass, *Psychosis and Power,* 6–9.

3. S. Freud, *Group Psychology and the Analysis of the Ego,* 139–42; *The Origins of Psychoanalysis,* 2–5.

4. Bion, *Experiences in Groups,* 9–11; Bettelheim, "Individual and Mass Behavior," 419–21. See also Brenner, *The Mind in Conflict;* Breznitz, *The Denial of Stress.*

5. On this subject see Ferenczi, "Stages in the Development of the Sense of Reality"; S. Freud, *Notes upon a Case of Obsessional Neurosis.*

6. Markus and Kitayama, *Culture and the Self,* 230–34, and "A Collective Fear of the Collective," 569–72.

7. Alford, *Melanie Klein,* 53; Benjamin, *The Bonds of Love;* Bion, *Experiences in Groups,* 4–11.

8. Alford, *Melanie Klein,* 52, 54.

9. On this subject see Smith, *The Ethnic Origins of Nations;* Anderson, *Imagined Communities;* Gellner, *Nations and Nationalism;* Geertz, *Old Societies and New States.*

10. Weber, *The Sociology of Religion,* 166; Berry and Wernick, *Shadow of Spirit,* 62.

11. Ajami, *The Arab Predicament,* 28–31; Ansari, "The Islamic Militants in Egyptian Politics," 140–43; Lanternari, *The Religions of the Oppressed,* 3–5; Marty and Appleby, *Fundamentalisms and the State,* 11–13; Rapoport, "Messianic Sanctions for Terror," 196–99; Lieberman, "Race and Ethnicity," 23; Silberman, *Between Past and Present,* 13–17.

12. Ajami, "The End of Pan-Arabism," 356–59, and *The Arab Predicament,* 6–8; Farah, *Pan-Arabism and Arab Nationalism,* 2–5.

13. Al-Turabi, "The New Wave of Islamic Awakening"; Qalada, al-Mismari Amin, et al., *Al-Tasamuh al-Dini,* 4–5; al-Naku'a, "How, from an Islamic Point of View," 14–16; Holmes, *The Anatomy of Antiliberalism,* 254.

14. Alford, *Melanie Klein,* 116.

15. Ibid., 61; Benjamin, *The Bonds of Love,* 10–11; Bion, *Experiences in Groups,* 3–4.

16. Alford, *Melanie Klein,* 68.

17. Bion, *Experiences in Groups,* 173, 189, 273.

18. Alford, *Melanie Klein,* 65.

19. Ibid., 15.

20. Berry, Poortinga, and Pandey, *Handbook of Cross-Cultural Psychology,* 86–88; Rhee et al., "Spontaneous Self-Descriptions," 149–51; Sampson, "The Debate on Individualism," 16–18; Triandis, Bontempo, and Villareal, "Individualism and Collectivism," 324–26; Berry et al., "Comparative Studies of Acculturative Stress," 508–10, and "Acculturation Attitudes in Plural Societies," 186–88; Tajfel, *Human Group and Social Categories,* 5–8; Tajfel and Turner, "An Integrative Theory of Intergroup Conflict," 83–85.

21. Ip and Bond, "Culture, Values, and the Spontaneous Self-Concept," 30–34; Kitayama and Karasawa, "Self: A Cultural Psychological Perspective," 159–63; Kitayama and Markus, *Emotion and Culture,* 4–6; Lebra, *Culture, Self, and Communication,* 2–4.

22. Khoury, *Urban Notables and Arab Nationalism,* 18–20; Khalidi, *Ottomanism and Arabism,* 54–56; Swedenburg, "The Role of the Palestinian Peasantry," 181–85; Johnson, *Islam and the Politics of Meaning in Palestinian Nationalism,* 8–11.

23. McLaurin, Peretz, and Snider, *Middle East Foreign Policy,* 210–11; Salamé, *The Foundations of the Arab State,* introduction; Haim, *Arab Nationalism,* 23–25; Owen, *The Middle East in the World Economy,* 154–56; Polk and Chambers, *Beginnings of Modernization in the Middle East,* 3–5; Udovitch, *The Islamic Middle East, 700–1900,* 2–4; Mosse, *The Nationalization of the Masses,* introduction.

24. Horton and Mendus, *Aspects of Toleration,* 3–8; Edwards and Mendus, *On Toleration,* introduction; Mendus, *Justifying Toleration,* 11–14; Gutmann, *Multiculturalism,* 19–21; Wolin, "Democracy, Difference and Re-Cognition," 467; Lucas, *The Principles of Politics,* 298–300; Ladd, *Community,* 79–81.

25. Bentham, "Fragment on Government," chap. 1, sec. 43; Klosko, "Presumptive Benefit," 242–44; Hart, "Are There Any Natural Rights?" 188–90; Rawls, "Legal Obligation and the Duty of Fair Play," 5–8; Walker, *Political Obligation,* 194–98; Beran, "In Defense of the Consent Theory," 258–60; Simmons, *Moral Principles and Political Obligation,* chaps. 2 and 3.

26. Oye, "Explaining Cooperation under Anarchy," 9–11; Hardin, "An Operational Analysis of 'Responsibility'," 51–53.

27. Podeh, *The Quest for Hegemony,* chap. 1; Hoch, "Near and Middle East Conflicts and Western Policies," 280; Hadar, "America's Moment in the Middle East," 95; Tétreault, "Gulf Winds," 23; Bahgat, "The Changing Economic and Political Environment in the Gulf Monarchies," 275–78; Zanoyan, "The Holiday

Ends in the Gulf," 3; Kemp, "Saudi Arabia Ends the Uncertainty"; Khalilzad, "The United States and the Persian Gulf," 110.

28. Entelis, *Islam, Democracy, and the State in North Africa,* introduction; Nagel and Olzak, "Ethnic Mobilization in New and Old States," 131–34; Smith, *The Ethnic Revival in the Modern World,* introduction.

29. Alwan, "The New Strive for Life," 1, 8–11; al-Naku'a, "How, from an Islamic Point of View," 11–12.

30. Kymlicka, *Liberalism, Community, and Culture,* introduction.

31. Rhee et al., "Spontaneous Self-Descriptions," 143–45; Sampson, "The Debate on Individualism," 16–19; Shweder and Bourne, "Does the Concept of the Person Vary Cross-Culturally?" 158–61; Triandis, Bontempo, and Villareal, "Individualism and Collectivism," 334–36.

32. Markus et al., *Of Selves and Selfways,* introduction; Markus, Mullally, and Kitayama, "Selfways," 14–16; Marsella, DeVos, and Hsu, *Culture and Self,* 3–5; Miller, "Culture and the Development of Everyday Social Explanation," 962–65, and "Theoretical Issues in Cultural Psychology," 86–88.

33. Church and Lonner, "The Cross-Cultural Perspective in the Study of Personality," 33–35; Greenfield, "Independence and Interdependence," 33–36; Guisinger and Blatt, "Individuality and Relatedness," 105–8; Hallowell, *Culture and Experience,* 3–6; Heider, *The Psychology of Interpersonal Relationships,* introduction.

34. Rorty, "The Hidden Politics of Cultural Identification," 158; Woolf, *A Room of One's Own,* 36; Tversky and Kahneman, "Judgment under Uncertainty," 1124–28; Fearon and Laitin, "Explaining Interethnic Cooperation," 715–19; Gellner, "Nationalism in the Vacuum," 243–48; Levey, "Equality, Autonomy, and Cultural Rights," 216–19.

Chapter 5. Arab Minorities: Individuals' Fear Absorbed in Groups' Anxieties

1. Walzer, "On Toleration"; Tully, *Strange Multiplicity,* 22–28; Taylor, "The Politics of Recognition," chap. 1.

2. Gurr and Moore, "Ethnopolitical Rebellion," 1080–89; Gurr and Scarritt, "Minorities at Risk," 401–5; Hannan, "The Dynamics of Ethnic Boundaries in Modern States," 253–56.

3. Brass, *Ethnicity and Nationalism,* 6–9; Lebra, *Culture, Self, and Communication,* chap. 2.

4. Smith, *The Ethnic Revival in the Modern World,* 2–5, and *The Ethnic Origins of Nations,* 11–14; Dawes, "Social Dilemmas," 191–93; Dawes et al., "Organizing Groups for Collective Action," 1173–75; Hwang and Burgers, "Properties of Trust," 69–72; Johnson-George and Swap, "Measurement of Specific Interpersonal Trust," 317.

5. S. Freud, *Civilization and Its Discontents,* 14–18, and *Why War?* 203–15.

6. Allport, *The Individual and His Religion,* 132; Allport and Ross, "Personal Religious Orientation and Prejudice," 433–36.

7. Horowitz, *Ethnic Groups in Conflict,* chap. 1; Jalali and Lipset, "Racial and Ethnic Conflicts," 585–86; Jenkins and Schmeidl, "Flight from Violence," 64–66; Muller and Weede, "Cross-National Variation in Political Violence," 624–26; Nagel and Olzak, "Ethnic Mobilization in New and Old States," 127–30.

8. Luciani, *The Arab State,* introduction; Anderson, "Liberalism, Islam, and the Arab State," 441; Salamé, *Democracy without Democrats,* chap. 2.

9. Dawn, *From Ottomanism to Arabism,* 9–11.

10. Kramer, *Arab Awakening and Islamic Revival,* 19–22; Eickelman and Piscatori, *Muslim Politics,* 68–70; Euben, "Premodern, Antimodern, or Postmodern?"; Falk, "Religion and Politics," 97; Ahmed, *Postmodernism and Islam,* 13; Cohen, *The Fundamentalist Phenomenon,* 151–53; Marty, and Appleby, *Fundamentalism Observed,* 19–23. See also Berry and Wernick, *Shadow of Spirit,* and Arendt, "What Is Authority?"

11. Weber, *The Sociology of Religion,* introduction; Shweder and LeVine, *Culture Theory,* 160–64; Triandis, "The Self and Social Behavior in Differing Cultural Contexts," 516–19; Wylie, *Measuring Self-Concept,* 3–6.

12. Lindsay-Hartz, "Contrasting Experiences of Shame and Guilt," 691–95; Lutz and White, "The Anthropology of Emotions," 432–35.

13. Hobsbawm and Ranger, *The Invention of Tradition,* chap. 1.

14. Ignatieff, *Blood and Belonging,* 33–34; Kumar, "Civil Society," 376–78; Kuper, "The Sovereign Territorial State," 74–76. On this subject see also Zalewski and Enloe, "Questions about Identity in International Relations"; Ajami, *The Arab Predicament;* Ansari, "The Islamic Militants in Egyptian Politics," 129–34; Armstrong, *Holy War.*

15. McIntosh, "The Economy of Desire," 406–8; "Cathexes and Their Objects in the Thought of Sigmund Freud," 680–82; and *Self, Person, World,* introduction.

16. Gutmann, "The Subjective Politics of Power," 570–71, 613–15; Iyengar, *Is Anyone Responsible?* 4–8; Schafer, "The Loving and Beloved Superego," 23–25.

17. Schafer, "The Loving and Beloved Superego," 27.

18. Ibid., 28.

19. Lebra, *Culture, Self, and Communication,* chap. 1; Lewin, *A Dynamic Theory of Personality,* introduction.

20. Cantor, "From Thought to Behavior," 735–38, and "Life Task Problem Solving," 241–43; Cantor and Kihlstrom, *Personality and Social Intelligence,* 3–5; Church and Lonner, "The Cross-Cultural Perspective in the Study of Personality," 60–62.

21. For more details about these concepts, see Church and Lonner, "The Cross-Cultural Perspective in the Study of Personality," 40–52.

22. Leventhal, Zimmerman, and Gutmann, "Compliance: A Self-Regulation Perspective," 3–8; Maslow, *Religions, Values, and Peak-Experiences,* chap. 1; Maton, "The Stress-Buffering Role of Spiritual Support," 311–12; Maton and Wells, "Religion as a Community Resource for Well-Being," 178–80; Nilsen, *Re-*

ligion and Personality Integration, 34–36; Quackenbush, "Comparison and Contrast between Belief System Theory and Cognitive Theory," 316–18.

23. Gerth and Mills, *From Max Weber,* 77–79; Weber, *The Protestant Ethic,* introduction.

24. Lichter, Rothman, and Lichter, *The Media Elite,* 36–39.

25. Salomon, "Predispositions about Learning from Print and Television," 122–25.

26. Schudson, *The Power of News,* 27–29.

27. Schafer, "The Loving and Beloved Superego."

28. Reich, *The Mass Psychology of Fascism,* 31–33; Lothane, "The Primacy of Love," 3–4, and "Love and Destructiveness," 2–9.

29. S. Freud, *Group Psychology and the Analysis of the Ego,* 23, 69.

30. Ibid., 74.

31. Ibid.

32. Veenhoven, "Questions on Happiness," 7–9; Wong, "Personal Meaning and Successful Aging," 516–17; Triandis, McCusker, and Hui, "Multimethod Probes on Individualism and Collectivism," 1006–9.

33. Freud, *Group Psychology and the Analysis of the Ego,* 85.

34. Ibid., 91.

35. Danielson and Engle, *After Identity,* chap. 1.

36. W. Brown, *States of Injury,* chap. 7; D. Cooper, *Power in Struggle,* 13–15; Dahl, *A Preface to Democratic Theory,* introduction.

37. Guinier, *The Tyranny of the Majority,* 4–8; Hirst, *Associative Democracy,* 35–38.

38. On this subject see Butler, *Gender Trouble,* and *Bodies That Matter;* Danielson and Engle, *After Identity.*

39. Kymlicka, *Liberalism, Community, and Culture,* chap. 1.

40. S. Freud, *Group Psychology and the Analysis of the Ego,* 94, 108.

41. Ibid., 110.

42. Ibid., 113, 116.

Chapter 6. Religion: Appeasing Psychological Fear and Creating Political Instability

1. Bellah et al., *Individualism and Commitment in American Life,* 5–9; McGuire, *Religion: The Social Context,* 22–25; Allport, *The Individual and His Religion,* 8–11; Allport and Ross, "Personal Religious Orientation and Prejudice," 432–35; Berger and Luckmann, *The Social Construction of Reality,* 33–36; Bergin, "Psychotherapy and Religious Values," 96–99; Bergin and Jensen, "Religiosity of Psychotherapists," 3–7; Beutler, "Values, Beliefs, Religion, and the Persuasive Influence of Psychotherapy," 432–35.

2. S. Freud, *Totem and Taboo,* introduction; *Group Psychology and the Analysis of the Ego,* 104–5; *The Future of an Illusion,* 23–25; and *Civilization and Its Discontents,* 81–83, 85.

3. BeitHallahmi and Argyle, *The Psychology of Religious Behavior, Belief, and Experience,* chap. 1; Hexham and Poewe, *New Religion as Global Cultures,* 3–7; Bruce, *Religion and Modernization,* 43–45; Burke, "Religion and Secularization," 293–95; Chaves, "Secularization as Declining Religious Authority," 749–52.

4. S. Freud, *Notes upon a Case of Obsessional Neurosis,* 231–34.

5. Ferenczi, "Stages in the Development of the Sense of Reality," and *The Clinical Diary,* 80–82; S. Freud, *Three Essays on the Theory of Sexuality,* 171, 186.

6. Ferenczi, *The Clinical Diary,* 83.

7. S. Freud, *Notes upon a Case of Obsessional Neurosis,* 234.

8. S. Freud, *Totem and Taboo,* 91.

9. Bergson, *The Two Sources of Morality and Religion,* 21–23; Gellner, *Postmodernism, Reason, and Religion,* 12–16; Hourani, *Arabic Thought in the Liberal Age,* 144.

10. On this subject see Greenfeld, *Nationalism;* Kramer, *Arab Awakening and Islamic Revival;* Nasr, *Mawdudi and the Making of Islamic Revivalism;* Eickelman and Piscatori, *Muslim Politics;* Euben, "Premodern, Antimodern, or Postmodern?"

11. Lawrence, *Defenders of God,* 232; Falk, "Religion and Politics," 380; Ahmed, *Postmodernism and Islam,* 13; Hassan, "The Burgeoning of Islamic Fundamentalism"; Cohen, *The Fundamentalist Phenomenon,* 151–55; Voll, "Fundamentalism in the Sunni Arab World," 340–48.

12. Kerr, *Islamic Reform,* 8–11; Berry and Wernick, *Shadow of Spirit,* 3–5; Connolly, "Beyond Good and Evil," 370; Parsons, "Religion in Modern Pluralistic Society," 141–45; Parsons, *The System of Modern Societies,* 3–5; Smith, *The Meaning and End of Religion,* 12–14; Thomas et al., *Institutional Structure,* introduction.

13. McGuire, *Religion: The Social Context;* chap. 1; Allport, *The Individual and His Religion,* 14–19; Allport and Ross, "Personal Religious Orientation and Prejudice," 432–36; Berger and Luckmann, *The Social Construction of Reality,* 3–6; Bergin, "Values and Religious Issues," 399–402; Csikszentmihalyi, *The Evolving Self,* 36–38; Dow, "Universal Aspects of Symbolic Healing," 56–66.

14. Wilson and Filsinger, "Religiosity and Marital Adjustment," 147–49; Gartner, Larson, and Allen, "Religious Commitment and Mental Health," 21–24; Gorsuch and Smith, "Attribution of Responsibility to God," 348–52; Pargament et al., "God Help Me," 794–98; Pargament et al., "Religion and the Problem-Solving Process," 901–4.

15. Pargament et al., "God Help Me," 819–22.

16. Durkheim, *The Elementary Forms of Religious Life,* introduction; *On Morality and Society,* 15–19; and *The Problem of Religion and the Duality of Human Nature,* chap. 1; Gellner, "Holism and Individualism in History and Sociology," 73–75; Hund, "Are Social Facts Real?" 270–76.

17. Al-Turabi, "The New Wave of Islamic Awakening," 9–10; Qalada, al-

Mismari Amin, et al., *Al-Tasamuh al-Dini,* 4–5; al-Naku'a, "How, from an Islamic Point of View," 7–9.

18. Hertel and Donahue, "Parental Influences on God Images among Children," 189–92; Hilbert, "Anomie and the Moral Regulation of Reality," 1–13.

19. S. Freud, *Civilization and Its Discontents,* 86–88; Markus and Kitayama, "Culture and the Self," 224–28, and "A Collective Fear of the Collective," 568–71; Markus, Kitayama, and Heiman, "Culture and Basic Psychological Principles," introduction; Markus et al., *Of Selves and Selfways,* 3–8.

20. S. Freud, *Totem and Taboo* and *The Future of an Illusion,* introduction.

21. Jung, *Modern Man in Search of a Soul;* Kilbourne and Richardson, "Psychotherapy and New Religions," 237–40; Maton, "The Stress-Buffering Role of Spiritual Support," 310–12; Maton and Wells, "Religion as a Community Resource for Well-Being," 190–93; Nilsen, *Religion and Personality Integration,* chap. 1.

22. S. Freud, *The Future of an Illusion,* 19–21.

23. Deleuze and Guattari, *Anti-Oedipus,* 5–8.

24. Gorsuch and Smith, "Attribution of Responsibility to God," 340–45; Pargament et al., "God Help Me," 802–5; Pargament and Hahn, "God and the Just World," 199–203.

25. Schaefer and Gorsuch, "Psychological Adjustment and Religiousness," 44–48; Spilka and Schmidt, "General Attribution Theory for the Psychology of Religion," 326–29.

26. Allport, *The Individual and His Religion,* introduction; Allport and Ross, "Personal Religious Orientation and Prejudice," 438–41.

27. Eickelman, "Muslim Politics," 17–42; Tessler, "The Origins of Popular Support," 93–99, 121–25.

28. Appleby, *Spokesmen for the Despised,* chap. 1.

Chapter 7. Fear, the Self, and Arab Culture

1. Marsella, DeVos, and Hsu, *Culture and Self,* 3–6; Miller, "Culture and the Development of Everyday Social Explanation," 961–64.

2. S. Freud, *Group Psychology,* 70–72. See also *The Ego and the Id; The Future of an Illusion; Civilization and Its Discontents; Why War?* 205–9.

3. Neisser and Jopling, *The Conceptual Self in Context,* 13–19; Miller, "Theoretical Issues in Cultural Psychology," 85–89.

4. On this subject see Alford, *Melanie Klein;* Diener and Diener, "Cross-Cultural Correlates of Life Satisfaction and Self-Esteem," 659–62; Diener, Diener, and Diener, "Factors Predicting the Subjective Well-Being of Nations," 853–55; Diener, Sandvik, and Pavot, "Happiness Is the Frequency," 125–28; Triandis, McCusker, and Hui, "Multi-Method Probes on Individualism and Collectivism," 1012–16.

5. Kitayama and Karasawa, "Self: A Cultural Psychological Perspective," 160–

63; Kitayama and Markus, *Emotion and Culture,* chap. 1; Lebra, *Culture, Self, and Communication,* introduction.

6. Simon, "Human Nature in Politics," 295–98; Fiske and Taylor, "Social Cognition," 16–19.

7. Lindblom, *Politics and Markets,* introduction.

8. On this subject see Laclau and Mouffe, *Hegemony and Socialist Strategy;* Skocpol, "Bringing the State Back In"; McLennan, *Pluralism;* McClure, "On the Subject of Rights"; McGowan, *Postmodernism and Its Critics;* Minow, "Justice Engendered," 10–16, 91–94; Phillips, *Democracy and Difference* and *The Politics of Presence.*

9. Guisinger and Blatt, "Individuality and Relatedness," 106–9; Hallowell, *Culture and Experience,* 13–16; Heider, *The Psychology of Interpersonal Relationships,* chap. 1.

10. Nagel and Olzak, "Ethnic Mobilization in New and Old States," 129–32.

11. Fairbairn, "Synopsis of an Object Relations Theory of Personality," 224–25; Fast, "Object Relations," 189–93; Fenichel, "Neurotic Acting Out," 197–201; A. Freud, *The Ego and the Mechanisms of Defense,* introduction.

12. Juni, "The Role of the Object in Drive Cathexis and Object Relations," 431–38.

13. Meissner, "Theories of Personality and Psychopathology," 632–38.

14. Cousins, "Culture and Self-Perception in Japan and the United States," 124–29; Enriquez, "Developing a Filipino Psychology," 163, 165; Hattie, *Self-Concept,* chap. 1; Hofstede, *Culture's Consequences,* 26–29; Ip and Bond, "Culture, Values, and the Spontaneous Self-Concept," 14–23.

15. Hobsbawm and Ranger, *The Invention of Tradition,* chap. 1.

16. Chodorow, *The Reproduction of Mothering,* introduction.

17. Marcuse, *Eros and Civilization,* 8–13; Mitchell, *Psycho-Analysis and Feminism,* introduction; Moi, *The Kristeva Reader,* chap. 1.

18. Markus and Kitayama, "A Collective Fear of the Collective," 570–76, and "Culture and the Self," 229–35; Markus, Kitayama, and Heiman, "Culture and Basic Psychological Principles," introduction.

19. Shweder and Bourne, "Does the Concept of the Person Vary Cross-Culturally?" 158–63; Triandis, Bontempo, and Villareal, "Individualism and Collectivism," 323–26; Berry et al., "Comparative Studies of Acculturative Stress," 509–11; Berry et al., "Acculturation Attitudes in Plural Societies," 185–89.

20. Ferenczi, "Stages in the Development of the Sense of Reality," introduction.

21. Salomon, "Predispositions about Learning from Print and Television," 119–23; Schafer, "The Loving and Beloved Superego," 8–11; Schudson, *The Power of News,* 16–21.

22. Brown, "The Effects of Intergroup Similarity," 21–33; Diener and Diener, "Cross-Cultural Correlates of Life," 653–63; Diener, Diener, and Diener, "Factors Predicting the Subjective Well-Being of Nations," 859–63; Diener, Sandvik, and

Pavot, "Happiness Is the Frequency," 119–40; Klopf, *Intercultural Encounters,* introduction.

23. Young, *Justice and the Politics of Difference,* chap. 1, and "Gender as Seriality," 713–38.

24. Bickford, *The Dissonance of Democracy,* 5–9; Bordo, "Feminism, Postmodernism, and Gender Skepticism," 21–25.

25. Guinier, *The Tyranny of the Majority,* 92; Hirst, *Associative Democracy,* introduction; Eisenberg, *Reconstructing Political Pluralism,* 6–11; Kymlicka, *Liberalism, Community, and Culture,* chap. 1.

26. Guinier, *The Tyranny of the Majority,* 104.

27. Walzer, *Thick and Thin,* chap. 1; Walzer, "On Toleration," introduction.

28. Demarco, *A Coherence Theory in Ethics,* 3–12; Ellis, *Coherence and Verification in Ethics,* 43–48; Holyoak and Thagard, *Mental Leaps,* 5–10; Hurley, *Natural Reasons,* 3–9; Johnson, *Moral Imagination,* 18–21; Kunda, "The Case for Motivated Inference," 480–94; Lakoff, *Moral Politics,* 14–18; Lichter, Rothman, and Lichter, *The Media Elite,* introduction.

29. Walzer, *Thick and Thin,* 3, 21.

30. Ibid., 81.

31. Ibid., 103.

Bibliography

Abed, S. "Islam and Democracy." In *Democracy, War, and Peace in the Middle East,* ed. David Garnham and Mark Tessler, 116–32. Bloomington: Indiana University Press, 1995.

Ahmed, Akbar S. "Ethnic Cleansing: A Metaphor for Our Time?" *Ethnic and Racial Studies* 18 (1995): 3–25.

———. *Postmodernism and Islam: Predicament and Promise.* London: Routledge, 1992.

Ajami, Fouad. *The Arab Predicament: Arab Political Thought and Practice since 1967.* Rev. ed. Cambridge: Cambridge University Press, 1992.

———. "The End of Pan-Arabism." *Foreign Affairs* 57, no. 2 (1979): 355–73.

———. *The Vanished Imam: Musa al-Sadr and the Shi'a of Lebanon.* Ithaca: Cornell University Press, 1986.

Alford, C. Fred. *Group Psychology and Political Theory.* New Haven: Yale University Press, 1994.

———. *Melanie Klein and Critical Social Theory.* New Haven: Yale University Press, 1989.

Allport, Gordon W. *The Individual and His Religion: A Psychological Interpretation.* New York: Macmillan, 1950.

———. *The Nature of Prejudice.* Garden City, N.Y.: Doubleday, 1958.

Allport, Gordon W., and M. R. Ross. "Personal Religious Orientation and Prejudice." *Journal of Personality and Social Psychology* 5 (1967): 432–43.

al-Naku'a, Muhammad. "How, from an Islamic Point of View." *Al-Hayat* (London), March 17, 1993.

Alrawi, Karim. "Good-bye to the Enlightenment." *Index on Censorship* 23, nos. 1–2 (1994).

Al-Suwaidi, J. "Arab and Western Conceptions of Democracy: Evidence from a UAE Opinion Survey." In *Democracy, War, and Peace in the Middle East,* ed. David Garnham and Mark Tessler, 82–115. Bloomington: Indiana University Press, 1995.

Al-Turabi, Hassan. "The New Wave of Islamic Awakening." *Sunday Times of India,* January 30, 1994.

Alwan, Arif. "The New Strive for Life: Do the People of Iraq Need a Neutral State Whose Slogan Is Tolerance?" *Al-Hayat* (London), October 24, 1991.

Anderson, Benedict. *Imagined Communities: Reflections on the Origin and the Spread of Nationalism.* London: Verso, 1983.

Anderson, Lisa. "Liberalism, Islam, and the Arab State." *Dissent* 41 (fall 1994): 441.

Ansari, H. N. "The Islamic Militants in Egyptian Politics." *International Journal of Middle East Studies* 16 (1984): 123–44.

Appleby, R. Scott, ed. *Spokesmen for the Despised: Fundamentalist Leaders of the Middle East.* Chicago: University of Chicago Press, 1997.

Arendt, Hannah. "What Is Authority?" In *Between Past and Future: Eight Exercises in Political Thought.* New York: Penguin Books, 1968.

Armstrong, Karen. *Holy War.* London: Macmillan, 1988.

Bahgat, Gawdat. "The Changing Economic and Political Environment in the Gulf Monarchies." *Journal of Social, Political, and Economic Studies* 20 (1995): 271–88.

Balay, J., and H. Shevrin. "The Subliminal Psychodynamic Activation Method: A Critical Review." *American Psychologist* 43 (1988): 161–74.

Banks, Arthur S. *Cross National Time Series Data Archive.* Binghamton, N.Y.: Center for Comparative Political Research, 1990.

Barakat, Halim I. *The Arab World: Society, Culture, and State.* Berkeley: University of California Press, 1993.

Barth, Fredrik, ed. *Ethnic Groups and Boundaries.* Boston: Little, Brown, 1969.

Batatu, Hanna. *The Egyptian, Syrian, and Iraqi Revolutions.* Washington, D.C.: Center for Contemporary Arab Studies, Georgetown University, 1984.

Beck, Aaron T., Gary Emery, and Ruth L. Greenberg. *Anxiety Disorders and Phobias: A Cognitive Perspective.* New York: Basic Books, 1985.

BeitHallahmi, Benjamin, and Michael Argyle. *The Psychology of Religious Behavior, Belief, and Experience.* London: Routledge, 1997.

Bellah, Robert N., Richard Madsen, William M. Sullivan, Ann Swidler, and Steven M. Tipton. *Individualism and Commitment in American Life.* New York: Harper and Row, 1987.

Benjamin, Jessica. *The Bonds of Love: Psychoanalysis, Feminism, and the Problem of Domination.* New York: Pantheon, 1988.

Benson, Peter L., and Dorothy L. Williams. *Religion on Capitol Hill: Myths and Realities.* San Francisco: Harper and Row, 1982.

Bentham, Jeremy. "Fragment on Government." In *Works of Jeremy Bentham,* ed. John Bowring. Edinburgh: William Tait, 1838.

Beran, Harry. "In Defense of the Consent Theory of Political Obligation and Authority." *Ethics* 87, no. 3 (April 1977): 257–64.

Berger, Peter L., and Thomas Luckmann. *The Social Construction of Reality: A Treatise in the Sociology of Knowledge.* Garden City, N.Y.: Doubleday, 1966.

Bergin, A. E. "Psychotherapy and Religious Values." *Journal of Consulting and Clinical Psychology* 48 (1980): 95–105.

———. "Values and Religious Issues in Psychotherapy and Mental Health." *American Psychologist* 46 (1991): 394–403.

Bergin, A. E., and J. P. Jensen. "Religiosity of Psychotherapists: A National Survey." *Psychotherapy* 27 (1990): 3–7.

Bergson, Henri. *The Two Sources of Morality and Religion.* Trans. R. Ashley Audra and Cloudesley Brereton. 1935; rpt., Notre Dame, Ind.: University of Notre Dame Press, 1977.

Berry, J. W., U. Kim, T. Minde, and D. Mok. "Comparative Studies of Acculturative Stress." *International Migration Review* 21 (1987): 491–511.

Berry, J. W., U. Kim, S. Power, M. Young, and M. Bujaki. "Acculturation Attitudes in Plural Societies." *Applied Psychology: An International Review* 38 (1989): 185–206.

Berry, John W., Ype H. Poortinga, and Janak Pandey, eds. *Handbook of Cross-Cultural Psychology: Theoretical and Methodological Perspectives,* 3 vols. Boston: Allyn and Bacon, 1996.

Berry, Philippa, and Andrew Wernick, eds. *Shadow of Spirit: Postmodernism and Religion.* New York: Routledge, 1992.

Bettelheim, B. "Individual and Mass Behavior in Extreme Situations." *Journal of Abnormal and Social Psychology* 38 (1943): 417–45.

Beutler, L. E. "Values, Beliefs, Religion, and the Persuasive Influence of Psychotherapy." *Psychotherapy: Theory, Research, and Practice* 16 (1979): 432–40.

Bickford, Susan. *The Dissonance of Democracy: Listening, Conflict, and Citizenship.* Ithaca: Cornell University Press, 1996.

Bion, Wilfred R. *Experiences in Groups, and Other Papers.* New York: Basic, 1961.

Bollen, Kenneth A. *Structural Equations with Latent Variables.* New York: Wiley, 1989.

Bordo, Susan. "Feminism, Postmodernism, and Gender Skepticism." In *Feminism/Postmodernism,* ed. Linda J. Nicholson. New York: Routledge, 1990.

Boswell, Terry, and William J. Dixon. "Dependency and Rebellion." *American Sociological Review* 55 (1990): 540–59.

Brass, Paul R. *Ethnicity and Nationalism: Theory and Comparison.* Newbury Park, Calif.: Sage, 1991.

Brenner, Charles. *The Mind in Conflict.* New York: International Universities Press, 1982.

Breznitz, Shlomo. *The Denial of Stress.* New York: International Universities Press, 1983.

Brown, R. J. "The Effects of Intergroup Similarity and Cooperative vs. Competitive Orientation on Intergroup Discrimination." *British Journal of Social Psychology* 23 (1984): 21–33.

Brown, Wendy. *States of Injury: Power and Freedom in Late Modernity.* Princeton: Princeton University Press, 1995.

Bruce, Steve, ed. *Religion and Modernization: Sociologists and Historians Debate the Secularization Thesis.* New York: Oxford University Press, 1992.

Brumberg, Daniel. "Comparative Reform Strategies in the Arab World." In *Politi-*

cal Liberalization and Democratization in the Arab World, ed. Rex Brynen and Bahgat Korany. Boulder, Colo.: Lynne Rienner Press, 1995.

Brunner, Jose. *Freud and the Politics of Psychoanalysis.* Cambridge: Basil Blackwell, 1995.

Burke, Peter. "Religion and Secularization." *New Cambridge Modern History* 13 (1979): 293–317.

Butler, Judith. *Bodies That Matter.* New York: Routledge, 1993.

———. *Gender Trouble.* New York: Routledge, 1990.

Calhoun, Craig. "Social Theory and the Politics of Identity." In *Social Theory and the Politics of Identity,* ed. Craig Calhoun. Oxford: Blackwell, 1994.

Cantor, N. "From Thought to Behavior: 'Having' and 'Doing' in the Study of Personality and Cognition." *American Psychologist* 45 (1990): 735–50.

———. "Life Task Problem Solving: Situational Affordances and Personal Needs." *Personality and Social Psychology Bulletin* 20 (1994): 235–43.

Cantor, N., and J. F. Kihlstrom. *Personality and Social Intelligence.* Englewood Cliffs, N.J.: Prentice Hall, 1987.

Casey, E. *Remembering: A Phenomenological Study.* Bloomington: Indiana University Press, 1987.

Chaves, Mark. "Secularization as Declining Religious Authority." *Social Forces* 72 (1994): 749–74.

Chodorow, Nancy. *The Reproduction of Mothering.* New Haven, Conn.: Yale University Press, 1978.

Chomsky, Noam. *In Reading of Father Giraldo's Documentation of the Reign of Terror.* From the Website about terror. May 1995, Cambridge, Mass.

Church, A. T., and W. J. Lonner. "The Cross-Cultural Perspective in the Study of Personality: Rationale and Current Research." *Journal of Cross-Cultural Psychology* 29, no. 1 (1998): 32–62.

Cohen, Norman J., ed. *The Fundamentalist Phenomenon.* Grand Rapids, Mich.: William B. Eerdmans, 1991.

Connolly, William. "Beyond Good and Evil: The Ethical Sensibility of Michel Foucault." *Political Theory* 21 (1993): 37–64.

Connor, S. R. "Measurement of Denial in the Terminally Ill: A Critical Review." *Hospice Journal* 2 (1986): 51–67.

Connor, Walker. "A Nation Is a Nation, Is a State, Is an Ethnic Group." *Ethnic and Racial Studies* 1 (1978): 377–400.

———. "The Politics of Ethnonationalism." *Journal of International Affairs* 27 (1973): 1–21.

Cooper, Davina. *Power in Struggle.* New York: New York University Press, 1995.

Cooper, S. H. "The Empirical Study of Defensive Process: A Review." In *Interface of Psychoanalysis and Psychology,* ed. J. W. Barron, M. N. Eagle, and D. L. Wolitzky, 327–46. Washington, D.C.: American Psychological Association, 1992.

Cousins, N. "Denial: Are Sharper Definitions Needed?" *Journal of the American Medical Association* 248 (1982): 210–12.

Cousins, S. D. "Culture and Self-Perception in Japan and the United States." *Journal of Personality and Social Psychology* 56 (1989): 124–31.

Cramer, P. "The Defense Mechanisms Inventory: A Review of Research and Discussion of the Scales." *Journal of Personality Assessment* 52 (1988): 142–64.

Csikszentmihalyi, M. *The Evolving Self: A Psychology for the Third Millennium.* New York: HarperCollins, 1993.

Dahl, Robert A. *A Preface to Democratic Theory.* Chicago: University of Chicago Press, 1956.

Dallmayr, Fred. *Margins of Political Discourse.* Albany: SUNY Press, 1989.

———. "Modernity in the Crossfire: Comments on the Postmodern Turn." In *Postmodern Contentions: Epochs, Politics, Space,* ed. John Paul Jones III, Wolfgang Natter, and Theodore R. Schatzki. New York: Guilford Press, 1993.

Danielson, Dan, and Karen Engle. *After Identity: A Reader in Law and Culture.* New York: Routledge, 1995.

Davis, P. J. "Repression and the Inaccessibility of Affective Memories." *Journal of Personality and Social Psychology* 52 (1987): 155–62.

Dawes, R. M. "Social Dilemmas." *Annual Review of Psychology* 31 (1980): 169–93.

Dawes, R. M., J. M. Orbell, R. T. Simmons, and A.J.C. Van de Draget. "Organizing Groups for Collective Action." *American Political Science Review* 80 (1986): 1171–85.

Dawn, C. Ernest. *From Ottomanism to Arabism: Essays on the Origins of Arab Nationalism.* Urbana: University of Illinois Press, 1973.

Deininger, Klaus, and Lyn Squire. "A New Data Set Measuring Income Inequality." *World Bank Economic Review* 10 (1996): 565–91.

Deleuze, Gilles, and Félix Guattari. *Anti-Oedipus: Capitalism and Schizophrenia.* Trans. Robert Hurley, Mark Seem, and Helen R. Lane. New York: Viking, 1977; rpt. Minneapolis: University of Minnesota Press, 1983.

Demarco, J. P. *A Coherence Theory in Ethics.* Amsterdam: Rodopi, 1994.

Dennett, D. *Consciousness Explained.* London: Penguin, 1991.

Diener, E., and M. Diener. "Cross-Cultural Correlates of Life Satisfaction and Self-Esteem." *Journal of Personality and Social Psychology* 68 (1995): 653–63.

Diener, E., M. Diener, and C. Diener. "Factors Predicting the Subjective Well-Being of Nations." *Journal of Personality and Social Psychology* 69 (1995): 851–64.

Diener, E., E. Sandvik, and W. Pavot. "Happiness Is the Frequency, Not the Intensity, of Positive vs. Negative Affect." In *Subjective Well-Being: An Interdisciplinary Perspective,* ed. E. Strack, M. Argyle, and N. Schwarz. Elmsford, N.Y.: Pergamon, 1991.

Dinnerstein, Dorothy. *The Mermaid and the Minotaur.* New York: Harper and Row, 1976.

Donahue, M. J. "Intrinsic and Extrinsic Religiousness: Review and Meta-Analysis." *Journal of Personality and Social Psychology* 48 (1985): 400–419.

Dow, J. "Universal Aspects of Symbolic Healing: A Theoretical Synthesis." *American Anthropologist* 88 (1966): 56–69.

Dryzek, John S. "Political Inclusion and the Dynamics of Democratization." *American Political Science Review* 90 (1996): 475–87.

Durkheim, E. *The Elementary Forms of Religious Life.* 1915; rpt., London: Allen and Unwin, 1984.

———. *On Morality and Society.* 5:1–44. (Originally published 1913). Chicago: University of Chicago Press, 1973.

———. "The Problem of Religion and the Duality of Human Nature." In *The Elementary Forms of Religious Life,* trans. Joseph Ward Swain. Glencoe, Ill.: Free Press, 1947.

Edwards, David, and Susan Mendus, eds. *On Toleration.* Oxford: Clarendon Press, 1987.

Eickelman, Dale F. "Muslim Politics: The Prospects for Democracy in North Africa and the Middle East." In *Islam, Democracy, and the State in North Africa,* ed. John Entelis. Bloomington: Indiana University Press, 1997.

Eickelman, Dale F., and James Piscatori. *Muslim Politics.* Princeton: Princeton University Press, 1996.

Eisenberg, Avigail I. *Reconstructing Political Pluralism.* Albany: SUNY Press, 1995.

Eisenstadt, S. N., and Stein Rokkan, eds. *Building States and Nations,* vol. 2. Beverly Hills, Calif.: Sage, 1975.

Ellis, R. E. *Coherence and Verification in Ethics.* Lanhan, Md.: University Press of America, 1992.

Elster, Jon. *Political Psychology.* Cambridge: Cambridge University Press, 1993.

Enriquez, V. "Developing a Filipino Psychology." In *Indigenous Psychologies: Research and Experience in Cultural Context,* ed. U. Kim and J. W. Berry. Newbury Park, Calif.: Sage, 1993.

Entelis, John, ed. *Islam, Democracy, and the State in North Africa.* Bloomington: Indiana University Press, 1997.

Erxleben, J., and J. A. Cates. "Systemic Treatment of Multiple Personality: Response to a Chronic Disorder." *American Journal of Psychotherapy* 45 (1991): 269–78.

Esman, Milton J. *International Organizations and Ethnic Conflict.* Ithaca: Cornell University Press, 1995.

Euben, Roxanne L. "Premodern, Antimodern, or Postmodern? Islamic and Western Critiques of Modernity." *Review of Politics* (summer 1997).

Fairbairn, W.R.D. "Synopsis of an Object Relations Theory of Personality." *International Journal of Psychoanalysis* 44 (1963): 224–25.

Falk, Richard. "Religion and Politics: Verging on the Postmodern." *Alternatives* 8 (1988): 380.

Farah, Tawfic, ed. *Pan-Arabism and Arab Nationalism: The Continuing Debate.* Boulder, Colo.: Westview, 1987.

Fast, I. "Object Relations: Toward a Relational Model of the Mind." In *Interface of Psychoanalysis and Psychology,* ed. J. W. Barron, M. N. Eagle, and D. L. Wolitzky. Washington, D.C.: American Psychological Association, 1992.

Fearon, James D., and David D. Laitin. *A Cross-Sectional Study of Large-Scale Ethnic Violence in the Postwar Period.* Department of Political Science, University of Chicago, 1997.

———. "Explaining Interethnic Cooperation." *American Political Science Review* 90, no. 4 (1996): 715–35.

Fenichel, O. "Critique of Death Instinct." *Imago* 21 (1935): 458–66.

———. "Neurotic Acting Out." *Psychoanalytic Review* 32 (1945): 197–206.

Ferenczi, Sándor. "Stages in the Development of the Sense of Reality." In *First Contributions to Psycho-analysis,* trans. Sándor Ferenczi and Ernest Jones. 1952; rpt., New York: Brunner/Mazel, 1980.

Fiske, S., and S. Taylor. "Social Cognition." *Peace and Conflict Studies* 1, no. 1 (December 1994): 64–82.

Flax, Jane. *Thinking Fragments.* Berkeley: University of California Press, 1990.

Foucault, Michel. *Madness and Civilization.* New York: Random House, 1965.

Francisco, Ronald A. "The Relationship between Coercion and Protest." *Journal of Conflict Resolution* 39 (1995): 263–82.

Freud, Anna. *The Ego and the Mechanisms of Defense.* 1937; rpt., New York: International Universities Press, 1966.

Freud, S. *Civilization and Its Discontents.* Standard Edition. 1930.

———. *The Ego and the Id.* Standard Edition. 1923.

———. *The Future of an Illusion.* Standard Edition. 1927.

———. *Group Psychology and the Analysis of the Ego.* Standard Edition. 1921.

———. *The Infantile Genital Organization: An Interpolation into the Theory of Sexuality.* Standard Edition. 1923.

———. *Introductory Lectures on Psycho-Analysis.* Standard Edition. 1917.

———. *On Narcissism: An Introduction.* Standard Edition. 1914.

———. *Notes upon a Case of Obsessional Neurosis.* Standard Edition. 1909.

———. *The Origins of Psychoanalysis.* Garden City, N.Y.: Doubleday, 1954.

———. *The Psychoneuroses of Defense.* Standard Edition. 1894.

———. *Three Essays on the Theory of Sexuality.* Standard Edition. 1905.

———. *Totem and Taboo.* Standard Edition. 1913.

———. *Why War?* Standard Edition. 1932.

Fromkin, David. *A Peace to End All Peace.* New York: Avon Books, 1989.

Fromm, Erich. *Escape from Freedom.* New York: Holt, Rinehart and Winston, 1941.

Gartner, J., D. Larson, and G. D. Allen. "Religious Commitment and Mental Health: A Review of the Empirical Literature." *Journal of Psychology and Theology* 19 (1991): 6–25.

Geertz, Clifford, ed. *Old Societies and New States: The Quest for Modernity in Asia and Africa.* New York: Free Press, 1963.

Gellner, Ernest. "Holism and Individualism in History and Sociology." In *Theories of History,* ed. P. Gardiner. Oxford: Oxford University Press, 1959.

———. "Nationalism in the Vacuum." In *Thinking Theoretically about Soviet Nationalities,* ed. Alexander J. Motyl. New York: Columbia University Press, 1992.

———. *Nations and Nationalism.* Ithaca: Cornell University Press, 1983.

———. *Postmodernism, Reason, and Religion.* London: Routledge, 1992.

Gelvin, James L. "Popular Mobilization and the Foundations of Mass Politics in Syria, 1918–1920." Ph.D. diss., Harvard University, 1992.

Gerth, H. H., and C. Wright Mills, eds. *From Max Weber: Essays in Sociology.* 1900; rpt., New York: Oxford University Press, 1946.

Gillett, G. "Multiple Personality and Irrationality." *Philosophical Psychology* 4 (1991): 103–18.

Glass, James. *Delusion.* Chicago: University of Chicago Press, 1985.

———. *Psychosis and Power: Threats to Democracy in the Self and the Group.* Ithaca: Cornell University Press, 1995.

Glover, J. *The Philosophy and Psychology of Personal Identity.* Harmondsworth: Penguin, 1988.

Gorsuch, R. L, and C. Smith. "Attribution of Responsibility to God: An Interaction of Religious Beliefs and Outcomes." *Journal for the Scientific Study of Religion* 22 (1983): 340–52.

Graham, George. "Consensus." In *Social Science Concepts,* ed. Giovanni Sartori. Beverly Hills, Calif.: Sage, 1984.

Greenfeld, Liah. *Nationalism: Five Roads to Modernity.* Cambridge: Harvard University Press, 1992.

Greenfield, Patricia M. "Independence and Interdependence as Developmental Scripts: Implications for Theory, Research, and Practice." In *Cross-Cultural Roots of Minority Child Development,* ed. Patricia M. Greenfield and Rodney R. Cocking. Hillsdale, N.J.: L. Erlbaum, 1994.

Greenstein, Fred I. "Political Psychology: A Pluralistic Universe." In *Handbook of Political Psychology.* ed. Jeanne N. Knutson. San Francisco: Jossey-Bass, 1973.

Grunbaum, Adolf. *The Foundations of Psychoanalysis.* Berkeley: University of California Press, 1984.

Guinier, Lani. *The Tyranny of the Majority.* New York: Free Press, 1994.

Guisinger, S., and Blatt, S. J. "Individuality and Relatedness: Evolution of a Fundamental Dialect." *American Psychologist* 49 (1994): 104–11.

Gurr, Ted Robert, and Will H. Moore. "Ethnopolitical Rebellion: A Cross-Sectional Analysis of the 1980s with Risk Assessments for the 1990s." *American Journal of Political Science* 41 (1997): 1079–1103.

Gurr, Ted Robert, and James R. Scarritt. "Minorities at Risk: A Global Survey." *Human Rights Quarterly* 11 (1989): 375–405.

Gusfield, Joseph. *The Culture of Public Problems*. Chicago: University of Chicago Press, 1981.

Gutmann, Amy ed. *Multiculturalism: Examining the Politics of Recognition*. Princeton: Princeton University Press, 1994.

Gutmann, D. "The Subjective Politics of Power: The Dilemma of Post-Superego Man." *Social Research* (winter 1973): 570–616.

Hacking, I. *Rewriting the Soul: Multiple Personality and the Sciences of Memory*. Princeton: Princeton University Press, 1995.

———. "Two Souls in One Body." *Critical Inquiry* 17 (1991): 838–67.

Hadar, Leon T. "America's Moment in the Middle East." *Current History* 95 (January 1996).

Haim, Sylvia G., ed. *Arab Nationalism: An Anthology*. Berkeley: University of California Press, 1962.

Hallowell, A. I. *Culture and Experience*. Philadelphia: University of Pennsylvania Press, 1955.

Hannan, Michael T. "The Dynamics of Ethnic Boundaries in Modern States." In *National Development and the World System*, ed. John Meyer and Michael T. Hannan. Chicago: University of Chicago Press, 1979.

Hardin, Garret. "An Operational Analysis of 'Responsibility'." In *Managing the Commons*, ed. Garret Hardin and John Baden. New York: Freeman, 1977.

Hart, H. L. A. "Are There Any Natural Rights?" *Philosophical Review* 64, no. 2 (April 1955): 175–91.

Hassan, Riffat. "The Burgeoning of Islamic Fundamentalism: Toward an Understanding of the Phenomenon." In *The Fundamentalist Phenomenon*, ed. Norman J. Cohen, 151–71. Grand Rapids, Mich.: William B. Erdmans Co., 1991.

Hattie, John. *Self-Concept*. Hillsdale, N.J.: L. Erlbaum, 1992.

Hechter, Michael. "Nationalism as Group Solidarity." *Ethnic and Racial Studies* 10 (1987): 415–26.

Heelas, Paul, Scott Lash, and Paul Morris, eds. *Detraditionalization: Critical Reflections on Authority and Identity*. Oxford: Blackwell, 1996.

Heider, E. *The Psychology of Interpersonal Relationships*. New York: Wiley, 1958.

Heine, S. J., and Lehman, D. R. "Cultural Variation in Unrealistic Optimism: Does the West Feel More Invulnerable than the East?" *Journal of Personality and Social Psychology* 68 (1995): 595–607.

Hermann, Margaret G. *An Interdisciplinary Adventure: The Research Training Group on the Role of Cognition in Collective Political Decision Making*. Mershon Center, Ohio State University, 1997.

———, ed. *Political Psychology*. San Francisco: Jossey-Bass, 1986.

Hertel, Bradley R., and Michael J. Donahue. "Parental Influences on God Images among Children: Testing Durkheim's Metaphoric Parallelism." *Journal for the Scientific Study of Religion* 34 (1995): 186–99.

Hexham, Irving, and Karla Poewe. *New Religion as Global Cultures: Making the Human Sacred.* Denver, Colo.: Westview, 1997.

Hilbert, Richard A. "Anomie and the Moral Regulation of Reality: The Durkheimian Tradition in Modern Relief." *Sociological Theory* 4 (1986): 1–19.

Hilgard, E. "Human Motives and the Concept of the Self." *American Psychologist* 4 (1949): 374–82.

Hirst, Paul. *Associative Democracy.* Amherst: University of Massachusetts Press, 1994.

Hobsbawm, Eric, and Terence Ranger, eds. *The Invention of Tradition.* Cambridge: Cambridge University Press, 1983.

Hoch, Martin. "Near and Middle East Conflicts and Western Policies." *Aussen Politik* 46 (1995): 280.

Hofstede, Erlbaum G. *Culture's Consequences.* Beverly Hills, Calif.: Sage, 1980.

Holmes, Stephen. *The Anatomy of Antiliberalism.* Cambridge: Harvard University Press, 1993.

———. *Passions and Constraint.* Chicago: University of Chicago Press, 1995.

Holyoak, K. J., and Thagard, P. *Mental Leaps: Analogy in Creative Thought.* Cambridge: MIT Press/Bradford Books, 1995.

Hopwood, Derek, *Egypt: Politics and Society, 1945–90.* London: HarperCollins Academic, 1991.

Horowitz, Donald L. *Ethnic Groups in Conflict.* Berkeley: University of California Press, 1985.

Horton, John, and Susan Mendus, eds. *Aspects of Toleration.* London: Methuen, 1985.

Hourani, Albert. *Arabic Thought in the Liberal Age.* Cambridge: Cambridge University Press, 1983.

Huber, E. R. *Verfassung.* Hamburg: Hanseatische Verlagsanstalt, 1937.

Hudson, Michael. *Arab Politics: The Search for Legitimacy.* New Haven: Yale University Press, 1977.

Hughes, M. W. "Personal Identity: A Defense of Locke." *Philosophy* 50 (1975): 169–87.

Hund, J. "Are Social Facts Real?" *British Journal of Sociology* 33 (1982): 270–78.

———. "Sociologism." In *Perspectives on Psychologism,* ed. Mark A. Notturno. New York: E. J. Brill, 1989.

Hurewitz, J. C., ed. and trans. *The Middle East and North Africa in World Politics: A Documentary Record.* New Haven: Yale University Press, 1979.

Hurley, S. L. *Natural Reasons: Personality and Polity.* New York: Oxford University Press, 1989.

Hwang, P., and W. P. Burgers. "Properties of Trust: An Analytical View." *Organizational Behavior and Human Decision Processes* 69, no. 1 (1997): 67–73.

Ignatieff, Michael. *Blood and Belonging: Journeys into the New Nationalism.* New York: Noonday Press, 1993.

Ihilevich, D., and G. C. Gleser. *Defenses in Psychotherapy: The Clinical Applica-*

tion of the Defense Mechanisms Inventory. Owosso, Mich.: DMI Associates, 1991.

Ip, G.W.M., and M. H. Bond. "Culture, Values, and the Spontaneous Self-Concept." Asian Journal of Psychology 1, no. 1 (1995): 29–35.

Iyengar, Shanto. Is Anyone Responsible? Chicago: University of Chicago Press, 1991.

Jalali, Rita, and Seymour Martin Lipset. "Racial and Ethnic Conflicts: A Global Perspective." Political Science Quarterly 4 (1992–93): 585–606.

Jenkins, J. Craig, and Susanne Schmeidl. "Flight from Violence: The Origins and Implications of the World Refugee Crisis." Sociological Focus 28 (1995): 63–82.

Johnson, M. L. Moral Imagination: Implications of Cognitive Science for Ethics. Chicago: University of Chicago Press, 1993.

Johnson, Nels. Islam and the Politics of Meaning in Palestinian Nationalism. London: Kegan Paul International, 1982.

Johnson, P. A History of the Jews. New York: Harper Perennial, 1987.

Johnson-George, C., and W. Swap. "Measurement of Specific Interpersonal Trust: Construction and Validation of a Scale to Assess Trust in a Specific Other." Journal of Personality and Social Psychology 43 (1982): 1036–57.

Jung, C. G. Modern Man in Search of a Soul. New York: Harcourt, Brace, 1936.

Juni, S. "Remorse as a Derivative Psychoanalytic Construct." American Journal of Psychoanalysis 51 (1991): 71–81.

———. "The Role of the Object in Drive Cathexis and Object Relations." Journal of Psychology 126 (1992): 429–42.

Juni, S., B. Katz, B., and W. Hamburger. "Identification with Aggression vs. Turning against the Self: An Empirical Study of Turn-of-the-Century European Jewish Humor." Current Psychology 14 (1996): 313–27.

Kaldor, Mary. "Cosmopolitanism vs. Nationalism: The New Divide." In Europe's New Nationalism, ed. Richard Caplan and John Feffer. New York: Oxford University Press, 1996.

Kemp, Peter. "Saudi Arabia Ends the Uncertainty." MEED 40 (January 12, 1996).

Kerr, Malcolm H. Islamic Reform: The Political and Legal Theories of Muhammad 'Abduh and Rashid Rida. Berkeley: University of California Press, 1966.

Khalidi, Rashid. "Ottomanism and Arabism in Syria before 1914: A Reassessment." In The Origins of Arab Nationalism, ed. Rashid Khalidi et al. New York: Columbia University Press, 1991.

Khalilzad, Zalmay. "The United States and the Persian Gulf: Preventing Regional Hegemony." Survival 37 (1995): 110.

Khashan, Hilal. Arabs at the Crossroads: Political Identity and Nationalism. Gainesville: University Press of Florida, 2000.

Khoury, Philip S. Urban Notables and Arab Nationalism: The Politics of Damascus, 1880–1920. Cambridge: Cambridge University Press, 1983.

Kilbourne, B., and J. T. Richardson. "Psychotherapy and New Religions in a Pluralistic Society." *American Psychologist* 39 (1984): 237–51.

Kitayama, S., and M. Karasawa. "Self: A Cultural Psychological Perspective." *Japanese Journal of Experimental Social Psychology* 35 (1995): 113–65.

Kitayama, S., and H. R. Markus, eds. *Emotion and Culture: Empirical Studies of Mutual Influence.* Washington, D.C.: American Psychological Association, 1994.

Kittrie, Nicholas N. *The War against Authority: From the Crisis of Legitimacy to a New Social Order.* Baltimore: Johns Hopkins University Press, 1995.

Klopf, W. K. *Intercultural Encounters: The Fundamentals of Intercultural Communication.* Englewood, Colo.: Morton, 1987.

Klosko, George. "Presumptive Benefit, Fairness, and Political Obligation." *Philosophy and Public Affairs* 16, no. 3 (summer 1987): 241–59.

Kluft, R. "The Postunification Treatment of Multiple Personality Disorder: First Findings." *American Journal of Psychotherapy* 42 (1988): 212–28.

Kockelmans, Joseph J. *Edmund Husserl's Phenomenological Psychology: A Historico-Critical Study.* Translated by Benno Jager. Atlantic Highlands, N.J.: Humanities Press, 1978.

Koopmans, Ruud. *Democracy from Below.* Boulder, Colo.: Westview, 1995.

Korsgaard, C. M. "Personal Identity and the Unity of Agency: A Kantian Response to Parfit." *Philosophy and Public Affairs* 18 (1988): 101–32.

Kramer, Martin. *Arab Awakening and Islamic Revival: The Politics of Ideas in the Middle East.* New Brunswick, N.J.: Transaction, 1996.

Kressel, Neil Jeffrey, ed. *Political Psychology: Classic and Contemporary Readings.* New York: Paragon House, 1993.

Kriesi, Hanspeter. "The Political Opportunity Structure of New Social Movements: Its Impact on Their Mobilization." In *The Politics of Social Protest,* ed. J. Craig Jenkins and Bett Klandermans. Minneapolis: University of Minnesota Press, 1995.

Kristeva, Julia. *Black Sun: Depression and Melancholia.* New York: Columbia University Press, 1989.

———. *Powers of Horror: An Essay on Abjection.* New York: Columbia University Press, 1982.

Kuhn, M. T., and T. McPartland. "An Empirical Investigation of Self-Attitudes." *U.S. Sociological Review* 19 (1954): 68–76.

Kukathas, Chandran. "Are There Any Cultural Rights?" *Political Theory* 20, no. 1 (1992): 105–39.

Kumar, Kishan. "Civil Society: An Inquiry into the Usefulness of an Historical Term." *British Journal of Sociology* 44 (1993): 375–94.

Kunda, Z. "The Case for Motivated Inference." *Psychological Bulletin* 108 (1990): 480–98.

Kuper, Leo. "The Sovereign Territorial State: The Right to Genocide." In *Human*

Rights in the World Community: Issues and Actions, ed. Richard Pierre Claude and Burns H. Weston. Philadelphia: University of Pennsylvania Press, 1992.

Kurtz, Lester. *Gods in the Global Village: The World's Religions in Sociological Perspective.* Thousand Oaks, Calif.: Pine Forge Press, 1995.

Kymlicka, Will. *Liberalism, Community, and Culture.* Oxford: Oxford University Press, 1989.

Laclau, Ernesto, and Chantal Mouffe. *Hegemony and Socialist Strategy.* London: Verso, 1985.

Ladd, John. "Elements of Justice." In *Community,* ed. Carl J. Friedrich. New York: Liberal Arts Press, 1959.

Laing, R. D. *The Politics of Experience.* New York: Ballantine, 1967.

Lakoff, G. *Moral Politics: What Conservatives Know that Liberals Don't.* Chicago: University of Chicago Press, 1996.

Lanternari, V. *The Religions of the Oppressed: A Study of Modern Messianic Cults.* New York: Knopf, 1963.

Lawrence, Bruce. *Defenders of God.* San Francisco: Harper and Row, 1989.

Le Bon, G. *The Crowd: A Study of the Popular Mind.* London: T. F. Unwin, 1897.

Lebra, T. S. *Culture, Self, and Communication.* Ann Arbor: University of Michigan Press, 1992.

Lecher, Jean. "Social Structure and Political Stability: Comparative Evidence from the Algerian, Syrian, and Iraqi Cases." In *The Arab State,* ed. Giacomo Luciani. Berkeley: University of California Press, 1990.

Leventhal, H., R. Zimmerman, and M. Gutmann. "Compliance: A Self-Regulation Perspective." In *Handbook of Behavioral Medicine,* ed. W. D. Gentry. New York: Guilford, 1984.

Levey, Geoffrey Brahm. "Equality, Autonomy, and Cultural Rights." *Political Theory* 25, no. 2 (1997): 215–48.

Lewin, K. *A Dynamic Theory of Personality.* New York: McGraw-Hill, 1935.

Lewis, H. "The Role of Shame in Depression over the Life Span." In *The Role of Shame in Symptom Formation,* ed. H. Lewis. Hillsdale, N.J.: L. Erlbaum, 1987.

———. *Shame and Guilt in Neurosis.* New York: International University Press, 1971.

Lichter, S. Robert, Stanley Rothman, and Linda S. Lichter. *The Media Elite: America's New Power Brokers.* Bethesda, Md.: Adler and Adler, 1986.

Lichtman, Richard. *The Production of Desire.* New York: Free Press, 1982.

Lieberman, Lawrence. "Race and Ethnicity: Overlapping Meanings." *Anthropology News Network* 1 (1993): 3–4, 23.

Lindblom, Charles E. *Politics and Markets.* New York: Basic Books, 1977.

Lindsay-Hartz, J. "Contrasting Experiences of Shame and Guilt." *American Behavioral Scientist* 27 (1984): 689–704.

Locke, J. *An Essay Concerning Human Understanding.* 1690; rpt. Glasgow: Collins, 1984.

Loewald, Hans. *Sublimation: Inquiries into Theoretical Psychoanalysis.* New Haven, Conn.: Yale University Press, 1988.

Loewenstein, Rudolph M. "Developments in the Theory of Transference in the Last Fifty Years." *International Journal of Psycho-Analysis* 50 (1969): 583–88.

Lothane, Z. "Dialogues Are for Dyads." *Issues in Ego Psychology* 5 (1982): 19–24.

———. "Love and Destructiveness." *Academy Forum* 31, no. 4: (1987): 2–9.

———. "The Primacy of Love: Love Ethics vs. Hermeneutics." *Academy Forum* 31, no. 1 (1987): 3–4.

Lucas, J. R. *The Principles of Politics.* Oxford: Clarendon Press, 1985.

Luciani, Giacomo, ed. *The Arab State.* Berkeley: University of California Press, 1990.

Lutz, C., and G. White. "The Anthropology of Emotions." *Annual Review of Anthropology* 15 (1986): 405–36.

McClure, Kirstie. "On the Subject of Rights: Pluralism, Plurality, and Political Identity." In *Dimensions of Radical Democracy,* ed. Chantal Mouffe. London: Verso, 1992.

McGowan, John. *Postmodernism and Its Critics.* Ithaca: Cornell University Press, 1991.

McGuire, Meredith B. *Religion: The Social Context.* Belmont, Calif.: Wadsworth, 1981.

McIntosh, Donald. "Cathexes and Their Objects in the Thought of Sigmund Freud." *Journal of the American Psychoanalytic Association* 41 (1993): 679–709.

———. "The Economy of Desire: Psychic Energy as a Purely Psychological Concept." *Psychoanalysis and Contemporary Thought* 9 (1986): 405–35.

———. "Max Weber as a Critical Theorist." *Theory and Society* 12 (1983): 69–109.

———. *Self, Person, World: The Interplay of Conscious and Unconscious in Human Life.* Evanston, Ill.: Northwestern University Press, 1995.

McLaurin, R. D., Don Peretz, and Lewis W. Snider. *Middle East Foreign Policy: Issues and Processes.* New York: Praeger, 1982.

McLennan, Gregor. *Pluralism.* Minneapolis: University of Minnesota Press, 1995.

Marcuse, Herbert. *Eros and Civilization.* 1955; rpt., Boston: Beacon, 1991.

Markus, H. R., and S. A. Kitayama. "A Collective Fear of the Collective: Implications for Selves and Theories of Selves." *Personality and Social Psychology Bulletin* 20, no. 5 (1994): 568–79.

———. "The Cultural Construction of Self and Emotion: Implications for Social Behavior." In *Emotion and Culture: Empirical Studies of Mutual Influence,* ed. S. Kitayama and H. R. Markus. Washington, D.C.: American Psychological Association, 1994.

———. "Culture and the Self: Implications for Cognition, Emotion, and Motivation." *Psychological Review* 98 (1991): 224–53.

Markus, H. R., S. Kitayama, and R. J. Heiman. "Culture and Basic Psychological Principles." In *Social Psychology: Handbook of Basic Principles*, ed. E. T. Higgins and A. W. Kruglanski. New York: Guilford. 1996.

Markus, H. R., P. R. Mullally, and S. Kitayama. "Selfways: Diversity in Modes of Cultural Participation." In *The Conceptual Self in Context*, ed. U. Neisser and D. Jopling. New York: Cambridge University Press, 1997.

Markus, H. R., S. Kitayama, P. Mullally, T. Masuda, and S. Fryberg. *Of Selves and Selfways: Patterns of Individuality and Uniformity in Identity.* Stanford: Stanford University Press, 1997.

Marsella, A., G. DeVos, and E. K. Hsu. *Culture and Self.* London: Tavistock, 1985.

Marty, Martin E., and R. Scott Appleby, eds. *Fundamentalisms and the State: Remaking Polities, Economies, and Militance.* Chicago: University of Chicago Press, 1993.

———. *Fundamentalism Observed.* Chicago: University of Chicago Press, 1991.

Maslow, A. H. *Religions, Values, and Peak-Experiences.* New York: Viking, 1971.

Maton, K. I. "The Stress-Buffering Role of Spiritual Support: Cross-Sectional and Prospective Investigations." *Journal for the Scientific Study of Religion* 28 (1989): 310–23.

Maton, K. I., and E. A. Wells. "Religion as a Community Resource for Well-Being: Prevention, Healing and Empowerment Pathways." *Journal of Social Issues* 51 (1995): 177–93.

Meissner, U. W. "Theories of Personality and Psychopathology: Classical Psychoanalysis." In *Comprehensive Textbook of Psychiatry*, vol. 1, ed. H. I. Kaplan, A. M. Freedman, and B. J. Sadock. London: Williams and Wilkins, 1980.

Mendus, Susan, ed. *Justifying Toleration.* Cambridge: Cambridge University Press, 1988.

Miller, J. G. "Culture and the Development of Everyday Social Explanation." *Journal of Personality and Social Psychology* 46 (1984): 961–78.

———. "Theoretical Issues in Cultural Psychology." In *Handbook of Cross-Cultural Psychology: Theoretical and Methodological Perspectives*, vol. 1, ed. J. W. Berry, Y. H. Poortinga, and J. Pandey. Boston: Allyn and Bacon, 1996.

Minow, Martha. "Justice Engendered." *Harvard Law Review* 101 (1987): 10–95.

Mitchell, Juliet. *Psycho-Analysis and Feminism.* New York: Random House, 1974.

Modell, A. "A Narcissistic Defense against Affects and the Illusion of Self-Sufficiency." *International Journal of Psychoanalysis* 56 (1975): 275–82.

Moi, Toril, ed. *The Kristeva Reader.* New York: Columbia University Press, 1986.

Money-Kyrle, Roger R. E. *Psychoanalysis and Politics: A Contribution to the Psychology of Politics and Morals.* New York: Norton, 1958.

Mosse, George L. *The Nationalization of the Masses: Political Symbolism and Mass Movements in Germany from the Napoleonic Wars through the Third Reich.* New York: Howard Fertig, 1975.

Muller, Edward, and Eric Weede. "Cross-National Variation in Political Violence." *Journal of Conflict Resolution* 34 (1990): 624–51.

Nagel, Joane, and Susan Olzak. "Ethnic Mobilization in New and Old States: An Extension of the Competition Model." *Social Problems* 30 (1982): 127–43.

Najjar, Fawzi. "The Debates on Islam and Secularism in Egypt." *Arab Studies Quarterly* 18, no. 2 (1996).

Nasr, Seyyed Val Reza. *Mawdudi and the Making of Islamic Revivalism*. Oxford: Oxford University Press, 1996.

Neisser, U., and D. Jopling, eds. *The Conceptual Self in Context*. New York: Cambridge University Press, 1997.

Nilsen, E. A. *Religion and Personality Integration*. Stockholm: Uppsala University, 1980.

Norbert, Elias. *The Civilizing Process*. Cambridge, Mass.: Basil Blackwell, 1994.

Norman, O. *Life against Death*. New York: Vintage, 1959.

Owen, Roger. *The Middle East in the World Economy, 1800–1914*. London: Methuen, 1981.

Oye, Kenneth A. "Explaining Cooperation under Anarchy: Hypotheses and Strategies." In *Cooperation under Anarchy*, ed. Kenneth A. Oye. Princeton, N.J.: Princeton University Press, 1986.

Paloutzian, Raymond F. *Invitation to the Psychology of Religion*. 2d ed. Needham Heights, Mass.: Allyn and Bacon, 1996.

Parfit, D. "Personal Identity." *Philosophical Review* 80 (1971): 3–27.

———. *Reasons and Persons*. Oxford: Clarendon, 1984.

Pargament, K. I. and J. Hahn. "God and the Just World: Causal and Coping Attributes in Health Situations." *Journal for the Scientific Study of Religion* 25 (1968): 193–207.

Pargament, K. I., J. Kennell, W. Hathaway, N. Gravengoed, J. Newman, and W. Jones. "Religion and the Problem-Solving Process: Three Styles of Coping." *Journal for the Scientific Study of Religion* 27 (1988): 90–104.

Pargament, K. I., D. S. Ensing, K. Falgout, H. Olsen, B. Reilly, I. Van Haitsma, and R. Warren. "God Help Me: Religious Coping Efforts as Predictors of the Outcome of Negative Life Events." *American Journal of Community Psychology* 18 (1990): 793–823.

Parsons, Talcott. "Religion in Modern Pluralistic Society." *Review of Religious Research* 7 (1966): 125–46.

———. *The System of Modern Societies*. Englewood Cliffs, N.J.: Prentice Hall, 1971.

Pennebaker, James W., Dario Paez, and Bernard Rime, eds. *Collective Memory of Political Events: Social Psychological Perspective*. Mainz, Del.: L. Erlbaum, 1997.

Perthes, Volker. "The Private Sector, Economic Liberalization, and the Prospects for Democratization: The Case of Syria and Some Other Arab Countries." In

Democracy without Democrats, ed. Ghassan Salamé. London: I. B. Tauris, 1994.

Pettit, Philip. *The Common Mind: An Essay on Psychology, Society, and Politics.* New York: Oxford University Press. 1996.

Phillips, Anne. *Democracy and Difference.* University Park: Pennsylvania State University Press, 1993.

———. *The Politics of Presence.* Oxford: Oxford University Press, 1995.

Pipes, Daniel. *The Hidden Hand: Middle East Fears of Conspiracy.* New York: St. Martin's Press, 1996.

Podeh, Elie. *The Quest for Hegemony in the Arab World: The Struggle over the Baghdad Pact.* Leiden: E. J. Brill, 1995.

Poliakov, L. *The Aryan Myth: A History of Racist and Nationalist Ideas in Europe.* New York: New American Library, 1971.

Polk, William R., and Richard L. Chambers, eds. *Beginnings of Modernization in the Middle East: The Nineteenth Century.* Chicago: University of Chicago Press, 1968.

Qalada, W. Suleyman, H.A.M. al-Mismari Amin, et al. *Al-Tasamuh al-Dini wa al-Tafahum Bayn al-Mu'taqadat.* Trans. Kanan Makiya. Cairo: Union of Arab Lawyers, 1986.

Quackenbush, R. L. "Comparison and Contrast between Belief System Theory and Cognitive Theory." *Journal of Psychology* 123 (1989): 315–28.

Ramachandran, V. S. "Anosognosia in Parietal Lobe Syndrome." *Consciousness and Cognition* 4 (1995): 22–51.

Rapoport, D. C. "Messianic Sanctions for Terror." *Comparative Politics* 20 (January 1988): 195–213.

Rawls, John. "Legal Obligation and the Duty of Fair Play." In *Law and Philosophy,* ed. Sidney Hook. New York: New York University Press, 1964.

Reich, Wilhelm. *The Mass Psychology of Fascism.* New York: Farrar, Straus and Giroux, 1970.

———. *Power: A New Social Analysis.* New York: Barnes and Noble, 1942.

Reiff, Philip. *Freud: The Mind of the Moralist.* Garden City, N.Y.: Doubleday, 1961.

Rhee, E., J. Uleman, H. Lee, and R. Roman. "Spontaneous Self-Descriptions and Ethnic Identities in Individualistic and Collectivistic Cultures." *Journal of Personality and Social Psychology* 69, no. 1 (1995): 142–52.

Rorty, Amelie Oksenberg. "The Hidden Politics of Cultural Identification." *Political Theory* 22 (February 1994): 158.

Roth, Guenther, and Claus Wittich, eds. *Economy and Society.* 1923; rpt., New York: Bedminster Press, 1968.

Said, Edward W. *Orientalism.* New York: Pantheon Books, 1978.

Salamé, Ghassan, ed. 1994. *Democracy without Democrats.* London: I. B. Tauris, 1994.

———. *The Foundations of the Arab State.* London: Croom Helm, 1987.

Salem, Paul. *Bitter Legacy: Ideology and Politics in the Arab World.* Syracuse, N.Y.: Syracuse University Press, 1994.

Salomon, G. "Predispositions about Learning from Print and Television." *Journal of Communication* 34 (1984): 119–35.

Sampson, E. E. "The Debate on Individualism: Indigenous Psychologies of the Individual and Their Role in Personal and Societal Functioning." *American Psychologist* 43 (1988): 15.

Schaefer, A., and R. L. Gorsuch. "Psychological Adjustment and Religiousness: The Multivariate Belief-Motivation Theory of Religiousness." *Journal for the Scientific Study of Religion* 30 (1991): 44–81.

Schafer, Roy. "The Loving and Beloved Superego." *Psychoanalytic Study of the Child* 15 (1960): 31–47.

———. "The Mechanisms of Defense." *International Journal of Psychoanalysis* 49 (1968): 49–62.

Schechtman, M. "Personhood and Personal Identity." *Journal of Philosophy* 87 (1990): 71–92.

———. "The Same and the Same: Two Views of Psychological Continuity." *American Philosophical Quarterly* 31 (1994): 199–212.

———. "The Truth about Memory." *Philosophical Psychology* 7 (1994): 3–18.

Scheff, T., and S. Retzinger. *Emotions and Violence: Shame and Rage in Destructive Conflicts.* Lexington, Mass.: Lexington Books, 1991.

Schudson, Michael. *The Power of News.* Cambridge: Harvard University Press, 1995.

Shweder, Richard A., and L. Bourne. "Does the Concept of the Person Vary Cross-Culturally?" In *Culture Theory: Essays on Mind, Self and Emotion,* ed. Richard A. Shweder and Robert A. LeVine. Cambridge: Cambridge University Press, 1984.

Shweder, Richard A., and Robert A. LeVine, eds. *Culture Theory: Essays on Mind, Self and Emotion.* Cambridge: Cambridge University Press, 1984.

Shoemaker, S. "Persons and Their Pasts." *American Philosophical Quarterly* 7 (1970).

Silberman, Neil. *Between Past and Present: Archaeology, Ideology, and Nationalism in the Modern Middle East.* New York: Anchor Books, 1990.

Silverman, L. H. "The Subliminal Psychodynamic Activation Method: Overview and Comprehensive Listing of Studies." In *Empirical Studies of Psychoanalytical Theories,* vol. 1, ed. Joseph Masling. Hillsdale, N.J.: L. Erlbaum, 1983.

Simmons, A. J. *Moral Principles and Political Obligation.* Princeton: Princeton University Press, 1979.

Simon, H. "Human Nature in Politics: The Dialogue of Psychology with Political Science." *American Political Science Review* 79 (1985): 293–305.

Skocpol, Theda. "Bringing the State Back In." In *Bringing the State Back In,* ed. Peter B. Evans, Dietrich Rueschemeyer, and Theda Skocpol. Cambridge: Cambridge University Press, 1985.

Smith, Anthony D. *The Ethnic Origins of Nations.* Oxford: Blackwell, 1986.
———. *The Ethnic Revival in the Modern World.* Cambridge: Cambridge University Press, 1981.
Smith, Wilfrid C. *The Meaning and End of Religion: A New Approach to the Relations of Mankind.* New York: Mentor, 1964.
Spilka, B. P., and G. Schmidt. "General Attribution Theory for the Psychology of Religion: The Influence of Event Character on Attribution to God." *Journal for the Scientific Study of Religion* 22 (1983): 326–40.
Stein, Maurice R., Arthur J. Vidich, and David Manning White, eds. *Identity and Anxiety.* New York: Free Press, 1960.
Strentz, T. "The Stockholm Syndrome: Law Enforcement and Ego Defenses of the Hostage." *Annals of the New York Academy of Sciences* 34 (1980): 312–19.
Swanton, C. *Freedom: A Coherence Theory.* Indianapolis: Hackett, 1992.
Swedenburg, Ted. "The Role of the Palestinian Peasantry in the Great Revolt (1936–1939)." In *Islam, Politics, and Social Movements,* ed. Edmund Burke III and Ira M. Lapidus. Berkeley: University of California Press, 1988.
Tajfel, H. *Human Group and Social Categories.* Cambridge: Cambridge University Press, 1981.
Tajfel, H., and J. C. Turner. "An Integrative Theory of Intergroup Conflict." In *The Social Psychology of Intergroup Relations,* ed. W. G. Austin and S. Worchel. Pacific Grove, Calif.: Brooks/Cole, 1979.
Taylor, Charles. "The Politics of Recognition." In *Multiculturalism: Examining the Politics of Recognition,* ed. Amy Gutmann. Princeton: Princeton University Press, 1994.
Tessler, M. "The Origins of Popular Support for Islamist Movements: A Political Economy Analysis." In *Islam, Democracy, and the State in North Africa,* ed. John Entelis. Bloomington: Indiana University Press, 1997.
Tétreault, Mary Ann. "Gulf Winds: Inclement Political Weather in the Arabian Peninsula." *Current History* 95 (January 1996): 23.
Thagard, P. *Conceptual Revolutions.* Princeton: Princeton University Press, 1992.
———. "Explanatory Coherence." *Behavioral and Brain Sciences* 12 (1989): 435–67.
———. *Mind: Introduction to Cognitive Science.* Cambridge: MIT Press, 1996.
Thagard, P., C. Eliasmith, P. Rusnock, and C. P. Shelly. "Knowledge and Coherence." In *Common Sense, Reasoning, and Rationality,* ed. R. Euo. New York: Oxford University Press, 2000.
Thomas, George M., John W. Meyer, Francisco O. Ramirez, and John Boli. *Institutional Structure: Constituting State, Society and the Individual.* London: Sage, 1987.
Triandis, H. C. "The Self and Social Behavior in Differing Cultural Contexts." *Psychological Review* 93 (1989): 506–20.
Triandis, H. C., R. Bontempo, and M. Villareal. "Individualism and Collectivism:

Crosscultural Perspectives on Self-Ingroup Relationships." *Journal of Personality and Social Psychology* 54 (1988): 323–38.

Triandis, H. C., C. McCusker, and C. H. Hui. "Multi-method Probes on Individualism and Collectivism." *Journal of Personality and Social Psychology* 59 (1990): 1006–20.

Tully, James. *Strange Multiplicity: Constitutionalism in an Age of Diversity.* New York: Cambridge University Press, 1995.

Tunick, Mark. *Practices and Principles: Approaches to Ethical and Legal Judgment.* Princeton: Princeton University Press, 1998.

Tversky, Amos, and Daniel Kahneman. "Judgment under Uncertainty." *Science* 185 (1974): 1124–31.

Udovitch, A. L., ed. *The Islamic Middle East, 700–1900.* Princeton, N.J.: Darwin Press, 1981.

Vaillant, G. E. *Ego Mechanisms of Defense: A Guide for Clinicians and Researchers.* Washington, D.C.: American Psychiatric Press, 1992.

Veenhoven, R. "Questions on Happiness: Classical Topics, Modern Answers, Blind Spots." In *Subjective Well-Being: An Interdisciplinary Perspective,* ed. F. Strack, M. Argyle, and N. Schwarz. Elmsford, N.Y.: Pergamon, 1991.

Vinacke, W. Edgar. *Foundations of Psychology.* New York: Van Nostrand Reinhold, 1968.

Voll, John O. "Fundamentalism in the Sunni Arab World: Egypt and the Sudan." In *Fundamentalism Observed,* ed. Martin E. Marty and R. Scott Appleby. Chicago: University of Chicago Press, 1991.

Walker, A.D.M. "Political Obligation and the Argument from Gratitude." *Philosophy and Public Affairs* 17, no. 3 (summer 1988): 192, 205, 207.

Wallerstein, Immanuel. *The Capitalist Economy.* Cambridge: Cambridge University Press, 1979.

Walzer, Michael. *Thick and Thin: Moral Argument at Home and Abroad.* Notre Dame: University of Notre Dame Press, 1994.

———. "On Toleration: Spheres of Justice." In *A Defense of Pluralism and Equality.* New York: Basic Books, 1983.

Weber, Max. *Economy and Society: An Outline of Interpretive Sociology.* 2 vols. Berkeley: University of California Press, 1978.

———. *The Protestant Ethic and the Spirit of Capitalism.* Trans. Talcott Parsons. New York: Charles Scribner's Sons, 1946.

———. *The Sociology of Religion.* Trans. Ephraim Fischoff. Boston: Beacon Press, 1964.

Whitebook, Joel. *Perversion and Utopia: A Study in Psychoanalysis and Critical Theory.* Cambridge: MIT Press, 1995.

Wilson, Margaret R., and Erik E. Filsinger. "Religiosity and Marital Adjustment: Multidimensional Interrelationships." *Journal of Marriage and the Family* 48 (1986): 147–51.

Wituski, Deborah M. "Bridging a Disciplinary Divide: The Summer Institute in

Political Psychology." *PS: Political Science and Politics* 31, no. 2 (1998): 221–26.

Wolin, Sheldon. "Democracy, Difference, and Re-Cognition." *Political Theory* 21 (August 1993): 467.

Wong, P. T. P. "Personal Meaning and Successful Aging." *Canadian Psychology* 30 (1989): 516–17.

Woolf, Virginia. *A Room of One's Own.* New York: Harcourt Brace Jovanovich, 1981.

Wylie, R. C. *Measuring Self-Concept.* Lincoln: University of Nebraska Press, 1989.

Yapp, M. E. *The Near East since the First World War.* London: Longman, 1991.

Young, Iris Marion. "Gender as Seriality: Thinking about Women as a Social Collective." *Signs* 19 (1994): 713–38.

———. *Justice and the Politics of Difference.* Princeton: Princeton University Press, 1990.

Zalewski, Marysia, and Cynthia Enloe. "Questions about Identity in International Relations." In *International Relations Theory Today,* ed. Ken Booth and Steve Smith. Oxford: Blackwell, 1995.

Zamir, Meir. *The Formation of Modern Lebanon.* Ithaca: Cornell University Press, 1985.

Zanoyan, Vahan. "The Holiday Ends in the Gulf." *Foreign Affairs* 74 (1995): 3.

Index

Absolutism, religious, 110

Abstraction, process of, 50

Acting out (psychology), 10, 58

Adam and Eve, story of, 25

Afghanistan: American retaliation against, 5, 6; fundamentalism in, 65

Africans, 90; tribalism of, 141

Agency, in social psychology, 87–88

Aggression: in Arab culture, 41; children's, 34; in death instinct, 17, 18; defense mechanisms against, 58; Freud on, 110; irrational, 86; minorities' toleration of, 151; in paranoia, 24; sexual, 25

Aggressors, identification with, 58–59

Alarm (psychology), 14

'Alawites, 90, 137

Alford, C. Fred, 138; *Melanie Klein and Critical Social Theory,* 136, 137

Algeria: fundamentalism in, 112, 128; hatemongering in, 141; nationalism in, 139; regionalism in, 78; religious minorities of, 64; violence in, 106, 117, 137

Ali Bin Abi Talib, 6

Alienation: habit of, 22; media-based, 97

Allport, Gordon, 127

Al-Qaeda, ix

Altruism, 3

Alwan, Arif, 79

Anger, ancient, 6

Anxiety: children's, 30; in civil strife, 15; collective, 15; depressive, 30; deprivation-based, 31; in ethnic groups, 13; frustration-based, 31; of illegitimacy, 56; in Iraqi-Kuwaiti conflict, 19; of minorities, 89; original, 133; paranoid, 23; persecutory, 22, 30; political, 14–15; in

psychology, 14; role in identity, 49; role in violence, 9; separation, 124, 125; sociocultural climate of, 7; Western, 74. *See also* Death anxiety

Anxiety, political: as motivation system, ix; role in September 11 attacks, ix

Arabism: essentials of, 68; pan-, 65; as political ideology, 66

Arab-Israeli war, popular support for, 142

Arabs: children, 34, 110, 121; communication among, 39; concept of God, 121; consumption of mass media, 96–97; cultural models for, 142–43; dislocated, 55; educated, 46; fear of non-Arabs, 145; frustration among, 32; migration by, 39; mutual recognition among, 68; non-OPEC, 11–12; paranoid-schizoid positions of, 141; political responsibilities of, 4; psyche of, 92; psychic disintegration of, 140; psychological adaptations of, ix; psychosomatic fears of, 20; religious happiness of, 125; religious rituals of, 127; self-discipline of, 95; toleration of authoritarianism, 129; urban, 144; use of language, 144; wealthy, 46; youth, 4, 27, 96–97. *See also* Elites, Arab; Groups, Arab; Minorities, Arab

Arab world: autocracy in, 130; boundaries in, 21; Communism in, 12, 63; corruption in, 9–10, 27; cultural reconciliation in, 141; cynicism in, 80; decolonization in, 42; economy of, 11; effect of Soviet collapse on, 38, 63; foundations of fear in, 21; fundamentalism in, 64–65, 117, 120, 128; group conflict in, 101, 134; group identity in, 91, 116; as identity framework, 66; Marxist factions in, 72;

Michel G. Nehme is professor and dean of the faculty of political science, public administration, and diplomacy at the Notre Dame University, Lebanon.